CUTTING TO THE POINT

Other Books by Desmond Fennell

Politics and Culture

The State of the Nation: Ireland since the '60s (1983)
Cuireadh chun na Tríú Réabhlóide (1984)
*Beyond Nationalism: The Struggle against Provinciality
in the Modern World* (1985)
Nice People and Rednecks: Ireland in the 1980s (1986)
The Revision of Irish Nationalism (1989)
Heresy: The Battle of Ideas in Modern Ireland (1993)
*Uncertain Dawn: Hiroshima and the Beginning
of Postwestern Civilisation* (1996)
*Dreams of Oranges: An Eyewitness Account of
the Fall of Communist East Germany* (1996)
The Postwestern Condition: Between Chaos and Civilisation (1999)

Travel

Mainly in Wonder (1960)
A Connacht Journey (1987)
Bloomsway: A Day in the Life of Dublin (1990)

Religion

The Changing Face of Catholic Ireland (ed.) (1968)
Irish Catholics and Freedom since 1916: A Humanist Essay (1984)
Savvy and the Preaching of the Gospel (2003)

Literature

Whatever You Say, Say Nothing: Why Seamus Heaney Is No. 1 (1991)

Autobiography

The Turning Point: My Sweden Year and After (2001)

History

The Revision of European History (2003)

CUTTING TO THE POINT

Essays and Objections
1994–2003

Desmond Fennell

The Liffey Press

Published by
The Liffey Press Ltd
Ashbrook House, 10 Main Street
Raheny, Dublin 5, Ireland
www.theliffeypress.com

A catalogue record of this book is
available from the British Library.

ISBN 1-904148-35-2

Front cover painting by Graham Knuttel,
reproduced with the kind permission of the artist

Printed in the Republic of Ireland by Colour Books Ltd.

Contents

About the Author

Born in Belfast in 1929, Desmond Fennell attended school in Dublin, where he learned Latin and Greek, and in the Leaving Cert won first place in French and German. He studied history, economics and languages at University College Dublin and Trinity College, and worked on his MA in Modern History at Bonn University. In 1991, the National University of Ireland awarded him its highest degree in the humanities (D. Litt.) for his published work. He has lived and worked in Spain, Germany, Sweden, the USA and Italy — adding three more languages to his repertoire — and has travelled in Asia. Living in Conamara from 1968 to 1979, he was active in the "Gaeltacht revolution" which changed the nature of the Irish language movement. His journalism, 1969–75, rethinking the nationalist approach to the Northern problem laid the intellectual basis for the peace process of the 1990s. From 1976 to 1982, he taught History and Politics at University College Galway, and from 1982 to 1993, English Writing at the Dublin Institute of Technology. His books and journalism have dealt with contemporary culture and politics, travel, religion, history and literature. Since 1997, Desmond Fennell has lived in Anguillara on Lake Bracciano, near Rome.

For Miriam

About the Author

Born in Belfast in 1929, Desmond Fennell attended school in Dublin, where he learned Latin and Greek, and in the Leaving Cert won first place in French and German. He studied history, economics and languages at University College Dublin and Trinity College, and worked on his MA in Modern History at Bonn University. In 1991, the National University of Ireland awarded him its highest degree in the humanities (D. Litt.) for his published work. He has lived and worked in Spain, Germany, Sweden, the USA and Italy — adding three more languages to his repertoire — and has travelled in Asia. Living in Conamara from 1968 to 1979, he was active in the "Gaeltacht revolution" which changed the nature of the Irish language movement. His journalism, 1969–75, rethinking the nationalist approach to the Northern problem laid the intellectual basis for the peace process of the 1990s. From 1976 to 1982, he taught History and Politics at University College Galway, and from 1982 to 1993, English Writing at the Dublin Institute of Technology. His books and journalism have dealt with contemporary culture and politics, travel, religion, history and literature. Since 1997, Desmond Fennell has lived in Anguillara on Lake Bracciano, near Rome.

For Miriam

Preface

Ten years have passed since I last presented a collection of essays, in *Heresy: The Battle of Ideas in Modern Ireland*. This new collection of my shorter writings is a diary of sorts. Except for my two stays in the US, mainly in Washington state, between April 1994 and the end of January 1996, it reflects fairly well both the course of my life since 1994 and what was happening, around the turn of the millennium, in Ireland and in the West generally. The personal and the broader dimensions of my American sojourns were recorded in the book published after my return to Dublin and now out of print: *Uncertain Dawn: Hiroshima and the Beginning of Postwestern Civilisation*. But the present book is also in the nature of an anthology, which means that my readers are invited to pick and choose as suits their palates. I believe that all of them will find meat to their taste; I have had their palates in mind when selecting the contents.

The opening piece on Graham Knuttel and the long essay, from 1995, on proposals for a federal Ireland, relate back to happy experiences in the 1960s and 1970s respectively — I mean, in the first case, my years as an art critic in Dublin, in the second, my participation in an eruption of thought and debate about better structures of government for Ireland.

Throughout my life, painting has been for me a rich source of contemplation and inspiration. I was lucky to be involved, as a critic, in the last exciting period of this art in Dublin. In great measure, the excitement was due to the contention between three groups with quite different visions of what painting should be: the Royal Hibernian Academy, the Living Art and the Independents. The Living Art, which had developed out of the Paris connection and which now included abstract painting as its vanguard, had won out over the Academy and was riding high. It had a feminine flavour, due to its large number of women members, its decoratively pleasing quality and its appeal to sentiment. The Living Art had also, as compared with the broadly nationalist and nativist quality of the Academy, an Anglo-Irish tinge. The younger painters who formed the Independent Artists were challenging its ascendancy. Aggressively figurative in opposition to the abstractionist element of the Living Art, their work echoed German Expressionism, had a masculine flavour, and a vaguely Dublin-Republican inspiration. While James White championed the Living Art, I batted for the Independents; but my deflating criticism of some Living Art fashionables led the Academy to perceive me as a friend and to invite me to lecture. However, while the contention of the schools was fun, my deepest pleasure came from the comradeship I established with almost the entire Dublin painting community. That was principally because the general tone of my criticism showed the high value I set on the painting art; but it was also because I managed to win a reputation for honesty and fairness that transcended factionalism. I particularly enjoyed the game many artists played of being totally indifferent to what "the critics" said, while in fact rushing to read what I wrote of them in the latest edition of *Hibernia* or the *Evening Press*, and not minding to let me know, one way or another, of their duplicity, and smiling with me at the negative or positive tones I had used.

If the piece on Graham Knuttel is an incidental echo of those years, "Federal Proposals for a Northern Solution" — presented here for the first time to Irish readers — is a deliberate monument to a high period of Irish political thought. I say that with the notes and bibliography especially in mind. The period in question lasted from 1968 to the publication of Tom Barrington's *The Irish Administrative System* in 1980. Its central theme was self-government — within the Republic, in Ireland as a whole, and in the Gaeltacht. Its general aim was to increase the democracy,

representativeness and humaneness of Irish governmental structures. With regard to the Gaeltacht, there was the additional
special aim of enabling it to survive. I have given an account of
this movement of creative thinking and popular education — for
such, in its various strands, it was — in Chapters 3 and 4 of my
Beyond Nationalism (1985). Sufficient to recall here that it was
begun with regard to the Republic by Charles McCarthy and Tom
Barrington; with regard to Northern Ireland by Ronald Bunting
and myself; to all of Ireland by Dáithí Ó Conaill; and with regard
to the Gaeltacht by the twin "revolutionary" movements of the
early 1970s in South Conamara. All these strands came together in
the Athlone conference of June 1973 that launched my *Sketches of
the New Ireland*. The creative circle was symbolically completed in
1974 by the Conamara delegation that went to meet Tom Barrington to discuss a Gaeltacht regional government embracing the
Irish-speaking communities from Gaoth Dobhair to Dún Chaoin.
The movement as a whole constituted the first concerted effort by
Irishmen to devise other structures of government for Ireland
than those imposed by Britain through the centuries and given
their final shape between 1898 and 1920.

In its form, "Federal Proposals" is an academic article written
for an academic journal, as it happened a Canadian one. Because
this required me to give precise references, to add ample notes
and append a relevant bibliography, it serves well the purpose for
which I have included it here. But generally speaking, I am not at
home with the academic article, nor with the academic style of
book, in their conventional Ameranglian form, which applies also
in Ireland. (Much of the writing by academics on the Continent is
done without giving detailed references for every second statement and a compulsory display, by reference, quotation or bibliography, that one is up to date with the latest — or with all! —
publications on the subject.) Even in "Federal Proposals", I con-
travene an unwritten rule of academic writing in English by citing
personal experience and openly drawing on it.

The only other instance in the book of an article written specifically for academic publication in an English-speaking country is
"Irish Studies in the United States", published in the same year,
1995. The three essays on Irish literary topics, beginning with "A
Provincial Passion" in 1997, started out as papers read at literary
festivals in Tralee, Clogher (County Tyrone) and Foxford, respectively. Two of them were subsequently dressed in collar and tie for
American academic journals, but they ended up, relaxed and at
home, in Christopher O'Rourke's literary magazine, *InCognito*, in
Dublin. Whatever I am writing, my aim is always, and uniquely, to
express, in clear language and logical sequence, some new truth or
truths that I have perceived by thinking or learned by experience
and reflection. If, in the course of so doing, I display less than
comprehensive knowledge of the subject, or even make minor
errors of fact, so be it. I have made it my business to know that the
main point I am making is new, and to equip myself with knowledge sufficient to ground and support the truth of it.

Underlying my responses to Irish Studies in the US, and, in
2000, to Irish literary studies in Italy — and almost explicit in the
latter part of "A Provincial Passion" — is surprise that there is
studious foreign interest in the Irish literature of the past half-
century and now. When foreign interest in modern Irish literature
began, with Joyce, Yeats, Synge and O'Casey, it was easily under-
standable. Those writers illuminated the human condition, as did
Beckett, later. My surprise is that foreign studious interest has
continued after our literature — apart from some of the poetry —
has long ceased to do that, or has been doing so only very rarely
and in a minor way. I think this persisting attention is in part due
to an established habit not critically re-examined. But the main
reason is probably the fillip given to interest in things Irish by the
war in the North, the politics connected with it, and the emergence, in this context, of the much publicised "Northern poets".

In 1980, at the First International Conference on Minority
Languages held at the University of Glasgow, I read a paper on

"Can a Shrinking Linguistic Minority Be Saved? Lessons from the Irish Experience". The experience referred to was in part my own in the Conamara Gaeltacht from 1968 to 1979. At the conference I met Sture Ureland, a Swede who was Professor of Linguistics at Mannheim University. In the following years, a friendship developed which led to Sture inviting me to speak at several of the seminars or conferences on linguistics which he organised. That is the background to the essay "The European Dialect of *Lingua Humana*" and the formal paper "A Critical Look at the Charter for Regional and Minority Languages". In both cases, as in two previous instances, Sture had me take part not — obviously — as a professional linguist, but as a professional of language and as one who had special knowledge of the linguistic situation on the Celtic Fringe. My contributions, like those of the other participants, were destined for publication in Germany; but the only conditions imposed on them were that, when they were presented for publication, they should be on a disc in Word and arranged in numbered paragraphs!

"The West's Campaign for Mastery of the World", my lecture last year at the American University of Rome, came about because an Irishwoman, Dr Breda Ennis, was in charge of the Distinguished Lectures series for 2002 and invited me to contribute. In view of the suggestive coincidence of the lecture's title with the lead-up to the American invasion of Iraq, a friend remarked afterwards that I had ventured "into the lions' den". In fact, however, in what I had to say, I was not engaged in moralising, let alone in finger-pointing; I was describing a European historical process of several centuries' duration that was now reaching a culmination in Europe Overseas.[1] Perhaps for that reason, while some metaphorical eyebrows were raised in the subsequent discussion — I had of

---

[1] For this term, referring to areas of European settlement overseas — Europe's *Magna Graecia* — and in particular the USA, see my *The Revision of European History* (Athol Books, 2003), pp. 62, 79.

necessity said things about the United States that diverged from its conventional self-image — the reception was civil and I was taken to a good dinner afterwards in Trastevere.

How could I present a collection of my "recent writings" without including a number of articles published in *The Irish Times*? My association with that paper, in the form of occasional contributions to it, has been on and off continuous since the late 1950s. People who are unaware of this, but who know of the clash between the paper's general line on Irish affairs and my own ideas about Ireland, are sometimes surprised that I figure repeatedly in its pages with articles or letters to the editor. Apart from old association, there are several explanations. In the first place, a substantial ideological clash has existed only since the 1970s. Second, I have testified on more than one occasion how, long before that, Jack White, as features editor and as friend, gave me my *entrée* to Dublin English-language journalism; and I have told how Douglas Gageby, as editor, was for me a contributor's dream. Conor Brady, succeeding him, never left me in doubt of how he valued my contributions. But these happy personal relationships apart, the simple fact of the past thirty years is that *The Irish Times* and I have had use for each other. I find in it the best Irish platform for expressing, occasionally, what I think about this or that. The paper's editors, for their part, have been intelligent enough to know that filling their paper exclusively with articles that toe the party line would bore people. So, both for that reason, and because it shows *The Irish Times* can still be broad-minded in the old Liberal manner, they see benefit in my stylish heretical intrusions — as in limited unorthodox intrusions by some others.

Talking of heresy brings me back to the collection of essays, with that title, which preceded this one. It prompts me to tell my readers what has principally changed in my life since that book was published ten years ago. In the last chapter of *The Turning*

Point,[2] where I discuss the 1990s autobiographically, I omitted to mention this change. I have ceased to be an active social idealist with regard to Ireland or to the world generally. By an "active social idealist", I mean someone who, having a conception of an ideal state of national or human affairs, and believing that it can be achieved in the foreseeable future, works for that. Nine years or so ago, I ceased to believe that the ideal I envisaged could be achieved in the foreseeable future, and consequently ceased to work for it.

I had first presented my ideal in a comprehensive, programmatic form in *Beyond Nationalism*, in 1985. That book brought together the hopes I had been entertaining and developing since the 1960s. The completion of the Irish Revolution is obviously a central value for the writer, and he is still clearly hoping that this will occur in the foreseeable future, in an Ireland that is intellectually self-determining, culturally self-shaping, economically self-sustaining, and democratically self-governing in all its parts — an Irish "community of communities". He believes, too, clearly, that there can be a "Europe of Regions" and movement towards a "world community of communities". Much the same themes appear, three years later, in my contribution to Richard Kearney's *Beyond the Frontiers*. Then, in the last chapter of *Heresy*, they are listed as "values" I had been working for since the 1960s and I mention several other Irish thinkers as companions in what I define as "national thought". By that I meant thought centred on the welfare of Ireland as a nation and, as an adjunct, on the restructuring of the surrounding world in a manner favourable to that welfare.

Rereading those pages now, I see that I had already lost belief in the possibility of my ideal being realised in the foreseeable future. I see this in the tone of dying fall, in the recognition that

---

[2] *The Turning Point: My Sweden Year and After*, Dublin, Sanas Press, 2001 (distributed by Veritas).

national thinking is blocked from effectiveness by the anti-national ideology that had come to ascendancy in Dublin, and, finally, in my exhortation that we "national thinkers" continue, nevertheless, to form a thinking and communicating underground. But if it is evident that my belief in ideal possibility had already crumbled then — in 1993 — my full realisation of this was delayed until my American sojourns of 1994–96. In the new vision of the contemporary reality that these gave me, I saw and accepted as fact that, throughout the entire West, movement towards the ideal was barred by the deadening reality of the consumerist empire.

As I write this, I am aware of a strange thing. I realise that the decline of my active social idealism with regard to Ireland and to the world coincided with the end of serious faith in the ideals that Communism stood for, but in practice had betrayed. (I have recorded in *Dreams of Oranges* how, in Communist East Germany in 1990, I witnessed the sad acceptance by surviving believers that those ideals, which they had made their own, had no practical future.) More strikingly still, my loss of belief in ideal possibility coincided with the generally disheartening effect of that Communist despair. I mean the simultaneous dissolution throughout the West of any serious intellectual and political challenge[3] to the liberal consumerist system that had been ordained by American power and was being upheld by it. This system had been declaring itself, throughout the West and in Ireland, to be in fact the ideal life finally realised: the goal and end of western history, the goal, indeed, of all history. Thenceforth, to its detriment, it could proclaim that without being contested from within or without by any persuasive alternative vision.

---

[3] The Green movement has not managed to constitute such a challenge, partly because it has not appealed to a need widely felt by the consumers, partly because its programme has proved in great part assimilable by the liberal consumerist system.

As I said, the coincidence of my own loss of belief with the general one is strange. I have traced above how, in my own case, it had a local and personal causation. But at the same time, it was part of a general phenomenon that had a causation of its own. Once again, it appears, as in 1968, in my move with wife and children from a big city to a cultural-ethnic periphery — in our case, Gaelic-speaking Conamara — I was caught up in the *Zeitgeist* and obeying it. Obviously, moreover, my belief in an ideal possibility for my own country and for the world that would transcend the present order of things was an occurrence in me of the general belief in "unlimited possibility" that characterised those famous Sixties. The *Zeitgeist* gave that belief its term, and then, as the 1980s moved towards their end, decreed another kind of mindset which affected, along with millions of minds, my own. Doubtless, underlying what I call the *Zeitgeist* and its shifts, there is another, more concrete historical causation and dictation. But even if there is, the question that these experiences raise regarding the reality of my personal existence and freedom is, to say the least, disturbing.

Be that as it may — what more can I say? — the end of my active social idealism did not leave me destitute or sad. I found a new fulfilment in my new perception, truer than my previous perception, of how things are in the world and consequently in Ireland. And if it is true that my active social idealism has ended, it is not the case — it now occurs to me — that I have ceased entirely to be an active idealist. I have found myself ever more animated by that residual idealism which I express at the very end of *Heresy*. It can be found implicit in this new collection in "Anglo-American Ireland Is Becoming Culturally Invisible" and "The Irish Problem with Thought". No longer directed towards the general or social, it limits its hope to the personal and individual, and to the faculties of observation, perception and free thought which every Irish man and woman possesses.

For the record and for those who might be interested, some of the pieces which I include in this book, and which were previously published in an American academic journal or in *The Irish Times* were slightly altered — or in the latter case slightly cut — on the printed page. Generally speaking, I have given them here in their original form, and when a title was altered — as regularly occurs in a newspaper — I have used my original title. I say "generally speaking", for if I found at the distance of some years that a text, no matter where published, contained an unclear or infelicitous phrase or sentence, I have not hesitated to amend it. My priority has been to present clearly to the reader, in each instance, what I was meaning to say at the time.

I have mentioned Christopher O'Rourke and his *InCognito* magazine. I mention him here again, along with the *Irish Political Review*, in order to thank both of them for the facilitating hospitality of their pages. I also thank my daughter Kate for the research she did regarding dates of previous publication where I had not recorded these. Finally, my thanks to Brian Langan of The Liffey Press for his attentive and sensitive editing.

Desmond Fennell
Anguillara
August 2003

Essays and Objections
1994–2003

Images that Hold and Scare Us

From New Works by Knuttel, *a catalogue of the Duke Gallery, Dublin, 1994*

Since 1987, when he became a workaholic instead of an alcoholic, Graham Knuttel's paintings have been astounding Dublin and winning an international clientele from Hollywood to
Milan. Born in Dublin in 1954, Knuttel takes his name from a
German grandfather and a father who lived in England and
served in the RAF. The father occasionally figures in the son's
paintings as a red-uniformed "military man". Sometimes, too,
Graham's own angular shape appears, or his daughter or wife —
his wife usually in conjunction with Mr Punch, the artist's alter
ego. "I can discern my mood," he says, "by painting Punch and
finding out how he feels on that day."

In Knuttel's work, drawing and colours are combined with
images of persons or things, not in order to render the visible
world as we see it, but to provide pleasure and entertainment by
playing with it. Perspective and the actual look of things are
disregarded. If a town is to be shown "in the background", it is
shown at the top of the picture, without receding effect, and by an
image of buildings which is more like a stage-set than buildings as
they actually appear. In the still-lifes, as in the peopled paintings,
images "stand for" things, rather than simulate them. The image
of an empty bottle with a label reading "Dark Black Rum" or "Vin
Rouge" is simply information — with whatever implications we
wish to draw from it — that such a bottle is standing on the table.
The fish that are a frequent theme are stylised fish, more alive in
their quirky way than real fish. (In all this there is something of
the "alienation effect" of Brechtian theatre: actors acting their
parts simply as presenters of the characters and the story — not

pretending that they are the characters.) Colours are used expressionistically; chosen not because that press or wall or face might actually be that colour, but because that colour, placed there, pleases, helps to give the picture harmony and mood, and occasionally points to a detail of the story.

The deepest pleasure that Knuttel's paintings give the viewer is that of being fascinated and held, and this effect, not surprisingly, comes mainly from the underlying element — the drawing. The present writer is reminded of what a contemplative Catholic priest said to him in an open-air market in India, when we were suddenly faced by an image of a Hindu god, a face gazing weirdly, semi-humanly, from an animal form: "The distortion is a device to induce contemplation." In the bustle of the market-place, the grotesque, staring face stopped and held us, thereby producing in the commotion of our thoughts and feelings a pleasurable pause, a concentrated emptiness. Knuttel's paintings do this, not only by the overall design but also, particularly, by the mutually cancelling directions of lines and movements within it — the direction of pointing noses cancelled by the lines of gaze, the direction of arms contradicting that of bodies, a group of wilful birds or fish displaying contested forward movement. These are devices of tense stasis commanding stillness in the viewer.

In the paintings with human figures, the dramatic cross purposes of line are usually intensified by suggested, emotional cross purposes in the persons represented. To begin with, they are men and women in a general state of being at odds, either with life itself or with respectable, conventional life. A look or a posture conveys unease and solitariness; arms reach self-protectively across chests. Often, in addition, the ambience and dress, the hairdos and demeanour are those of low-life, so that the group as a whole conveys social and emotional alienation. But as if a state of being fundamentally "at variance" were not enough, these alienated individuals are presented to us in moments of acute social disjunction and tension; moments when something sharply separating has happened, and something malign may be about to happen. No face looks directly at another face, eyes brood or squint warily, lips purse or curl, chins jut. Visible emotion and other tell-tale signs point backwards or forwards to violent words, or threaten violent action. Here what is being rendered pictorially is, in the first instance, a psychological moment. No doubt but that Knuttel's men and women have souls, intense souls, and that these are his chief interest in them. And the depicted psychical moment fascinates us because something we fear deeply pulses in it. Not "evil" vaguely, but that particular, most fundamental evil, that worst thing for humans: the morbid opposite of social at-oneness, by whatever name we call it.

Yet, as we shudder at this sight of lowering disharmony or repressed, interpersonal malice, we also smile because we see that it is not for real, that the painter and his actors, Mr Punch and his puppets, are doing this to scare us! In short, it is entertainment; and as we take in the visual delight of the harmonious, gleaming colours we may suspect that it was for the sake of these — so that we might contemplate them and be filled by them — that we were held, fascinated and emptied. Graham Knuttel says: "My main interest is in colours and the differing relationships between them. I work intuitively, but I have noticed certain external rhythms I am influenced by, such as the changing seasons. Earth colours I find I use to the best during the autumn months, the colours of nature — red oranges, browns. Winter comes in colder, bleaker. I find my research goes to reds, black, dark blue. And so on through the seasons. As each year goes on, my research and observation of colours develops."

If I have dwelt on Knuttel's images of individual alienation and social discord, that is because these are his most typical vehicles for exerting fascination and delivering harmonious colour. But images of discord are not his only vehicle, and it is interesting watching for the Knuttel who allows the at-oneness of his pictorial compositions to carry over into his subjects. This is the Knuttel of the still-lifes, of some bird and fish paintings, female nudes, and occasional images of two human figures. In the still-lifes, line, colour and reflected light issue calm declarations. A female nude is at one with herself or, playfully, with nature — as a sky-sun is reflected in a breast-sun, two peaks outside a window correspond with buttocks prone within, or the curve of a hill reflects a bottom-curve. Or again, a man and woman experience a moment of fragile togetherness, timorously, surprised.

Of course, much — perhaps most — of what we see in Knuttel's paintings, as we peer into them and think about them, has come to be there simply through the artist's instinctual pursuit of the good finished work, rather than by conscious intent. He says: "I try not to concern myself overly with intellectual reasoning or planning. As a hard-working painter, my concerns are mainly technical, practical and immediate. My concern is to paint the picture first and think about it afterwards. That way I can progress in a proper manner. Above all I try to speak with my own voice and see with my own eyes."

1995

Irish Studies in the United States

Éire-Ireland *(St Paul, Minnesota), Spring 1995*

I want to offer some thoughts about the condition of Irish Studies in the United States based on my attendance at the last national meeting of the American Conference for Irish Studies (ACIS) in Omaha, Nebraska, and an examination of the programme for the three previous national meetings. My perspective is that of an Irishman living in Ireland who, prior to the Omaha conference, had no direct experience of Irish Studies in the United States. Well aware of the limited basis for my comments, I offer them in the hope that they may nevertheless be of some interest to the Irish Studies community in North America.

As far as I know, Ireland is the only European country to enjoy the favour in American academe of having a widespread, inter-disciplinary course of studies devoted to its life and culture. This surprises me, and makes me, as an Irishman, feel privileged. Its uniqueness apart, however, the existence of Irish Studies in the United States affords an Irishman who attends one of its conferences the pleasure of meeting people who value his homeland, and who have applied their minds to aspects of its life and culture. That pleasure, mingled with the sense of privilege I have alluded to, was my first reaction to the Omaha conference.

My second was surprise that the three-day conference was so heavily weighted towards literature. By my count, leaving Irish-American topics aside, sixty-three of the ninety-one papers on Irish topics concerned Irish literature — more specifically, apart from three papers, Irish literature in English. I had understood that, Irish-American studies apart, the intended theme of Irish Studies was Irish life and culture. I had been told that the

founders of ACIS had managed to carry this through at national
conferences by having plenary sessions at which everyone, whatever their subject, heard lectures on various aspects of Ireland
past and present. True, I had also heard that in practice, in American colleges, an Irish Studies course generally entailed literature,
history, and perhaps some "other matters"; and I had gathered
that the sheer number of papers submitted and accepted had
made the original interdisciplinary sharing at national conferences
largely impractical. But I was not prepared for the heavy preponderance of literary studies that I found in Omaha.

Later I was to discover that the number of literary studies was
unusually great. Even so, this preponderance did raise the question, which nothing I subsequently discovered silenced, whether,
things being as they are, Irish Studies might acquire a more
coherent structure and purpose from a differently defining title,
say, "Irish (or English Irish)[1] Literature in Context". Then the
other matters studied, including history and contemporary
events, might be specifically organised to supply social context to
the literary studies. That the literature needs such context, and
interpretation relating to it, goes without saying, and American
literary specialists try to supply both. But to acquire the requisite
knowledge, they must study Irish life and culture — engage in the
relevant "Irish studies". And as things stand, the question again
arises: does Irish Studies at college or at conference level provide
for this?

At Omaha, this question was acutely raised for me with regard
to the contemporary period 1960–1994. I asked myself whether
this Irish Studies conference, in which literature predominated,
was displaying real knowledge of Irish life and culture during

---

[1] Sharing the growing unhappiness with the term "Anglo-Irish" to describe Irish
literature in English, I had opted for a solution on the lines of French Canadian,
German Swiss, Swedish Finnish, etc.; namely, "English Irish", accompanied by
"Gaelic Irish" to describe the other current.

that period — which, willy-nilly, I knew at first hand. Through the medium of a few American individuals and papers it was; but my impression was that generally it was not.

I leave aside two broadly informative, plenary lectures by Irish visitors. The conference delivered statements about Ireland in the period since 1960 in four forms: through ten papers on non-literary topics, thirty-seven literary papers (out of the total of sixty-three), question-and-answer sessions and informal conversation. Of the ten papers that directly tackled contemporary Ireland, four concerned politics, two social matters. There was nothing on religious affairs; on the Irish economy, except a paper on publishing; the non-literary arts, apart from two papers on film; constitutional and legal matters; or ideas and ideology in Ireland, apart from a paper on historiography. The five papers I heard were well-informed.

Thirty-six of the thirty-seven literary papers were directed to imaginative literature — that is to say, to fictions: poetry, prose fiction, drama, in that order. Their statements about contemporary Ireland occurred when their authors dealt with matters of social reference and context, or used a text to make some point about Irish society. In most of the papers I heard or read, many of these statements were a little or considerably out of touch with contemporary Irish reality. The reason seemed to be that the literary specialists were relying for information about contemporary Ireland, not on adequate study of it, but rather on the literary text combined with representations culled from other Irish literary texts, from works of literary criticism or literature lectures, or from the mass media and hearsay. Moreover, some statements in question-and-answer sessions and in conversation, from people of various background and speciality, gave me the same impression. Together, the preponderance of papers on imaginative literature, and the statements about Ireland based on literary or other inadequate references, had the following, fascinating effect: I felt that much of the talk about contemporary Ireland in those three days was more about representations of my country than about its actuality.

My curiosity aroused by the Omaha meeting, I obtained and examined the programmes for the three previous national conferences. All in all, and including the papers concerning the Irish overseas, the picture presented by the four conference programmes was of an island producing literature, history and emigrants. By my reckoning, there were 408 papers on topics from Ireland, and of these, 240 were on literature or language, including 9 on Gaelic literature and 4 on the Gaelic language. That made the four-year percentage for literature and language 58.7, as against 69.5 for Omaha. The topics were poetry 88, prose fiction 77, drama 41, non-fiction 20, general 9, language 5. Of the 235 *literary* papers, 209 focused on the literature of the last hundred years.

History before 1960 was covered by 118 papers divided thematically as follows: political and social, including economic, 71; secular culture 34; church and religious matters 13. On intellectual history there was next to nothing. More than half the papers, 68, dealt with the period 1800–1922; there were 21 on eighteenth-century matters and 11 on history before 1500.

My classification was rough and ready. Some subjects were difficult to put in a slot. In the small minority of instances where a paper linked two different kinds of subject or two different periods, I classified now in one direction, now in another, letting the contradictions cancel out. My aim was simply to get a roughly accurate picture. Frequently I was fascinated by a title and wanted to get my hands on the paper. When I noticed three papers on Irish Studies curricula in American colleges — models for, versions of — and reflected that I had not read them or heard them discussed, and how little I knew, the foolhardiness of my intention to make the comments I am making struck me forcibly. Occasionally I was impressed by the benefit of having outsiders look at Irish matters: some papers came up with topics, or angles on topics, I had never encountered in Irish research. I regretted that, at least in the programmes I was examining, this outsider view had been used to make various, enlightening comparisons between Ireland and comparable countries — other small European nations or post-colonial countries in Africa or Asia. I came on a few literal reinforcements of my Omaha impression that, for the contemporary period, Irish Studies in the United States tends to focus on representations rather than reality. For example, in 1991, there were papers on "Images of Republicanism in Selected Contemporary Irish Novels" and on "Representing the IRA", but in all four programmes there was no mention of a paper on the IRA or on contemporary Irish republicanism, and I wondered when there last had been.

The contemporary period, dating from 1960, was covered by 176 papers in all and shows some interesting results. The topics divide as follows: literature and language 126, other arts 5, politics 14, church and religion 0, other social and cultural topics 24, ideas and ideology 3, constitutional or legal matters 0. The five "other arts" papers were about film. Other visual arts, music and the like, do not appear. Eleven of the fourteen "politics" papers concerned Northern Ireland, two the Republic's foreign policy. The internal politics of most of the country — one paper — hardly figure. The absence of any interest in church and religious affairs is remarkable and corresponds to their low showing in the historical studies. The coverage of ideas and ideology relates only to the controversy surrounding "historical revisionism". The low interest in ideas reflects the virtual absence of intellectual history from the historical studies.[2] (I was surprised to notice during my visit to the United States that the arrangements for the 1994 ACIS award for "best Irish Studies book" grouped "history of ideas" with literary criticism rather than history, in a section to be judged by

---

[2] In relation to this evident assumption that Irish intellectual history does not exist, see "The Irish Problem with Thought", pp. 222–31.

literary scholars, not historians or philosophers — as if ideas, exclaimed Old Europe within me, were a matter of literary aesthetics!) All in all, taking account of the meagre rating for economics, the spiritual and material forces which shape Irish life come a very distant second to intermediate phenomena: literature, language, miscellaneous social and cultural themes.

It is also instructive to review the topics of conference papers covering the period from 1922 to the present. For these years since Irish independence, we find a very big disproportion between literary and non-literary topics. The period 1922–60 adds 41 papers on literature and a mere 8 on history (5 political/social, 2 church/ religious) to the "contemporary" papers analysed above. Thus, at the four conferences under examination, papers on the period 1922–1994 were concerned with: literature and language 167, or 75 per cent; other topics 58, or 25 per cent. That figure for "other topics" represents a thin input, proportionally, on Irish life and culture, generally, during most of the twentieth century. But it was also a random input, not shaped by any guidance as to its function, and that brings me back to the suggestion I made earlier.

It may well be that the four conference programmes I have examined give a distorted view of Irish Studies in the United States. My American readers will know, and judge accordingly. But on the evidence just cited, and taking what it tells about Irish Studies as fairly representative, there would certainly seem to be a case for organising at least twentieth-century Irish Studies under the rubric "Irish Literature in Its Social Context" — "social context" being understood to include the full spectrum of twentieth-century Irish life and culture. This would mean that people doing twentieth-century Irish Studies, and therefore in the great bulk of cases, twentieth-century English Irish literature, also take a general, well-planned course in the Irish life and culture of this century.

My analysis of the subject-matter of four major Irish Studies conferences makes it not surprising that at Omaha I sensed a considerable out-of-touchness with contemporary Ireland. Basically, this had to do with certain essentialist conceptions of Ireland and things Irish which got embedded many years ago in Irish Studies circles. Either such conceptions were persisting intact as images of contemporary Ireland, or they had not been adequately replaced by fresh study of Ireland since the 1960s, or there was a bit of both. I am talking about notions, for example, of rurality, poverty, Irish nationalism, the church, the Irish family, the West of Ireland, sexual and drinking practices, the principal cultural forces, the Irish character, the Irish diaspora, the relation of Irish writers to their society. These old conceptions in their time were partly true, partly illusory. To some extent, they did not even originate from Irish life directly, but again, from fictive literature of one kind or another and writing that fed on it. But all of them, true or untrue, have been cherished, and have resisted change and replacement, because they belong to the foundational period — in the first half of this century — both of modern Irish cultural and political independence and of Irish Studies as we understand the term. So, they have persisted long after they were utterly, even glaringly invalid — and persisted not only in Irish Studies, or only in the United States. In Ireland, at least until some years ago, they could turn up in the most unexpected ways.

In the 1970s, when I was living in Gaelic-speaking South Connemara, my seven-year-old daughter showed me a landscape painting she had done in the local school. The landscape was typically Connemara. Noticing that the houses in it were thatched, and knowing that all of the forty houses we could see from ours had slated or tiled roofs, I asked her in Irish, "Why are the houses thatched?" "Because it's Connemara," she said. "That's how you do Connemara." But that is not to say that there are now no thatched roofs in Ireland; it is rather that, for a variety of reasons, they have almost disappeared in Connemara, their overall number has declined, and their geographical distribution has changed. Living in Ireland, it is fairly easy for one to know both those three facts and the reasons for them. However, for an American student of Irish literature, or of any branch of Irish Studies, it is not easy; it requires a deliberate act of learning. Even visits to Ireland, if they are mainly spent in libraries studying literary or historical texts, do not suffice. In short, with regard to any aspect of contemporary Irish life one can think of, the out-of-touchness I noticed in Omaha — and which I am sure extends beyond that gathering — was, *mutatis mutandis*, a matter of people believing that Connemara houses are thatched, or of their not being accurately informed about or understanding the new thatched-roof situation.

Perhaps the central foundational concept in Irish Studies was the uniqueness of Ireland in almost any respect one could think of. In Ireland for many years now, intellectuals have been in reaction against this and have been at pains to understand Ireland, comparatively, in various international contexts. The result has been to demolish many notions of the nation's uniqueness, to retain some critically, and to discover a few well-founded singularities which previously had not been noticed. But the underlying attitude has been one of critical scepticism toward the many supposed uniquenesses of the foundational period. It is my impression that this intellectual procedure, either the scepticism or the kind of analysis that follows from it, has not yet been adopted to the same extent in Irish Studies in the United States. By way of illustration, I will relate an anecdote from Omaha; it exemplifies not only this particular point, but also the more general misapplication of pre-1960s models to contemporary Ireland which I adverted to above.

A woman who works in the human sciences was telling me that Irish life revolved around family and community. Habituated to the scepticism I have mentioned, I said, "You think the family is more important to Irish people than to, say, Italian-Americans or Americans generally?" I was also thinking of "the family" in France or Spain, but kept my question relevant to what I assumed might be the woman's immediate experience. At the same time, my mind was racing sceptically towards "community", but I was brought up short by her response that "It is all in Arensberg and Kimball". My speechlessness was rendered irrelevant by the brief conversation ending — she had to leave. But I pondered for a while on that classic work she had mentioned, which studied rural — and, in a second edition, also town — society in County Clare in the early 1930s, and on the fact that she regarded it as an all-time picture of "family and community in Ireland", while for me it was a fine work in localised social archaeology. For good measure, let me add that, if my mind had got around to coping with the value set on "community" in Ireland, I would have thought, among other things, of the community of 670 people in Washington state where I had just spent five weeks, and which had so impressed me with its town council, and the "town ordinances" displayed on the main street. Led, intellectually, by Tom Barrington, I and others had struggled for years to have communities in Ireland accorded such dignity. All of which, of course, is not to say that family and community are of no account in contemporary Ireland!

A considerable number of the papers at Omaha — in most instances, literary papers — had a feminist slant in title and content. Without adverting to them particularly, let me just say that in American feminist studies relating to contemporary Ireland, out-of-touchness, when it occurs, arises not only from applying faulty archetypes or failing to replace them adequately; it arises also from American feminist ideology. Everyone knows that there is an American debate about that ideology's in-touchness or otherwise with respect to American women, or to women *tout court*. Leaving that aside, it must be obvious that American feminist studies in an Irish context will be seriously deficient in reality if they imagine that the condition of Irish women with regard to ideologically defined "women's issues" is tantamount to the condition of women in contemporary Ireland.

*

To identify obstacles to true perception is to be empowered to cope with them, and I hope that my pointing out such obstacles in the way of Irish Studies students will be found to be of such use. Let me conclude by mentioning an impediment which impinges unequally on both our countries, hindering mutual perception in contrasting ways. I refer to the media of mass communication, ranging from newspapers, magazines and radio to film, television, and, at the end of the line, books. Because of the great volume and variety of such representations of the United States that impinge on Ireland — authored mainly by Americans, but by some Irish people too — Irish students of things American can easily make mistakes. Faced with the great array of differing messages, they are likely to be unable to discriminate consistently between truth, half-truth and falsity, and to fall victim to some misperceptions of American life. For Irish Studies students in North America the corresponding situation is rather different. Because the number of representations relating to Ireland is small, misperceptions arising from quantity and variety can hardly occur, and it is the paucity, rather, of representations that gives rise to misapprehensions. It does this when a particular, forceful representation of Irish affairs is misleading and there arises nothing effectively to contradict it, or when a partial representation of Irish reality is, because of its rarity, overvalued and taken to represent more about Ireland than it does.

An instance of the first kind has been the reporting of the conflict in Northern Ireland by the mainstream media of the United States. Because this generally toed the line put out by the British, it gave rise to widespread misperceptions of the conflict among Americans, including some students of Irish affairs. An instance of taking a partial representation of things Irish to represent more than it does would occur if an ACIS member happened to imagine that the *Irish Literary Supplement* is more than a good review of Irish literature and took it, for example, to be a reliable guide to Ireland in modern times.

Something like this did happen with regard to *Whoredom in Kimmage,* by Rosemary Mahoney, which was published during my sojourn in the United States. What the book was marketed as, and consequently to some extent received as, was considerably more than, and different from, what the book actually is. *Whoredom in Kimmage* is an observant, if idiosyncratic travel essay set in the Irish social equivalents of Greenwich Village and La Conner, Washington (minus town council and ordinances). The book does not, as far as I can see, purport to be more than that. But it was marketed, and treated in the American media, as a major revelation or exposé of the condition of Irish women, of religion in Ireland, and the like. I hoped, vainly I'm sure, that this misrepresentation would not make readers of the book determined to find in it what was, in fact, not there![3]

---

[3] See, for comparison, "Irish Literary Studies in Italy" pp. 160–7.

Federal Proposals for a Northern Solution

Abbreviated from "Solutions to the Northern Ireland Problem: A Federal Ireland and Other Approaches" in The Canadian Journal of Irish Studies, *Vol. 21, No. 1, 1995. Because Canada is a federation, the Canadian editors were principally interested in federal proposals for a Northern solution. There was then no comprehensive account of this matter and, as far as I am aware, there is still none apart from this essay. Given the length of the notes to this essay, they are placed at the end of the essay (pp. 51–53) rather than as footnotes, as elsewhere in the book.*

Between 1969 and 1972, by a devious route, I came to the conviction that a federally united Ireland, along the lines proposed by Sinn Féin, would be the best solution for the Northern problem. By "best" I mean ideal. It would constitute full political justice for the peoples of Ireland and give the country the most democratic and efficient form of government it could practicably have. Until 1971–2, when Sinn Féin published and developed its proposals, the federal option had not been seriously suggested or discussed either as a solution for the Northern problem or in any other context. Eight years later, in 1979, a second federal scheme was published by Fine Gael, and much the same scheme was presented in abbreviated form as one of the options offered at the end of the *New Ireland Forum Report* (1984). I will discuss both these proposals. First, however, that "devious route" mentioned above.

In the decades after independence Irish nationalism identified two wrongs relating to Northern Ireland: the "unnatural" and anti-democratic partition of Ireland and the oppressive discrimination against Irish nationalists in the Six Counties. Its formula for righting these wrongs was a "united Ireland"; shorthand for a reunited independent Ireland which, though the shape of it was little discussed, was generally taken to mean an all-Ireland unitary state with a devolved government for Northern Ireland. Like other Irish nationalists at the time — about three-quarters of the inhabitants of Ireland — I accepted this view of the matter, unreflectively, as true and reasonable. But when, during the escalating conflict in the North from 1969 onwards, "peace with justice" became a cogent slogan, and nationalist leaders stated that only a united Ireland would ensure this, I sensed, and ultimately perceived, a flaw.

According to the nationalist reasoning, the war was being caused by the two abovementioned wrongs, and only a united Ireland, by removing them could bring justice and with it peace. But for my part, observing the Northern nationalist revolt and listening to the people involved in it, I realised that the oppression and wrong which they *felt* was not, primarily, either of those wrongs. It was, rather, another wrong, which was sensed more deeply and existentially. They felt and knew that they were Irish people — in the same sense exactly as the Irish of Wexford, Dublin and Kerry — and that this reality, their national and personal identity, was being denied and insulted daily by a British and Protestant system which was hostile to it. By the same token, what they were primarily struggling for, and what some of them willingly risked their bodily integrity, liberty and lives for, was the removal of that alien imposition and negation, and the recognition, with respect and honour, of who they were, so that they could live their lives freely and with dignity. That was their real demand.

When their leaders translated it into a demand for a united Ireland, they were of course, up to a point, representing it truly, inasmuch as an (independent) united Ireland — unitary or federal — would indeed mean the recognition of the national identity of the Six-County Irish. More: if it were a united Ireland which gave due recognition to the Britishness of the unionists, it would undoubtedly be the most just way of recognising their national identity. The Irish, living as they do throughout their entire ancestral territory, and forming as they do the great majority of its inhabitants, have a clear right to live in political union and independence. This is the paramount national or ethnic right in Ireland, and the Northern nationalists, the Six-County Irish, share in it. Within this context, the substantial Ulster British community, forming a local majority in a region of the island, have a subordinate right to recognition and self-determination. Full justice requires that both these rights be respected in political practice. However — and this was the decisive perception — while a united Ireland which recognised the Ulster British was the fully just way of recognising the national identity of the Six-County Irish, this recognition could also be given by constitutional and political structures which, though falling short of full justice, would be sufficiently just to bring peace. So the slogan "peace with justice" implicitly posed the question, "How much of the latter to achieve the former?" and the answer was "A reasonable amount, sufficient to provide dignity and a reasonably free life". Peace, after all, meant simply no warfare. Full justice could still be struggled for, and would be; but because it would then represent the difference, not between none and all, but between a reasonable amount and all, it would seem, to the great majority of those who now felt wronged, not worth dying or killing for, and would therefore be struggled for by ordinary political means.[1]

Applying the Peace Formula

It followed from the above that the formula for peace was, in general terms: *A symbolic, political, and administrative structure which recognises, to a sufficiently just degree, the Six-County Irish ("the Irish nation in Ulster") and the Ulster British.*[2] To that must be added the gloss that recognising a community means calling it by its proper name, and, in political terms, "letting it be", that is, guaranteeing it a secure autonomy.

The most pragmatic way of implementing that was through a British–Irish condominium (joint sovereignty) of Northern Ireland, in which the territory would be self-governing under London–Dublin supervision and have a constitution recognising its two communities by their ethnic names. Other potentially "sufficient" structures were the ethnic cantonisation of Northern Ireland within the United Kingdom, or an independent Northern Ireland with an appropriate constitution. A united Ireland, having due regard for the Ulster British, became in this context a "more-than-sufficient" structure, aimed at by nationalists whose priority was not peace simply, but "full justice and therefore a peace ending the national struggle once and for all". Combinations of nurture, temperament, location and class would decide whether any given Irish nationalist would pursue the sufficient, or the more-than-sufficient, version of the peace formula — or both simultaneously. In the end, of course, only the British government, supported by the Irish government, would decide whether any of the solutions mentioned would be implemented; and the fact is that more than twenty years of lethal conflict have passed without the British government sponsoring, or opening the way for, any of them.

At the start, in 1969, I advocated the cantonisation of the North into predominately nationalist or unionist districts with considerable powers, and got support, in all of Ireland, only from Ian Paisley's adjutant Major Ronald Bunting, a few days before he resigned. In 1971, I began, in the *Sunday Press* and elsewhere, to campaign for condominium and, a year later, the Social Democratic and Labour Party (SDLP) adopted "joint sovereignty" as policy. During the same period Provisional Sinn Féin proposed and developed its scheme of a four-province federal Ireland based on strong district government. It seemed to me that a scheme on those lines — I would want some minor modifications of the Sinn Féin plan — would be, for more reasons than one, the ideal solution for the Northern problem; more than sufficient for peace, of course, but of great benefit to all the inhabitants of Ireland.

Its merits lay not only in what it offered to the Six-County Irish and the Ulster British, but also in the fact that it would replace the over-centralised system of government in the Republic — the most centralised in Europe if not the world — with a multi-centred, far more democratic system that would serve the citizens better. No other proposed "Northern solution" offered change in the Republic's governmental system. For this combination of reasons I collaborated with Sinn Féin in the drafting of explanatory texts, particularly for the province of Connacht, where I was then living, and I published maps illustrating the proposed arrangements.[3] At the same time I was aware that there was only a tenuous possibility of a united Ireland of any kind being implemented in the short term, and almost no chance, if it were implemented, of this radical federal version being adopted. Consequently, the enterprise was more a matter of political education — of conveying to nationalist Ireland, and in some measure perhaps to unionist Ireland, that they *could*, if they so decided and Britain withdrew, organise the country in this highly desirable manner. There was also, however, a hope, call it no more, that the project might seize imaginations and galvanise desires to the point of creating the political will to realise it.

Misunderstandings of Federalism

Two misunderstandings must be weathered and dealt with in proposing a "federal" Ireland in nationalist Ireland. The first is the belief in some circles that a federal Ireland is not a united Ireland, but something else. This usually arises because "united" is conventionally taken to mean unitary. Consequently, when one is talking about a federal Ireland, it is often necessary to point out that the country can be united through a unitary or a federal state; that federally organised countries such as Germany, Switzerland, the USA and Canada are "united" countries; and that one is talking about and proposing, therefore, a *federally united* Ireland.

However, there are also people who believe that by a "federal" Ireland one means an Ireland with a devolved regional government in the North. This confusion has often occurred in relation to the suggestion, made on several occasions by de Valera, that a suitable arrangement for Irish unity would be to transfer to Dublin the powers with regard to the Northern Ireland Parliament which were vested in Westminster. Although it has occurred to no one, to my knowledge, to describe the United Kingdom of Great Britain and Northern Ireland as a "federation", this proposed transfer of Westminster's powers to Dublin is referred to, even in some reputable books, as a "federal" proposal. The confusion here derives from an overspill into Ireland of an erroneous British usage of the term *federal* which goes back to the 1870s. When Isaac Butt proposed Home-Rule-all-round (i.e. devolved parliaments for Ireland, Scotland and Wales), somebody called it "federal devolution". Because federation was a political system which the English knew little about, the misnomer stuck, the "devolution" part of it was ultimately dropped, and British politicians right through the twentieth century could be heard referring to Scottish or Welsh devolution as "federal".[4]

Prerequisites of a Federal Ireland

Obviously a federal Ireland would be possible only if Britain announced its intention of withdrawing from Ulster by a given date, and the political leaders of the Ulster British showed willingness to negotiate an all-Ireland state. Assuming, for the sake of argument, that both those conditions were met, an Irish federation would have several intrinsic prerequisites.

Firstly, like any federation it would need to be a *viable federal construct*. Since federations with two or three units have proved unstable and transitory, it would need to contain at least four units. None of the units should be of such a size or weight as to be actually or potentially dominant. Ideally they should correspond to historical social entities; failing that, they should be capable of becoming coherent social entities which would attract the adherence of their populations.

Secondly, in view of the fact that the Ulster British have long been opposed to participation in an independent Irish state, the federation must include a Northern unit with the maximum feasible powers, which would contain all of the Ulster British and in which they would form the majority. On this point, and on its consequences for the Six-County Irish, some explanatory comment is called for.

The inherited antagonism of the Ulster British to political association with an independent Ireland arises partly from their sense of ethnic (including religious) difference, but more perhaps from their feeling of insecurity as a colonial minority in Ireland, and their fear that within an all-Ireland political structure they would be swamped and dominated, and prevented from maintaining their distinct ethos and heritage. But they neither have nor feel security in their present situation. They feel insecure with regard to the Republic and its "irredentist" claims, and, within Northern Ireland itself, with regard to the substantial Irish nationalist minority. They also feel insecure *vis-à-vis* London. They have seen their devolved regional parliament, based on a Westminster Act of Parliament, suspended by London in 1972. Since then they have been increasingly in doubt about Britain's intentions towards them. Their cultural links with Britain are more with Scotland than with England, and they are keenly aware that most British people have little regard for them.

A federal Ireland containing a unit with the maximum feasible powers, which would include all of the Ulster British and in which they would form the majority, would go some distance towards alleviating these insecure and alienated feelings. In addition to the security provided by the constitutionally guaranteed provincial government, they would have the security deriving from participation in the federal government on the basis of a constitution agreed by them. Granted that this would entail political inclusion in an independent Ireland, it would offer the freest possible form of such inclusion: a form in which the Ulster British ethos and heritage would be constitutionally protected and the impingement of the rest of Ireland strictly limited. As a "compensation", moreover, for such inclusion, there would be a permanent end to nationalist rebellion in Ulster, and consequently to the violence against themselves, and the economic and social damage, which this entails. Then again, because the Belfast parliament — assuming it were located there — and the powers of self-government associated with it, would be anchored in the federal constitution, they could not be removed as were the devolved parliament and powers under London. Finally, whatever the scepticism or distance with which many Ulster British might approach a federally integrated Ireland, the fact is that they are regarded more as fellow countrymen in Ireland than in Britain, and are more "wanted" in Ireland than in the neighbouring island, if for no other reason than that their co-operation is needed to fulfil the most cherished aim of Irish nationalism.

Incidentally, the reason why I stipulate that the Northern or Ulster unit must contain all of the Ulster British is that their political leadership would be very likely to insist on this and to reject any notion of, say, a smaller unit which, by excluding some of their community towards the west and south, would result in a more predominately Protestant and British unit in East Ulster. Given that this would very probably be their attitude, it is pointless to speculate on such notional alternatives.

What, then, of the nationalist or Irish community who would be included as a minority in a Northern state equipped with the maximum feasible powers, and having an Ulster British majority? To some extent they would find a "guarantee of secure autonomy" through their participation in the autonomy of their nation — in Irish national independence and the federal government and constitution. But given their experience under the Stormont

Parliament, and generally over the past seventy years, that is certain not to be sufficient for them, and they would require some regional or local autonomy within the Northern federal unit. True, the circumstances would no longer be so fraught with as much tension and danger as heretofore. Because the Six-County Irish would no longer be under foreign rule and separated by partition from their fellow countrymen, they would no longer have these grounds for alienation from the Northern state. Their equal civil rights would be constitutionally guaranteed. Moreover, the Ulster British, having accepted the all-Ireland state, would no longer have an obsession with the "border", or regard the nationalist people as subversives plotting to drag them into an alien republic. All of these would be factors tending to ease intercommunal relations. Nevertheless, the Irish community would feel, justifiably, that their autonomy was not adequately secured unless they had guaranteed participation in the government of the Northern province. As to how this might be done, it could hardly be by means of that mandatory sharing of the executive power regardless of election results — called "power sharing" — which the Ulster British have been resolutely rejecting since it was tried and overthrown in 1973–4. To expect them to agree both to a federally united Ireland *and*, within their own federal unit, to a denial of "majority rule", would be too much. Other means of securing the Irish community's position would have to be found either through some arrangement in the provincial parliament, or through "territorial power-sharing" on a regional or local basis, such as I have mentioned above.

Consequently, as a *third* prerequisite an Irish federation must provide for the guaranteed participation of the Irish minority in the government of the Northern state by means other than executive power-sharing.

Fourthly, since the federation itself, by its all-Ireland nature, is an express recognition of the Irish community in Ulster, the federal Constitution must include a formal recognition of the British community in Ulster. This might be done by a form of words, or by allowing the Ulster British to hold British as well as Irish citizenship automatically, or to have some other symbolic link with Britain, or by a combination of such measures.

Fifthly, because the Ulster unit of the federation must have maximum feasible powers, all units of the federation must have similarly large powers.

Sixthly, and finally, because it would not be possible for Ireland to supply, immediately, the level of subvention to the Northern economy which is maintained by the United Kingdom, it would be necessary to have the agreement of Britain or the European Community or of both to subsidise the northern province for a stated number of years.

Given that the Republic of Ireland, covering four-fifths of the island, has maintained itself now for seventy years, it seems fair to say that an all-Ireland federation structured on the lines indicated, and agreed to by all concerned, would be a viable state. Other aspects of the Constitution, including the location of the federal capital, would be matters for negotiation among the federal units. It goes without saying that the method of government would be parliamentary democracy. A federal upper house or Senate, containing an equal number of representatives from each of the federal units, would replace the Republic's vocationally elected Senate and would probably have more effective powers of blocking legislation than the latter has. With regard to the law, the courts, and the electoral system, it would seem wise to retain, in general terms, the institutions with which people are at present familiar. The federal reorganisation of the country would in itself be sufficient novelty for the citizens to cope with. The Supreme Court would retain its powers of reviewing legislation in the light of the Constitution, and it would be well that the latter should carry forward, as fully as possible, the valuable and richly interpreted "Personal Rights" section of the 1937 Constitution — ideal, indeed, if the "new" Constitution could be, formally, the present one considerably amended.

Advantages of a Federal Ireland

As compared with other proposals for bringing peace with full justice to the North, a federal Ireland on the lines just indicated shares several advantages with a unitary Ireland providing substantial recognition to the Ulster British. An agreed united Ireland of *either* kind would constitute a triumph for democracy in Ireland as a whole. It would fulfil the ultimate aim of Irish political nationalism, thereby ending, without possibility of recurrence, the political violence arising from this and from British rule. (The only remaining possible source of such violence would be a diehard Ulster British minority.) More than any other arrangement, it would create conditions for permanent good relations between Ireland and Britain. Finally, it would benefit all of Ireland economically, and particularly the Six Counties. It would do this by facilitating a co-ordinated approach to infrastructure, co-ordinated and interacting industrial development, and a common approach in dealings with the European Community.

However, an Ireland united federally in the manner described would have advantages over a unitary state providing substantial recognition to the Ulster British. In the matter of regional self-government, the most a unitary state, whether British or Irish, can give to the Ulster British is devolution. As the majority in a federal unit, they would have a much greater degree of constitutional and psychological security. Then again, deviations from normal democratic practice which a unitary Ireland might offer as substitutes — weighted majorities or mandatory power-sharing in the central parliament — would be unnecessary in a federal arrangement. Finally, whereas a unitary state would not improve government throughout most of Ireland, a federation of the kind indicated i.e. having at least four units, would do so notably. The division of the country into several federal units would give the greater part of Ireland, which is now the Republic, a more democratic, pluralist and serviceable system of government than it now has.

A Two-State Federation

In 1979, the Fine Gael party published a scheme for a two-state federation based on the existing Republic and Northern Ireland. The proposal formed Parts IV–VI of the party's policy statement *Ireland — Our Future Together*. Much the same scheme, in abbreviated form, appeared again as Chapter 7 of the *Report of the New Ireland Forum* (1984), where it was presented as one of two "structural arrangements" which the Forum examined in addition to its preferred scheme, a unitary state. The New Ireland Forum was an Irish nationalist get-together representing the principal Dáil parties and the SDLP, but excluding Sinn Féin, which from May 1983 to early 1984 met in Dublin to examine the Northern question in depth and to work out a common approach. Both in the Fine Gael document and in the *Forum Report* the proposed scheme is "federal/confederal", that is to say, these two options are presented and certain explanatory distinctions made.

The *Forum Report* makes the distinction thus (7.3): "In a federation, residual power would rest with the central government. Certain powers would be vested in the two individual states. A confederation would comprise the two states which would delegate certain specified powers to a confederal government." The *Report* leaves the options open, but represents (7.6) the confederal arrangement as offering the possibility, if it were desired, of having "the powers held at the centre . . . relatively limited (for example, foreign policy, external and internal security policy and perhaps currency and monetary policy), requiring a less elaborate parliamentary structure [than the federal arrangement] at the confederal level." In either case, however, "unionists would have parallel British citizenship and could maintain special links with Britain."

The Fine Gael document, published five years earlier, comes down on the side of confederation. It states (80): "The distinction between 'federal' and 'confederal' is often a confused one, but the latter word seems most appropriate to describe the kind of provision for the delegation upwards of certain specific functions in the common interest that appears most relevant to the Irish case." Arguing that under such an arrangement the centre could have wide or quite limited powers, it poses for discussion (81):

a)   A Confederation with delegation of a fairly wide range of powers to the Confederal Government, not unlike in some respects the models that exist in the United States, Canada, Australia, etc., although with some specific difference; and limitations arising from Irish needs.

b)   A more limited delegation of functions to the Confederal Government, related particularly to two areas — security, and external representation — but extending to economic policy, which are intimately linked with the EEC, and where the main function of national governments is the implementation of EEC legislation.

The suggestion here that the division of powers as between the "confederal" government and the states could approximate to the arrangements in the United States, Canada, Australia, etc. seems to blur the practical distinction between federal and confederal to the point of insignificance.

Further on (113–4), the document proposes that either the confederal administration might be chosen directly by the people of the two states and be subject to a parliament similarly selected, or that its personnel might comprise members of the two state governments, with the portfolios being distributed equitably, and the post of foreign minister alternating between North and South. Within the Northern state (119–22), the nationalists must not, because of their minority position, be permanently excluded from the government, and perhaps therefore also from the confederal government. Some method must be found for including a due number of them in the state government, whether through executive power-sharing or the requirement — having the same effect

— that the executive must secure and retain a vote of confidence by a large majority of the state parliament. Finally, in the initial period, the Northern state would need subvention from such sources as the United Kingdom, the United States and the European Community (99–105).

As will be obvious, even from this brief and incomplete summary,[5] a great deal of painstaking and thoughtful work went into the preparation of this proposal. Its principal weakness, which it shares with the federal proposal in the *Forum Report*, is, unfortunately, a very basic one; namely, that the federation would consist of only two states, and these of markedly different size and weight. There is, of course, something to be said for basing an all-Ireland federation on two existing state structures which have considerable experience as administrative units, even if one of them has not so far proved to be a successful unit. But even on the most hopeful of assumptions the advantage of such an arrangement would be outweighed by its inherent flaws. The paragraph which introduces the Fine Gael proposal states:

> It has been objected that such a federation or confederation would be unbalanced and that there are no precedents for a successful bi-partite federation of this kind. We recognise that the imbalance in population between these two units, and the need to safeguard the unionist section (*sic*) of the community within the smaller unit, would pose problems, and that special measures would have to be devised to secure the success of such an arrangement. These measures would of course require some sacrifices by the Republic, in terms of sharing control over aspects of its affairs.

Since the "unionist section of the community" would continue to constitute 60 per cent of the population within the "Northern Ireland" state, it is difficult to understand what is meant there by "the need to safeguard it"; the possibility that there is a misprint for "nationalist section of the community" suggests itself. But leaving that aside, this passage does home in on the basic flaws in this federal programme.

In a book dealing with possible solutions to the Northern problem, J.C. Vile comments:

> No unit has survived with only two or three units of government at the lower level. It is indeed very unlikely that such a federation could survive because federal systems operate on the basis of the bargaining between shifting coalitions of groups, bringing about compromises because no single group or coalition of groups is in a continually dominant position. The danger of an irreconcilable confrontation between the units in a two-unit federation is so great that sooner or later it would lead to civil war, secession, or both.

Later, referring to the Fine Gael proposal, Vile says:

> Such an arrangement would seem to fly in the face of all the experience of federal systems, successful and unsuccessful. Two units, each dominated by a different communal majority, would seem almost inevitably to come into head-on conflict sooner or later, with none of the mechanisms available to mediate such conflict in federations with a larger and more varied collection of units. The problem of creating a federal government which would not be either totally dominated by one unit or totally deadlocked by the other seems to be insuperable. (Vile, 1982)

The objections arising from the "mathematics" of the arrangement are compounded when the two units in question, as in the Fine Gael and Forum proposals, have a recent history of sharp antagonism. In these circumstances, the imbalance between the states would easily reawaken the old phobia of the Protestant North about "domination by the South", while the Republic and its individual regions, after the initial euphoria, would soon be chafing at the disproportionate influence of a northern state comprising only one-fifth of the national territory and 30 per cent of the population.

Given these basic objections to the two-state proposal, its additional weaknesses need not detain us.[6] It is right in assuming that the transformation of Northern Ireland into a federal unit would not of itself make its politics normal, and that special measures would be required to guard against the continued exclusion of the nationalist minority from power. However, the prescription of one form or another of compulsory power-sharing in the state government would hardly fill the bill. As has already been suggested, the Ulster British could hardly be expected to accept both a "united Ireland" and, within the Northern state, compulsory power-sharing with the Irish community. The Fine Gael/Forum scheme makes no proposal about the location of the federal capital or the *names* of the two states — a difficult conundrum when one thinks of it. Neither does it offer any hope to those who might look to a federal Ireland for some reform of the Republic's top-heavy governmental system.

A Four-Province Federation

None of the criticisms I have made of the Fine Gael and Forum proposals can be made of the earlier, Sinn Féin scheme for a federation based on provincial parliaments in Ulster, Munster, Leinster and Connacht. First announced in general terms in August 1971, it was spelt out in some detail in June 1972 in an appendix to *Éire Nua* (1971), the Sinn Féin social and economic programme, and in a four-page leaflet "Peace with Justice".[7] The immediate inspiration, in the mind of one of its principal initiators, Dáithí Ó Conaill, was Switzerland, a country with which Mr Ó Conaill was familiar. A draft Charter of Rights, for inclusion in the federal Constitution, was published together with the governmental proposals.

According to Sinn Féin, the government structure of the New Ireland would consist of four levels: federal, provincial, regional, and district. The one-chamber federal parliament, Dáil Éireann, would have approximately 150 deputies, half of them elected by direct universal suffrage, and half in equal numbers from the four provincial parliaments. The federal parliament "would control all powers and functions essential to the good of the whole nation". It would elect a president who would be both prime minister and head of state, and he would nominate a government for election by the parliament. Members of the government would relinquish their seats in the parliament. The supreme court would be guardian of the constitution. National legislation could be initiated by federal parliament deputies, the federal government, a provincial parliament, or by referendum, and it could be adopted by the federal parliament, or by referendum in specified cases.

The establishment of Dáil Uladh (The Parliament of Ulster) would be the first step in the creation of the federation.

> By thus creating a Provincial Parliament for the nine counties of Ulster within a New Ireland, the partition system would be disestablished and the problem of the border removed. Dáil Uladh would be representative of Catholic and Protestant, Orange and Green, Left and Right. It would be an Ulster Parliament, for the Ulster people. The Unionist-oriented people of Ulster would have a working majority within the Province and would therefore have considerable control over their own affairs. That power would be the surest guarantee of their civil and religious liberties within a New Ireland.

Within each province, regional development councils of an administrative, non-legislative kind would "promote and co-ordinate the economic, social and cultural affairs of clearly defined economic regions". East and West Ulster are cited as two cases in point. The regional councils would be composed of representatives of the district councils and appointed experts. The elected district councils, taking decisions "with the minimum of control by Central Government" (surely this should be by the provincial governments?), would replace the two existing local government systems.

In the course of the 1970s, as Sinn Féin and affiliated promotional bodies in the four provinces published a large amount of explanatory literature, slight revisions were made and further details added. For example, in the eight-page multilingual pamphlet *Peace with Justice* (1977), Athlone, a town in the centre of Ireland, is named as the federal capital, and we read that the district councils "would exercise the maximum amount of governmental power consistent with justice and efficiency". From the start it was explained in the ancillary literature that the chief practical purpose of expanding the Ulster unit of the federation from the Six Counties to the whole of Ulster was, by altering the ratio between the two communities from 60–40 to about 55–45, to make possible and encourage "normal" politics; that is, the replacement of intercommunal confrontation by cross-communal alliances on the basis of shared class interest or social ideology. The closeness in numbers of the two communities would, Sinn Féin believed, promote this. There was no talk of compulsory power-sharing in government, no exclusion of "majority rule" by the Ulster British, but it was thought unlikely that they would rely on this for long. One way or the other, the Ulster Irish were to take their chance in the democratic process.

The Fine Gael document, in introducing its federal proposal (75), makes the following reference in brackets to the four-province proposal: "The idea of a four-province federation we dismiss as contrived, administratively cumbersome, and serving only to place the representatives of Ulster in an artificially small minority." That last phrase is unintelligible, and the comment as a whole unfortunately typical of the contemptuous and careless manner in which the Dublin establishment (political, journalistic and academic) "dismisses" any innovative ideas about Irish government which depart from British precedent, and particularly any proposals emanating from Sinn Féin.[8] A federation of the four provinces, far from being contrived, is something that springs naturally to mind if a federal organisation of Ireland is being considered. Although they are not administrative units, and are referred to nowadays mainly in the context of weather forecasts and some sporting contests, the provinces do constitute the major divisions of Ireland and correspond roughly to the North, South, East and West of the island. To an outsider such as Professor Northcote Parkinson, a noted European regionalist, they appear as the obvious major units if it is a matter of dividing the island regionally.[9] As for the four-province arrangement being "administratively cumbersome", the four-province federation, as outlined above, would enhance Irish democracy and substitute a multi-centred system of self-government, down to district levels, for the over-centralised, imperial state that now holds sway in most of the island. Apart from the benefits this would bring to the citizens of the Republic, their state's present monolithic structure is probably an additional, subconsciously working factor in the "un-uniteable-with" image which it presents to the Ulster British. Indeed, Parkinson, in a remark to the present writer at a conference on European regionalism in Copenhagen, suggested it was the principal factor. He said, "Your Ulster problem will be solved when you people in the Republic make Leinster, Munster and Connacht self-governing." Translating this thought into historical terms, one could say that the progressive centralisation of Irish government under the British regime from the mid-nineteenth century onwards was a major cause of "Ulster's" secession as Ireland moved towards independence. A positive feature of the Sinn Féin scheme is that its "offer to the Ulster unionists" includes the reversal and removal of this centralisation.

With regard to the internal aspects of the Ulster problem, the Sinn Féin scheme has three attractive features. It frees all the inhabitants of Northern Ireland from the narrow, murder-provoking confines of what might well be called their political prison, and offers them the adventure of a new, uncharted, all-

Ulster politics. If the Ulster British, for their part, could bring themselves to sacrifice their "secure" majority which has brought them no security, it would give them, as their political home in Ireland, the entirety of that Ulster from which they derive so much of their sense of identity. Finally, the reduction in the disparity of size between the two communities would render superfluous any special measures to ensure nationalist participation in government, and allow normal democracy, including "majority rule", however composed, to take its course.

It is impossible to be precise about the numerical sizes of the two ethnic communities in Northern Ireland, and *a fortiori* impossible to predict their exact size in a reunited Ulster. No Northern Ireland census has ever included a question requiring a choice between British and Irish nationality. Figures for religious adherence would give only a fair approximation (there seem to be some thousands of Catholic and non-religious unionists and a smaller number of Protestant and non-religious nationalists); but even religious adherence can at best only be roughly estimated. In recent years, 40:60 — or the numbers 600,000 to 900,000, in a population of just over one and a half million — have been used publicly to indicate the sizes of the nationalist/Irish and unionist/British communities, respectively. They are reasonably accurate, round-figure estimates.[10] If we add the Catholics and Protestants living in the three Ulster counties of the Republic, the number of Catholics becomes roughly 813,000, or 46 per cent of the total population of Ulster.

This estimate makes no claim to precision, but it does indicate that, in a united Ulster, while the unionist/British community would predominate, the two communities would be close in size. On the face of it, this would be unwelcome to the British community, especially when taken in conjunction with the widespread, though unfounded, belief among them that, within Northern Ireland itself, Catholics will outnumber Protestants in the foreseeable future. But the Sinn Féin scheme provides a compensating and reassuring factor. By means of the twin devices of the administrative region (see above) and the strong district councils, the British community would have firm, subordinate control of East Ulster where the great majority of them live. Similarly, of course, the Irish community would have subordinate control of West Ulster. However, these considerations would be of major importance only on the assumption that the unionist laager mentality would continue unabated, whereas the basic reasoning behind the nine-county Ulster notion is that, precisely because the two communities would be close in size, the majority/minority question would cease to be a major issue, and inter-communal confrontation would be replaced by a cross-communal politics of interest groups and social ideologies. Everything would depend on the Ulster British taking the risk of "mixing it" in Ireland and in Ulster for the sake of a secure home and future such as they can hardly have otherwise.

At the Sinn Féin Ardfheis (annual conference) in 1982, the party decided to abandon its federal policy. This major change was brought about chiefly by Northern, especially Belfast, delegates, supported by the Dublin city branches. The federal scheme had been generated principally in the Republic, and Belfast Sinn Féin had been unhappy for some time at the prospect of a continuing enclosure of Belfast and Northern nationalists in a Northern state, even if it were an enlarged and federal unit. They believed that the full direct weight of the entire nation would be required to hold the unionist/British community in check. Four years later, after a decision by Sinn Féin to recognise the Dáil and allow elected Sinn Féin candidates to take their seats in it, the party split, with the smaller body calling itself Republican Sinn Féin. In 1989–90, in the booklet *Éire Nua: A New Democracy*, this party re-affirmed, with additional detail, the four-province federal policy, thereby placing it once more, if very marginally, on the table of Irish politics.

The Sinn Féin scheme has a few defects and omissions which could easily be remedied. Even in its latest formulation, it is vague about the allocation of powers and functions as between the centre and the provinces, and does not indicate clearly that Ulster — and hence the other provinces — would have the maximum feasible powers. The financial aspects of the federation are insufficiently dealt with, and there is no mention of any express recognition of the Britishness of the Ulster British. While four seems to be an adequate number of federal units, it is only just adequate, and a good case could be made for increasing the number of units, to, say, six. It would be a better federation if Dublin and Belfast, with their surrounding areas, were additional federal units, much as Hamburg and Bremen form units of the German federation. Making Dublin a separate unit would benefit both Dublin and Leinster. When intercommunal relations in Ulster had improved and it no longer seemed imperative to have all the Ulster British in a single federal unit, Belfast might be given separate status — thereby increasing Ulster British representation in the Senate.

A difficulty with the Sinn Féin scheme is that none of the proposed federal units has any political or administrative existence. Though there have been instances of federal units being created when a federation was being founded (West Germany) or at a later stage (Canada), no federation, to my knowledge, has been established entirely *ex nihilo*. But this difficulty could be overcome, and the four provincial (or more) units established, if the political will to do so existed. The decisive practical weakness of the scheme is that it does not seem likely that the political will to undertake this radical political restructuring of Ireland could be found or mobilised, given the extreme conservatism of the Dublin political establishment and the lack of any notable popular pressure for this or any other kind of major change in the way the Republic is governed.

Vile, commenting on the Sinn Féin scheme, and comparing it with the Fine Gael proposal, has this to say:

> Intellectually the Sinn Féin proposal is subject to considera-
> bly fewer objections in terms of its four-unit structure, and
> if the political basis for such a proposal existed, it would be
> well worth discussion. At the moment I would imagine that
> few people would think that a constitutional convention
> could be called to give serious discussion to such an idea,
> and like the other long-term possibilities a great deal of
> political development would be necessary before such dis-
> cussion could be initiated. (Vile, 1982)

I believe that fairly sums up the matter, and in relation not only to
the Sinn Féin proposal but to any viable scheme of all-Ireland
federation. There is also the far from unimportant consideration
that the British commitment to withdraw, which would be a
necessary condition for a united Ireland of any kind, does not
seem likely.

A federation on the Sinn Féin lines — a genuinely Irish-made
state in keeping with the best contemporary thinking on decentralisation and communal self-government — is a noble aspiration.
While bringing peace and stability with full political justice to
Ireland, it would make it a refreshingly new and interesting country, and open the way for the creativity of its peoples in various
spheres. But given that the conditions for its creation, or indeed for
any form of united Ireland, do not exist and are not likely to exist
in the foreseeable future, it is necessary, in view of the urgency of
the Northern problem, to seek peace with a lesser but sufficient
measure of justice, by some other, less inspiring means.

Postscript: *The Good Friday Agreement of 1998 provided for a system of
government amounting in practice, if not juridically, to something like the joint
sovereignty first mooted at the beginning of the 1970s: an elected power-sharing
Assembly in Northern Ireland under British sovereignty, with some tenuous
all-Ireland institutions and a strong political and consultative input by Dublin.
But the Assembly has been experiencing an uncertain fate between existence
and suspension due to the enduring reluctance of the Ulster British to share
power with the Six-County Irish or to collaborate with the Republic in all-
Ireland matters.*

Notes

[1] The "new view" outlined here was developed progressively in three articles in *The Irish Times* during August 1969, in a weekly column in the *Sunday Press*, 1970–2, and in various newspapers and journals throughout the 1970s. It was presented in a summary form in Fennell (1983), and in a submission by the author to the New Ireland Forum in the same year. A fairly detailed account of its genesis and development can be found in Fennell (1989), and is included, with slight revision, in Fennell (1993).

[2] The "Irish" and "British" communities referred to here are coterminous with nationalists and unionists, respectively, but not exactly with Catholics and Protestants, because there are some Catholic unionists and a smaller number of Protestant nationalists. "Irish" and "British" refer, in other words, to those groups in Northern Ireland which identify, respectively, with the Irish nation or the British nation (the latter comprising Scots, English, Welsh and some Irish).

[3] The Republic of Ireland has no provision for regional, and only very limited provision for sub-regional or urban, self-government. In addition, the refusal of the numerous agencies of central government to organise their services, coherently, on a shared regional and district basis — each of them operates a separate territorial system — makes the public administration a jungle through which the citizen must struggle mapless. Together, this administrative chaos, and the centralised monolith frustrating regional initiative and enterprise, are a principal cause of the Republic's inability to generate a prosperous native economy; its high dependence on imported enterprise; and its recurrent waves of forced emigration. Since the 1960s the Republic's system of government has come under frequent sporadic criticism by individuals and groups. At the same time a considerable body of sustained critical analysis, accompanied by proposed alternatives, has been published, most of it by the Institute of Public Administration, Dublin. Tom Barrington, one of the founders of the Institute and its Director until 1977, has led the field with his many magisterial writings, some of them unsigned. See McCarthy, Charles, 1968, *The Distasteful Challenge*, Chapter 3, and, by Tom Barrington, *From Big Government to Local Government* (1975), *The Irish Administrative System* (1980), all published by the Institute; Barrington's Addendum to the *Report of the Devlin Commission* (1969, Dublin: Stationery Office); and, by Fennell, the two pamphlets *Build the Third Republic* (1972, Maoinis: Foilseacháin Mhaoinse), *Sketches of the New Ireland* with maps (1973, Galway: Association for the Advancement of

Self Government), and Fennell (1985), Chapters 3 and 4, including maps, where the author's participation in the Sinn Féin federal scheme is outlined. In 1990, the Government announced its intention of reforming local government and appointed an advisory committee chaired by Tom Barrington. This committee reported, recommending regional and district government as well as county, and all levels equipped with considerable devolved functions and powers. The Government has signalled a general willingness to implement these recommendations, but there is a pervasive scepticism that this will really happen.

[4] In Coupland (1954), p. 223, note, the author, dealing with the "federal devolution" proposals of the 1870s, makes the following illuminating comment:

> None of the proposals made now or later for devolution was strictly federal. Federalism is a division of power between the Central and Provincial Parliaments and Governments. The Centre and the Province is equally self-governing in the fields allotted to them. This is not the case in any of the devolution schemes. In all of them the Central (or Imperial) Parliament retains its sovereignty complete and unshared. The Provincial Governments are subordinate, not co-ordinate authorities. Their decisions can be over-ridden and their powers altered, or annulled, by the Central Parliament. The term federal, however, has been so commonly applied to the devolution scheme that it seems pedantic to abstain from its use in these pages.

[5] In view of the considerable part which Dr Garret FitzGerald played in the preparation of this document, it is not surprising that it deals at length with the economic advantages which would arise from some form of all-Ireland association, and, specifically, with the financial and economic aspects of a two-state federation.

[6] On similar grounds I omit discussion of Bristow (1982) which deals with the possible political arrangements, and the economic aspects of a two-state federation.

[7] *Éire Nua*, first published a year and a half previously, had outlined an economic and social programme and presupposed a unitary state. Consequently, when the appendix containing the federal scheme and a Draft Charter of Rights was added in a new edition, there were contradictions with the earlier text. These were superficially resolved in the "Peace with Justice" leaflet, which ranked thereafter as a summary restatement of

Éire Nua. I mention these details because the *Éire Nua* federal scheme is often referred to as "the *Éire Nua* programme", when it would be more accurately referred to as *Éire Nua* (revised version) or Mark Two.

[8] Bristow (1982) illustrates, with regard to Sinn Féin, how this attitude could lead not only to self-deception but to misinformation. The author (Associate Professor of Economics at Trinity College (Dublin) having dismissed the four-province option as "without merit" (144) and discussed two-state federation at some length, has this note at the end of the paper: "Practically nothing has been published on possible political solutions for united Ireland, though Fine Gael (1979) makes some reference to this question. This document is of broader interest in that it is the only recent, developed statement by an Irish political party on the issue of reunification."

[9] A map projecting a Europe of autonomous regions, which Parkinson published in the magazine *Profiles* (Brussels, 1975) showed Ireland divided into its four provinces.

[10] Curran (1984) and Compton (1985) estimate the Catholic percentage at 42 and 38 respectively.

Works Cited

Anglo-Irish Agreement, Dublin, Stationery Office, 1985.

Bristow, J., "All-Ireland Perspectives" in *Political Co-operation in Divided Societies: A Series of Papers Relevant to the Conflict in Northern Ireland*, ed. Desmond Rea, Dublin, Gill and Macmillan, 1982, pp. 137–155.

Compton, P.A., "An Evaluation of the Changing Religious Composition of the Population in Northern Ireland", *Economic and Social Review*, 16, 1985, pp. 201–224.

Compton, P.A. and Power P.J., "Estimates of the Religious Composition of Northern Ireland Government Districts in 1981 and Change in the Geographical Pattern of Religious Composition between 1971 and 1981", *Economic and Social Review*, 17, 1986, pp. 87–105.

Coupland, R., *Welsh and Scottish Nationalism*, London, Collins, 1954.

Curran, F., "Submission to the New Ireland Forum" in *New Ireland Forum*, Dublin, Stationery Office, 1984.

Fennell, D., *A New Nationalism for the New Ireland*, Monaghan: Comhairle Uladh, 1972.

Fennell, D., "A Federal Ireland", *Irish Times*, 22–24 February 1972.

Fennell, D., "What a Federal Ireland Means", *Sunday Press*, 4 June 1978.

Fennell, D., "Could Ulster's Advantage Lie in a Federal Ireland Shaped by Ulstermen?", *The Church of Ireland Gazette*, 9 February 1979.

Fennell, D., *The State of the Nation* (2nd ed., Chapter 4), Swords, Ward River Press, 1983.

Fennell, D., *Beyond Nationalism: The Struggle against Provinciality in the Modern World* (Chapter 3), Swords, Ward River Press, 1985.

Fennell, D., *The Revision of Irish Nationalism*, Dublin, Open Air, 1989.

Fennell, D., *Heresy: The Battle of Ideas in Modern Ireland*, Belfast, Blackstaff, 1993.

Fine Gael, *Ireland — Our Future Together*, 1979.

New Ireland Forum Report, Dublin, Stationery Office, 1984.

Sinn Féin, "Appendix" to *Éire Nua*, 1971.

Sinn Féin Poblachtach, *Éire Nua: A New Democracy*, 1990.

Vile, M.J.C., "Federation and Confederation: The Experience of the United States and the British Commonwealth" in *Political Co-operation*, ed. Desmond Rea, Dublin, Gill and Macmillan, 1982, pp. 216–28.

Law, Virtue and Individual Freedom

The Irish Times, *15 May 1996*

After returning from a long stay in the US, I have noticed that the legal restriction of individual and social freedom, which is very advanced there, is proceeding apace in our republic also. I mean a legal restriction of freedom which enters into the minutiae of everyday life, is promoted by politicians and the media, and supported by the active or passive consent of a majority of citizens.

Previously the matters in question were left to individual responsibility and discretion, or to people, formally or informally, making arrangements among themselves. To uphold the freedom of the individual, and of individuals acting collectively, was considered the right thing to do. It was a specifically liberal virtue based on the assumed tendency of human beings towards good behaviour, and as such it was considered appropriate for a liberal democracy. That underlying assumption seems to have been reversed.

In the name of higher virtue of various kinds, and in order to prevent the evils likely to result from people acting freely, it is now considered increasingly necessary to intrude the compulsive force of the State into our lives. In the teeth of scattered resistance, but with the new order winning steadily, the Liberal State we inherited is being replaced by an authoritarian power more intrusive in detail than any church, and backed by police and courts to boot.

I began to notice this trend in February when a report appeared in *The Irish Times* about the banning of smoking in bingo halls. Working-class women who played bingo regularly were complaining that "bingo is the only pleasure in our lives" and that smoking went with its "nail-biting tension". They had petitioned against the ban in vain. A few days ago, my growing awareness of what was happening peaked. I heard working-class adults and children in north Dublin being interviewed about legislation which will have the effect of virtually ending the children's habit of keeping horses. "What will the children do?" one adult asked, and I wondered, anxiously, what?

Between those two incidents, virtue rampaged. There was the campaign to make the reporting of child abuse mandatory for doctors and others, regardless of circumstances. A coming law was discussed which would end the age-old right of publicans to decide, at their discretion, who might not enter their pub. (There had been no popular demand for this law; on the contrary, there is widespread appreciation of how Irish publicans maintain their pub's amenity on their customers' behalf.) Next, a new law intruded into the management of restaurants. Restaurateurs were no longer to use their discretion in catering for their smoking and non-smoking customers. They were ordered, regardless of the circumstances on any given day or at any meal-time, always to keep at least half the tables free for non-smokers.

And then came the frantic announcements in all media that anyone wanting to marry validly must give three months' notice to some state official. We were told this had to do with providing for divorce, and it became clear what the push for divorce by the politicians and media, united, had really been about. The Power — as Tom Wolfe in *The Bonfire of the Vanities* calls the hybrid power that rules us now — wanted to take the management of marriage away from individuals and their churches, and to subject that, too, to its control.

All that occurred in a mere three months, and I draw attention to the trend for two reasons. First, so that we will be aware of what we are doing and choosing, and not fool ourselves, as we sometimes do, that we still set high value on the freedom of the individual or of individuals acting collectively. In order that justice and virtue of a higher order might be realised in Ireland, our local Power, and a sufficient number of us, want an authoritarian, virtuously intrusive State, not unlike Calvin's Geneva. And oddly, this seems to suit our mood and mentality better than America's, for there is nothing here like the organised resistance which there is there.

Second, I would suggest that, while we are getting what many of us want, we should not be naïve about it. The State which has taken on, aggressively, the role of moral teacher and improver is failing in the basics — and the resulting bad conscience may well be a reason for its frantic display of virtue in peripheral or trivial matters.

The freedom of the streets and of open spaces has been shrinking and continues to shrink, particularly for women and children. Respect for human life has conspicuously fallen, and the special respect for women and old people is almost gone: they are frequently beaten up, killed or raped. Young men, seeing no point in life, often end it. Drug dealers are permitted to walk the streets, plying their wares to hopeless youth and criminalising them. There is no space left in the crammed jails. Many children conceived recklessly by teenagers and young women are aborted or have anguished, warping childhoods. All these are developments of the last twenty or thirty years and are becoming permanent.

The point about this, the bitter pill for our rulers to swallow, is that it's all occurring while the State has more control over citizens' lives than ever before; more money and police than ever before; more power — having pushed the Church aside and delegitimised local social control — to teach and inculcate virtue and supply life with meaning. Faced with such fundamental failure in its dual role as orderer and moral teacher, there is nothing more natural than to make a great show of stopping women smoking in bingo halls, and poor children having horses, and publicans managing their pubs, and restaurateurs making their table arrangements, and people arranging privately to get married when they choose. Nothing more natural than to parade shocked horror about Sister Xaviera.[1]

But to be fair to the rulers, one must add that nothing is more natural, either, than for ordinary decent people, like *Irish Times* readers, to deduce from the righteous noise, and the busy compulsion to good behaviour, that they live in the most virtuous society Ireland has known, and to preen themselves.

Desmond Fennell's forthcoming book, written in Seattle, is Uncertain Dawn: Hiroshima and the Beginning of Postwestern Civilisation.

---

[1] A nun who worked in an orphanage in the "bad old days of de Valera's Ireland", and who allegedly — it was now being affirmed — had been cruel to a number of the children.

Cén Fáth "Tee Na Jee"?

Foinse, *17 Samhain 1996*

5 Samhain 1996

An tEagarthóir
Foinse

Adhuine uasail, — Le tamall anuas tá Raidió na Gaeltachta ag soláthar foclóra chuimsithigh do Ghaeilge labhartha ár linne. Níl ach máchail suntasach amháin ar an bhfoclóir seo: usáidtear na hainmneacha Béarla do litreacha na haibítre. Nil teanga Eorpach ar bith eile a úsáideann ainmneacha eachtranacha don aibítir, agus níl an Nua-Ghaeilge fásta suas i gceart mar theanga fad a ndéanann sí amhlaidh. Gach teanga eile bíonn ainmneacha ar na litreacha aici a fheileann dá foghraíocht féin.

Tá sé soiléir nach bhfeileann an fuaim Béarla "ee" do e na Gaeilge, ná "eye" don i, ná "you" don u, ná "see" agus "jee" do c agus g na Gaeilge nach bhfuaimnítear riamh mar sin. Maidir le "haitch", bain triail as an fuaim seo a litriú i nGaeilge!

Tá sé thar am go gcuirfí deireadh leis an rian gránna seo den choilíneachas ar ár dteanga. Bhí deis an-mhaith ag Teilifís na Gaeilge sampla a thabhairt ón tús — sampla a chuirfeadh le húire agus le snastacht a stíle agus a híomhá. Ach faraor, tá sí ag tabhairt "Tee na Jee" uirthi féin agus ag úsáid na n-ainmneacha Béarla eile do na litreacha. Smaoinigh, dá dtabharfadh na Sasanaigh "Bay Bay Tsay" (ón nGearmáinis) ar an BBC!

Ta liosta de na hainmneacha Gaeilge ar na litreacha — ainmneacha lena nglacann an Institiúid Teangeolaíochta agus An Gúm — le fáil ar an gcéad leathanach de *Graiméar Gaeilge na mBráithre Críostaí* (An Gúm, 1985). Tosaíonn sé le á, bé, cé agus leanann ar aghaidh go zae. Níor mhór an dua Gé Á Á, Í Ear Á, Vae Héis Eif, Ear Té É, agus Té na Gé a rá, ach bhainfeadh dínit leis.

Is mise, le meas,
DEASÚN FENNELL
Cuan Aoibhinn, BÁC 8

Making Nationalism Serve People

Written 29 January 1997 as first draft for a lecture on "Religion and Nationalism"
to be given in Letterkenny (see next item). A Christian ecumenical group had
requested it; and it seemed to me necessary — before getting around to the
relationship the group was interested in — to clarify "nationalism". I wanted to
separate it, for what it was, from the polemical accretions which obscured it.

I

Nationalism, like drink, worries some people all the time, but occasionally the worry extends to many, and there is a flurry of public talk about it. I mean nationalism as a general phenomenon, not just the nationalism of one's own nation or of another one, or the nationalism of other nations but not of one's own. These, too, have their worriers, some of whom talk as if they were concerned about nationalism as such; which they are not. At present due to the emergence of many new nationalisms in Central and Eastern Europe, and the movement towards Union in the European Community, there is once again a flurry of public talk about nationalism as such, the *ding an sich*.

Much of the talk is pointless because it stems from fuzzy ideas about nationalism and nation-states, and opposes nationalism to internationalism as if there were an intrinsic opposition. Insofar as it expresses worry about the existence of nationalism and a wish to get rid of it, it is wasted energy. The concern that underlies it would be more profitably directed to shaping or reshaping nationalism so that it would serve human needs much better than it has done hitherto. Thinking about this might, moreover, have a further benefit: it could offer a future to socialism which it otherwise lacks; a future linked to and developed from that formidable strain of socialist endeavour which was submerged by crude statism at the beginning of this century.

II

In the British *Independent on Sunday* last September, the well-known Polish journalist Ryszard Kapushinski made some acute observations about nationalism. He was writing about a crowd of refugees from the Somali civil war in a camp just across the Ethiopian border. It was a crowd mainly of women and children with a few old men, and they were "shouting at first chaotically and then in unison — a powerful, resonant chanting". Kapushinski was certain "that these women holding emaciated children to their parched breasts were demanding food and water. Maybe, I thought, their demands were fantastical and they were calling for meat and milk. Then I understood. The crowd was shouting 'Somaliland!'".

They were demanding independence from Somalia — the former Italian colony of that name, with its capital in Mogadishu, which in 1960 joined Somaliland to become the Republic of Somalia. They wanted to create a sovereign state with its capital not in Mogadishu but in Hargeisa. "'Independent Somaliland!' they shouted, with joy and rapture in their voices." Kapushinski continued:

> So the most important thing was neither bread nor water. And even though they were naked or half-naked, without shoes or shirts on their backs, they did not want our money, medicine or shelter . . . I thought about that powerful, dominating force (a sceptic might say obsession): the need to feel at home, to be independent, to lock oneself within the walls of one's own national, racial or cultural home. It seems that insofar as the twentieth century was one of ideology, the next might become the century of nationalism.

Leave aside that last, distracting contradistinction between ideology and nationalism. Kapushinski, in that passage, accurately depicts nationalism as the most powerful motivation of people, collectively, in modern times. It expresses a cause for which, above all else, people, male and female and in large numbers, are willing to risk death or life-long imprisonment. He also names the human spiritual need that is at the root of their motivation: the need to feel at home in the world, to have together a social space and life in the world in which they feel at home because they are able, there, to order their affairs in accordance with their shared values; as they see fit.

In a speech given recently in the US on the subject of "Home", in all its dimensions, Vaclav Havel said: "The category of 'home' belongs to what modern philosophers call 'the natural world'. . . . For everyone, home is a basic existential experience".

When the members of a nation, or an ethnic group, feel the lack of a social home in the world, and feel that this lack is both oppressive of their humanity and unjust, they develop a liberationist nationalism. When they have a national home and feel it threatened, they respond with a defensive nationalism or, if they have the power, with an expansionist one. Sometimes, too, when opportunity offers, a nationalism becomes expansionist through a combination of competitiveness and greed. The nation, or initially, more likely, its rulers, want more of the good thing they already have: a larger, better furnished, more splendid home in the world — a better home than their neighbours have.

A nation is a community of people who, in their own minds and to some degree in their neighbours', constitute a basic unit of mankind. It is one of the "peoples of the world" in the ancient and perennial meaning of the phrase; the group that directly and primarily mediates its members' relations with mankind and other nations. Forming a "we" within the world, it contains other "we's", other communities; it is by nature a community of communities and persons. It also feels associated, beyond itself, with broader communities of language, race or history. But even when, in one of its constituent regions or cities, the nation takes second place in consciousness, or when there is a strong surge of fellow feeling with one of those communities larger than the nation, the nation retains its primacy, subconsciously, as an existential fact.

Religion and Nationalism

Notes for lecture at Letterkenny Regional Technical College, County Donegal, 5 February 1997. The audience listened with interest, but afterwards the chairman told me, smilingly, they had been expecting a rather different lecture. I supposed he meant the theme in question as applied directly to the Northern conflict.

1. Permanent characteristics of "representative communities"

Since the beginning of history, there have been representative communities — communities with a normal mix of sexes, ages, occupations, etc. These have always felt themselves distinguished and bonded to a degree that set them off from other similar groups. Distinguishing and bonding factors: past history, language, religion, race, etc. In ancient cities, often the particular "god" of a city.

Also from the beginning of history, some largish representative communities have felt themselves distinguished and bonded to a degree that made them *representative units of mankind*. "Peoples, nations, of the world." Distinguishing and bonding factors: consciousness of shared history, of sharing same land. External, cultural ones: language, religion. "Our gods", "our God". *Albanach*, *Sasanach* in Donegal Irish, meaning "Presbyterian", "Church of Ireland" — the religious adherence taken as equivalent to nationality. These external, recognisable features induced within the forming nation a feeling of kinship, helpfulness, willingness to co-operate.

2. The situation in medieval Europe

Such spontaneously forming nations existed in medieval Europe. In the eighth century, the Venerable Bede wrote his *Ecclesiastical History of Britain and Especially of the Race of the English*. At the start, he mentions four peoples as inhabiting Britain. At the same time, the Gaels in Ireland were conscious of being Gaels.

These natural or spontaneous nations were casual communities made up of other communities, lordships, cities. Together with neighbouring nations, and without regard to "national boundaries" between them, they were ruled by a variety of dynastic dukes, barons, earls and kings. The sense of national belonging was mingled with a sense of being the subjects of these various family dynasties, and of loyalty to them; or to important city-states ruled by councils. (Or consider the Uí Néill within the Gaelic nation, the Hansa within the German.) These nations, often split among different rulers, were distinguished and bonded principally by language, dress, saints and customs. Until the Reformation they hadn't the means of distinguishing themselves by religion — except on the boundaries with Orthodoxy: Croats, Serbs; Poles, Russians.

3. Emergence of instinctive or unprogrammatic nationalism

From the fourteenth and fifteenth centuries on, in some European countries, a political movement which we would later recognise as nationalism began. Most notably in England, France, Castile and Sweden. Strong monarchs, engaged in conflict, began to make the nation the supreme and exclusive principle of social belonging, to draw firm boundaries around it, and to construct nation-states. Quote from Austria book:[1] in the Hundred Years War, the French and the English, "the two nationalistic whetstones of medieval Europe, proceeded to sharpen themselves against each other. The so-called Hundred Years War, which dragged on until 1453, was a patriotic as well as a dynastic war . . ."

4. Emergence of conscious, programmatic nationalism

By the eighteenth century, England and France were the two outstanding nation-states, and they were to become exemplary for

---

[1] Gordon Brook-Shepherd, _The Austrians: A Thousand-Year Odyssey_, Harper Collins, 1997.

the rest of Europe. In Germany, the philosopher Herder emphasised the people or *Volk*, bound by language, folklore and custom,
as the central fact of human history, and the French Revolution
declared and spread the doctrine of national sovereignty as the
fundamental right of peoples, superior to that of dynasties.

From then on, many European nations were made highly conscious of themselves by writers, thinkers and ambitious politicians, and these elites set out to make their nations into nation-
states like Britain and France. Differently than the nations where
nationalism had originally emerged, these nations now had a
conscious programme based on existing models. The word "nationalism" emerged to describe both that effort to make and become a nation-state *and* the programme of self-maintenance in a
competitive world which the established nation-states pursued.
So we can say that nationalism is *the enterprise of establishing and/or
maintaining a nation-state, based on an actual or imagined nation.*
Incidentally, maintaining a nation-state in a competitive world led
easily to external imperialism — in order to anticipate or guard
against, or gain some advantage over a rival, a threatening com-
petitor. I said "external imperialism", for the fact is that successful
nationalism — as we shall see — is also an internal imperialism.
London, Paris, over the rest of the English, French. So it is fair to
say that there are two kinds of nationalism: imperialist nationalism and liberationist nationalism — as long as we keep in mind
that the liberationist kind, when successful, always engages in
internal imperialism and goes over, when it can, into the external
kind.

5. A closer look at the nation-state, its construction and maintenance

A nation-state meant essentially the replacement of a spontaneous,
casual nation, whose people had a variety of strong allegiances,
by a nation organised as a single state which purported to be the

nation. Its subjects or citizens had an overriding sense of belonging to it, and being defined by it, to an almost exclusive degree. A nation-state, in short, meant a nation transformed into a state, and therefore recognisable as a nation. Cf. the United "Nations" — which must be states to get admitted!

The construction of a nation-state began with an *idea* of a particular nation as a people with certain cultural characteristics — a distinguishing and bonding "national culture" — inhabiting a certain territory — the "national territory" — and having their own sovereign state, whether monarchy or republic. The nationalist project consisted in making that idea into a reality.

6. Realising the national idea

Realising the national idea meant intensifying and diffusing the national cultural characteristics, and concentrating the power of the nation for the benefit of the state and the citizens. Removing all other allegiances. Destroying power and authority, whether of aristocrats, or councils, or foreign governments, which came between the individuals and the national state. Removing barriers to internal trade — including local legal systems. (France at the Revolution — many provincial *parléments*, 360 local legal systems wiped out). In short, creating a single national administration, economy and legal system to go with the single, distinctive "national culture".

7. The agent

Normally the agent of this transformation was the ruling elite of a nuclear national state — Southeast England, the Paris region, Prussia, Piedmont — that controlled part of the projected "national territory". In other words, a minority of the projected nation.

The instruments of the nuclear national state were of three kinds: (a) persuasion, soft and hard; (b) purging force — the hanging, shooting, imprisonment, banishment of cultural dissidents —

Jews in Spain, Catholics in England, Protestants in monarchical France, Catholics in revolutionary France; artillery, to demolish castles and city walls; and (c) education — certainly through schools, perhaps, if there were a state church, through religious preaching also; more recently, through mass media.

Sometimes, as with Garibaldi in Italy, the nuclear state was helped by freelance nationalist freedom-fighters. Sometimes, as in Ireland between the beginnings of Irish nationalism in the 1790s and the establishment of the Free State, there was no nuclear state in the sense I have defined it, and the persuasion (through popular agitation, parliamentary activity, etc.), physical force and education had to be carried out by an amateur or part-time nationalist elite, or combination of elites, working under the occupying power. Since there was no artillery, the nationalist freelances had to make do with swords or rifles. As Brendan Behan truly said, "the terrorist is the fellow with the small bomb".

8. Nationalism and the Christian conscience

Nationalism has only very occasionally troubled the Christian conscience. Nationalism was created by Christian nations. Often devout Christians led it or were its willing beneficiaries. The principal causes of clashes between the Christian, usually the Catholic conscience, and nationalism has arisen from nationalism becoming gradually, and especially during and after the French Revolution, an alternative religion which erected the nation into a false God. The principal occasions when the Christian conscience has clashed with nationalism have been (a) when the nationalist leadership (e.g. in Reformation England) called for a religious or ideological conformity that some Christians could not in conscience accept, or (b) engaged in a war that seemed unjust or that used unjust methods, or (c) when nationalist measures for the increase, at all costs, of national economic power have oppressed or injured the poor and the weak.

Revisionism

March 12, 1997
Boston, Mass.

To: Professor Nancy J. Curtin
Fordham University
Joint Editor of *Éire-Ireland*

A contribution to your "Notes and Queries" section

Dr Desmond Fennell writes:

On a brief visit to the US from Ireland I have happened on Professor Power's article "Revisionist Nationalism's Consolidation, Republicanism's Marginalization, and the Peace Process" in the current issue of *Éire-Ireland*. Often, this sweeping summation of a recent Irish history in which I have actively participated causes me to cheer. But the account is vitiated by the repeated use, without obvious or argued justification, of two or three ideological descriptions which are at variance with those in use in Ireland. I will confine myself to the most serious instance, the "revisionist nationalism" of the title, which is used throughout the text. Here the Irish reader is presented not only with a term not current in Ireland, but with an oxymoron. And the American reader is misled and confused.

In well-established Irish parlance, a "revisionist" means, roughly, "a writer (journalist, essayist or historian) from the Republic of Ireland who is unsympathetic to Irish nationalism, and its representations, in the past; hostile to traditional Irish nationalism in the present; and more or less sympathetic, in past and present, to the unionists (the Ulster British) and to British policy in Ireland". Hence, the oxymoron of "revisionist nationalism"!

Originally, and still today primarily, a "revisionist" was/is a re-interpreter of the Irish past in an anti-nationalist vein — a mode which surfaced, journalistically, in the 1960s, and academically in the 1970s. It is to be distinguished from the moderate and scholarly revision of the nationalist version of Irish history which began in the 1930s, and which was not, and is not, called "(historical) revisionism".

A quite distinct phenomenon, which Professor Power wrongly merges with revision*ism*, was the nationalist rethinking of the nationalist position on the North which began in August 1969, and in which, as it happens, I played a pioneering and continuing role.[1] This revised or neo-nationalism, developed separately from the contemporaneous revisionist campaign, was furthered most effectively by the SDLP, and consolidated in the *New Ireland Forum Report* of 1984. Its programme of accommodation between the Irish and British communities in a Northern Ireland linked with Britain has come to be more or less accepted by those revisionists who have not become, simply, apologists for the unionists.

Given that in history-writing, as Professor Power indicates, revisionism has not been "consolidated", but transcended by a more balanced "post-revisionism", a title which would have allowed him to tell the story much more clearly might be "Revisionism Transcended, Neo-Nationalism's Consolidation, Republicanism's Marginalisation, and the Peace Process". This is not to ignore that, in ordinary as distinct from politically sectarian parlance, Irish republicanism has always been a wing or current of Irish nationalism.

---

[1] See my *The Revision of Irish Nationalism*, Dublin, Open Air, 1989.

Crime, Society and Conscience

Review of Crime, Society and Conscience, *edited by Seán MacRéamoinn,*
Columba Press, published in The Irish Catholic, *27 February 1997*

Contrary to what its title suggests, this book — with contributions from the editor Seán MacRéamoinn and four others —
is not about the "crime problem". In the opening chapter,
MacRéamoinn sets the agenda by commenting on two phrases in
a recent statement by Archbishop Connell:

> I do not believe that we can succeed in revising present
> trends towards lawlessness and crime, unless we tackle the
> weakening of moral convictions which lies at the source of
> our current malaise. This is largely the responsibility of the
> Church. But the work of the Church is rendered more diffi-
> cult by sustained attack on its moral teaching in so many
> areas of public discourse . . .

MacRéamoinn agrees that a "weakening of moral convictions" lies
behind the crime explosion. He writes of "moral breakdown". But
tackling this, he believes, is not "largely the responsibility of the
Church". "The state and other secular agencies" must make good
the historical lack of a civic ethic in Ireland by inculcating "a sense
of what it means to be a good citizen".

It makes sense to approach the crime problem in moral terms.
MacRéamoinn's point about a civic ethic is valid, and is touched
on by Anne Looney, and emphasised by Garret FitzGerald, in
their respective contributions. But where the book is weak is in its
unreal depiction of the scenario in which the present moral crisis
is occurring: what that scenario is, and who and what have done,
and are doing, what, to make it so.

Human will and agency are absent here. The only personal
agents who appear, but mainly in the past, are the Catholic clergy,

doing various wrongheaded things. Otherwise, the causative agents, beginning with "moral breakdown", are abstract. For Anne Looney, it's television and consumerism, producing passive young people who want only "buzz". For the two contributing clergy, Seán Fagan and Terence McCaughey, it's technology and cultural change. All these produce problems to which the Church must adapt, and they give conscience, properly understood, a pre-eminent role. For Garret FitzGerald, it's individualism that wreaks social havoc.

All those impersonal forces have contributed. But the discussion would have gained much in realism if MacRéamoinn, in setting the agenda, had not omitted to comment on the last part of Archbishop Connell's statement: "The work of the Church is rendered more difficult by sustained attack on its moral teaching in so many areas of public discourse".

When the Archbishop refers to "sustained attack", is he talking about something that is really happening? If so, these attacks must have identifiable human agents. Who, what kinds of Irish people, make the attacks and why? Why especially, in a country that lacks a second-line moral defence in the form of a civic ethic?

If this matter, thrown up by the quotation, had been explored, instead of being ignored, the scenario of discussion might have widened to embrace the momentous decision by the rulers of the West — Dublin merely following in their wake — to end their support for Christian ethics and to promote a more profitable, non-Christian morality.

With this important human agency duly taken into account, the real setting of our moral crisis and crime explosion would have been brought into play. And the discussion would have achieved that realism in dealing with the world which Christians need.

Dismayed by the lack of realism in the book just reviewed — and not only there — regarding moral affairs and the Church in Ireland, I tried to remedy this by drawing on the insights I had acquired during my two recent stays in the US: the La Conner visit and the Seattle sojourn. Hence the two items that follow this book review.

Advice to the Catholic Church
Must be Realistic

Written for The Irish Times, *7 February 1997, but not published*

The Catholic bishops aren't short of advice! Tony Downes (January 28th) follows Joe Foyle. Like Mr Foyle, he criticises the Catholic Church's current manner of preaching the Gospel; but his criticism is different and he advocates improvements of a different kind.

Mr Downes advises the Church to accommodate its preaching to the present times. But his arguments for this course of action are based on his characterisation of the present age, and this is seriously flawed. Obviously, if we are to talk about what the Church — or any institution — should be doing or saying now, we need to know what sort of times these are in our part of the world. Mr Downes does not seem to know this.

He describes the western world today as "post-modern". Fair enough; it comes after the "modern". But his main emphasis is on this being an "age of transition". And that again is true, except that every age is, in some sense, a transition. With these empty phrases, Mr Downes misses the main distinguishing feature of the age. Far from being yet another mere "transition", it is a beginning such as comes rarely in history — the start, if we are lucky, of a new civilisation; or, if we are not lucky, of a chaotic dark age.

He writes that "traditional attitudes, values, concepts, life-styles . . . are increasingly questioned". "Questioned" is a demurely inaccurate way of saying that, in the past half-century, the set of values and moral rules which the West upheld for many centuries has been powerfully overthrown, and replaced by a new

set which hundreds of millions live by. Mr Downes must have heard of the West being armed with weapons of massacre, of its "youth revolution", its "sexual revolution", its "liberation of women from patriarchy" — and of the plethora of new laws which enforce these revolutions and liberations.

To be aware that we are living in a radically new departure, one needs only to note some of the new rules — about religion, the past, and interpersonal relations — which now hold good from Los Angeles to Berlin. "It is wrong to take guidance from the past or for the State to support Christian morality. An educated person doesn't need to know Latin. High-spending consumers, because they power the economy, are the most valuable members of society. Women are right to abort their babies if they wish, and people may divorce and remarry as often as they desire. All kinds of sexual association between consenting adults are legitimate and equally normal. Chastity is pathological. The massacre of innocent men, women and children is in certain circumstances legitimate. There is no difference between men's work and women's work. Age has no authority over youth, nor men over women. Girls who copulate and bear babies without committed fathers are to be specially cherished, never blamed. Human beings may be conceived in test-tubes. Some parts of living bodies are legitimately saleable."

Whether for good or ill, this post-western, non-Christian civilisation is the environment in which the Church now exists. Once again, as in its first three centuries, the rulers of the West endorse a worldview and a morality which are intrinsically hostile to Christianity; and most westerners find this acceptable. Advice to the Church that is not based on this perception of the present age is useless. Such advice is realistic and of possible use only if it takes account of this obtaining situation, and relates to what the Church, while remaining the Church, can actually do in these circumstances.

In the West for the foreseeable future — elsewhere the story varies — the Catholic Church is an awkwardly surviving cultural dinosaur. It embodies and transmits a transcendental faith in God made flesh in Jesus, and a way of life which arises from that faith. Simultaneously, the Church transmits the Judaeo-Christian and Graeco-Roman philosophy of man that shaped European civilisation. Because, in the present and foreseeable state of affairs, that gospel is absurd and that humanism irrelevant, the Church cannot, as Mr Downes wishes, please the rulers and opinion-makers of the West, and cannot, without itself being absurd, agree with them. To those many millions of decent, well-meaning people who adhere to the new, reigning worldview and rules of conduct, the Church must necessarily seem irrelevant or perverse.

When it does things that the consumerist preachers are also doing — when it calls for measures to help the poor, condemns the IRA, or mobilises aid for starving Africans — it will of course be praised. But where its discipline and its distinctive teaching, its sacred action and its clergy are concerned, the Catholic Church's normal lot will be caricature, smear and dismissal, inevitably.

Both for that reason, and because its access to media of mass communication is meagre, the Church will be unable to make itself known to most people. Even that "Catholic control" of many schools which worries our local consumerists will amount to little. Experience has shown that the mass media preachers can adequately counteract initial Christian influence on the young.

By and large, then, society will continue on its new, pagan way, governed by new, pagan rules. The possibilities open to the Catholic Church will be within this context. As it did in its first Roman centuries and in penal times in Ireland, it can and will continue to exist as a community of faith in Jesus, which is its main *raison d'être*. Freed from responsibility for the welfare of the West generally, and the Irish in particular, the Church can and will develop and innovate, theologically, philosophically, and liturgically. It will do this — as it has done before now in civilisations with which it was at odds — by observing attentively the new evolving life around it and reflecting on the Gospel in the light of this. While it cannot, by definition, join the non-Christian system, it can profit from it. Every new civilisation or new barbarism reveals new facets of human nature and of the ways of God.

There is, moreover, no limit, other than practical, to the works of charity which the Church can perform for the victims of the new order. And finally, in Ireland as elsewhere, the developing comradeship of Catholics with other Christians, and with religious Muslims and Jews, can continue to deepen.

Such, it seems to me, is the framework of realistic possibility within which, in the present circumstances, advice can be usefully offered to the Catholic Church, whether from within it or from without.

The Church in the World

Two articles, published in The Irish Catholic, *24 April and 1 May 1997. For an expanded treatment of the themes dealt with in these articles — and in the previous item — see my* Savvy and the Preaching of the Gospel, *Veritas, August 2003.*

1. Effective preaching needs knowledge of the world

Preaching the Gospel necessarily involves saying things about the world which the faithful inhabit. In this respect, I have had a difficulty for some time with the teaching Church in Ireland. While in matters of grassroots detail the clergy are evidently *au fait* with the temporal reality, they often seem naïve or hazy about the general circumstances of the times. This gets in the way as I listen to them or read them. It considerably lessens, for me, the effectiveness of their teaching.

My distress about this isn't primarily on my own account. Many years ago I was deeply impressed by something the German philosopher Josef Pieper wrote about prudence (in German, much better named *Klugheit* or "savvy"). Explaining why it is the virtue basic to all virtues, he wrote:

> Realisation of the good [making it actual in the world] presupposes knowledge of reality. He alone can do good who knows what things are like and what their situation is . . . So-called "good intention" and so-called "meaning well" by no means suffice. Realisation of the good presupposes that our actions [say, preaching the Gospel] are appropriate to the real situation, that is to the concrete realities which form the environment of the action; and that we therefore take this concrete reality seriously, with clear-eyed objectivity.

For a start, take the mass media. They very much "form the en-vironment of" Christian preaching, pastoral letters and so on, and Fr Tom Stack was writing last November [in his column in *The Irish Catholic*] about their relationship to the Church. He quoted Avery Dulles SJ on the "necessary tension" between the media and the Church due to their different aims and nature. True enough, but what Fr Stack did not go on to say — in his space he cannot say everything! — is that "necessary tension" does not mean necessary hostility. Many of us can remember when the media in Ireland were not hostile to the Catholic Church, and in Britain and the USA not hostile to Protestant religion. Specifically, in all three countries the media didn't oppose Christian morality, but on the contrary, were supportive of it.

Lurking therefore unsaid in Fr Stack's article were the follow-ing "facts of the present environment". Without any intrinsic necessity, the principal media on both sides of the Atlantic have become hostile to Christian morality — to the Christian "moral package" — and consequently to those who teach it. The principal media, on both sides of the Atlantic, adhere to and propagate a non-Christian set of rules of good, bad and neutral behaviour. The hostility of the Irish national media to Christian morality, and their propagation of a non-Christian code, is a local instance of this general western development. In the second half of this cen-tury a major change occurred in the moral history of the West.

It isn't that effective preaching of the Gospel always requires such "environmental facts" to be mentioned. It's that, together with other similar facts, they must be known clearly to the preacher, must colour what he says, and be available for spelling out when the occasion seems to require it. Such occasions aren't necessarily infrequent. The people who are being addressed are often blind to, or misinformed about, the environment in which they are being called on to realise the Christian good — and con-sequently, are incapable of doing so.

What is the specific nature and purpose of the pagan morality which the western media have been propagating? Fr Stack, in that article, suggested the answer when he wrote: "Religion is now the only challenge to the rationale of the consumer culture." The reigning, pagan morality is the morality of "consumer culture". Its purpose is to "grow" the Western economy — and insofar as profitable, the constituent national economies — by getting people to desire and buy goods and services. To this end, its basic principle is as follows: "It is right for you to go for and get any thing or person you desire, provided you don't — except when the law is outmoded and oppressive — break the civil law".

Obviously, the Church, by teaching Christian morality, hinders the consumerist programme. That is why "Catholic education" is something to be decried. That notorious *Irish Times* headline NEW BILL WILL COPPERFASTEN CHURCH CONTROL OF SCHOOLS was a cry of panic about their rivals from the consumerist preachers.

Those are some of the realities that form the environment in which the Church teaches in Ireland today. Another is that the consumerist morality, by helping to "grow" the international economy, has helped to make the Irish much better-off materially, and physically healthier and more long-lived, than they ever were. Add, finally, this fact of contemporary history which should lodge in the Church's awareness and condition its teaching: the long centuries have ended in which the rulers of the West, whether believers or not, saw virtue in upholding Christian morality and basing their laws on it. We are back, as it were, in a province of the pagan Roman Empire, and with no Emperor Constantine in prospect.

2. Has the Church chosen a hidden existence?

In an article in this paper last September, Fr Colin Garvey discussed the persistent attempt by powerful forces in Irish society to push the Church and religion out of public life. It is not surprising that this should be happening. Since the US Supreme Court, in 1963, ended organised Christian prayer in American public schools — or, more precisely, since the official endorsement of Hiroshima as a virtuous act — the trend throughout the West has been to refound society on non-Christian principles and to render religion a purely private affair.

But there is another side to the story in Ireland, a mysterious side. I mean the voluntary withdrawal of the Catholic Church and religion from the public sphere and from self-manifestation in daily life. And combined with that, a persistent refusal to counter the attempted exclusion by creative "intrusions" into the nation's life. All in all, something like a deliberate choice of a hidden existence.

The public Corpus Christi and May processions ceased. Happy occasions, they were the stuff of many treasured child-hood memories and of parish and civic pride. In the streets of Dublin, Hare Krishna became the only living evidence of religion.

With the onset of consumerism, Lenten fasting was brought to an end. This recurrent, sensible presence of religion in the minds, physical life, and conversation of the faithful was withdrawn. Christianity became perhaps the only religion, ever, not to include periodic fasting in its discipline. The "no meat on Friday" rule, which had immemorially been part of the routine of homes and restaurants, was annulled. Both measures, coming when they did and unasked for, seemed like a wish by the Church to accommo-date consumerism, to let it have unchallenged sway. In retrospect, it chimes with the recent withdrawal of Corpus Christi and other holydays from intrusion into weekday money-making and shop-ping by shifting these feasts to Sundays.

Consumerism sold itself as permission and as liberation — of youth, sexuality and women, and from penury and frugality. The Church responded in accordance with its stereotype in consumer-ist propaganda, by reiterating prohibition — of illicit sex, contra-ception, abortion, divorce, excess of all kinds — and by silence on liberation. On this great theme, so central to the Irish consciousness and memory, and now to a de-religionising crusade, the faithful were left without the Christian word. It was the theme crying out loud for the Church to make into the obtrusive, challenging core of its message to the nation — so easy, what else is the Gospel about? But the Church remained silent on liberation, as enslavement to materialism and sensuality proceeded.

Speaking predictably is one way for the Church to be inaudible. Talking like secular social workers is another. Largely through the media, a collective impression arose of priests and nuns, collectively, doing this. Hiding the light it was their vocation to shed, they could be heard agreeing with the consumerist cant that the growth of violence and robbery, and the spreading appetite for drugs, were caused by material deprivation. No surprise then, when the people marched against the drug-dealers and drove them from their streets, that the news bulletins carried no word of street missions, sprung up to fill the spiritual vacuum.

It is an old wisdom of the Church that people can be attached and attracted by catering to their temporal needs. The opportunities to do this change with changing circumstances. During the last twenty-five years it became the order of the day for every town to have a "festival". I have still to hear of one that, by Church initiative or otherwise, honours a saint. As the magazines and feature pages where non-journalists could place a thoughtful article melted away, Irish intellectuals found themselves without a periodic forum for reflection and debate. This might have suggested something.

As vocations to the religious orders decreased, large country houses without function became available to the Church. Years before the Tyrone Guthrie Centre for working writers and artists opened in Annaghmakerrig, it was proposed to Cardinal Conway that the Church establish such a centre. In the 1930s when Fianna Fáil in power found itself confronted with uniformly hostile national media, de Valera founded a daily newspaper so that his party's voice could be heard in print and its detractors refuted.

From the 1970s onwards, as the national media became ever more hostile to the Church, a similar initiative seemed obviously called for.

For any of these creative "interventions" in the life of the nation and in the interests of religion, money, if needed, would not have been lacking. The Church can mobilise millions for needy Africans.

All praise to the Conference of Religious, and to like-minded priests and nuns, who have worked alongside secular agencies to ensure that the material enrichment promoted by consumerism is more evenly spread. What I am talking about, and have no explanation for, is the voluntary process by which the Church has chosen to make itself and religion increasingly invisible, inaudible and insensible in Irish life.

Trains Are Heaven

Written 19 June 1997 and sent to The Irish Times *but not published. This long train journey was in fact a search for a new home, and resulted in my settling in Anguillara, near Rome, in September 1997.*

I have just returned from travelling much of Europe by train, and there is a lot to be said for that mode of travel when the trains are as good as they are in most of the Continent. Add to the comfortable seat with leg-room and the freedom to move around on board, the painless delivery into city centres, the certainty that in a few hours there will be "another train", and the adjacency of cheap hotels to stations. Make it heaven by travelling with one easily portable bag containing a collapsible umbrella. This has an extra advantage if you are alighting in France: for fear of bombs, they have suspended all baggage storage in stations.

In London's Victoria Station I had an experience which told me more about Britain's difficulty in relating to Europe than a score of speeches by Euro-sceptics. Victoria, as everyone knows, is the principal British railway station for travel to the Continent. Arriving there at 6pm, and wanting to buy a ticket to Vienna for the following morning, I discovered that the "International" ticket-offices had closed at five. On enquiring elsewhere in the station, I learned that a separate private company now ran that section and, as well as closing on weekdays at five, it closed on Saturday afternoons and Sundays.

At Ostende, and again when I changed at Cologne, every carriage was divided by a glass door into smoking and non-smoking. Reflecting on how a religion of bodily health has replaced the old religion of the West, it occurred to me that such arrangements are now the yardstick by which religious tolerance is to be measured, as one moves from country to country. Along the train route through Flanders, French, not so long ago dominant there, has been banished from public view. Only Dutch is to be seen ("Dutch" is now the official name for "Flemish"). The effect is to produce a visible continuum of quasi-German or German proper all the way from Ostende to Vienna. Dutch followed by *Deutsch*.

In Heidelberg people give you slightly different versions of why the Americans refrained from bombing the city — they wanted it for the American occupation headquarters or an air force general was sentimental about *The Student Prince*. The temple of that old student world is the Seppel near the Castle hill. So unpretentious as to be almost unnoticeable, it has remained scrupulously its old, plain self: no bar, just two rooms with long wooden tables incised with the initials of student generations. Only the walls, covered with old photos, cuttings, cartoons and fraternity emblems, going back more than a hundred years, show its sense of self. Visit it in the daytime to examine the walls, in the evening during term to see the students and to hear them singing.

Down a short, narrow side-street, a protruding sign "Sex Boutique" cut into my view of the lovely baroque church façade at the other end. The new civilisation and the old. A young Kurd I met told me he had been a policeman of Saddam Hussein's regime; that was why he was now in Heidelberg working in an American restaurant, sending money home to his family in Kurdistan. It is asparagus season; so my good Swedish friend, Sture Ureland, in nearby Nussloch, gave me tender stalks of it with slices of smoked raw ham for dinner in the sunny garden. In the Main valley, I remember from another time, every country inn in early summer was advertising *Spargel* with trout. I would eat it forever with either accompaniment. I wonder why it is so rare in Ireland.

At the Frankl in Mannheim, where Sture is a university professor, we drank with George Broderick, Manx linguist and old friend, who has made his career in Germany. A student of German folk songs, he has the fame of shocking people from

Mann and the Dublin Institute of Advanced Studies to the Seppel
in Heidelberg by singing some of the songs loudly with their Nazi
words. If you mention to anyone in Germany, apart from Mannheim, that you are going there, they ask with a look of dismay,
"Why Mannheim?" It is an industrial city, heavily destroyed in
the war, and rebuilt in a bleak modernity. Not a place I would
choose to live, but the fact that Alsace is a short distance away
across the border set me thinking.

In Munich it was a sensual pleasure to walk the central streets
in the warm sun, observing the gracious affluence — the abundant displays of fruits of the earth, the good clothes, the contented
people walking or sitting. In the West we are passing through a
remarkable moment, deserving to be treasured, of human material achievement. Munich still shows itself as the regal city of the
Bavarian kingdom — all those architectural perspectives, those
grandiose neo-classical buildings. The "National" Theatre means
"of Bavaria", not Germany. But my most lasting memory of
Munich — apart from the Lenbach Haus art gallery, of which
more anon — is a Sunday afternoon in the suburb of Solln, when
my friends Walter and Helga went off to fetch Helga's mother
home for a meal of *Spargel*. It was a cameo of civilisation as an
active force — how people are encouraged to civility by the man-
made environment.

It begins with the white block of flats in which Walter and
Helga live on the ground floor. The block is four storeys high, built
as three wings irregularly protruding; seven flats with verandas in
each wing; garages underground; grass extending all around; a
pond with ducks; a semi-circle of enclosing trees. The trees are the
edge of a small wood and you can enter it, go down steps to an iron
gate which you open with a private key, and emerge on a straight
road. A canal, with occasional wooden bridges, runs parallel, and
beyond the canal flows the broad river Isar.

On the river there were three canoes. The land between canal
and river was laid out as a park with paths. People were standing

on one of the canal bridges, looking upstream towards Munich, and joining them I soon saw what they were watching for. A log raft, with about thirty people sitting on it, was coming downstream to a weir, beyond which the water-level sloped rapidly for a few metres. As the raft slid wobbling, over and down, there was laughter and screaming. As it regained the flat water surface and moved towards and beneath us, we could hear the accordion music and the singing. It was the first of several such rafts, great entertainment! On the bridge, in a wooden niche, there was a statue of a saint, and beneath it: "This bridge was built in 1914, renovated in 1957, rebuilt 1985."

Walking in the direction the water was flowing, with cars and cyclists passing me, I came to a beer-garden, old refectory tables under trees. There was a place where you could get beer and salads, another for meat and bretzels, and from somewhere, people were carrying grilled fish on plates. The chef at the meat grill was dispensing half-chickens, pork ribs and cutlets. From the bridge to these tables, not an angry shout nor a blow struck; no cans, bottles or paper littering the ground.

It struck me that when the families and couples came here at a week-end in 1914 they were eating and drinking precisely the same things as today, and, apart from the cars and the clothes, it was the same scene. Such stability at Europe's heart is consoling.

Something that Vienna and Munich have in common is a great number of public benches and other seats for people simply to sit on. I recalled Seattle, where you will search in vain in the central streets for a place to sit; doubtless, because the city authorities believe that good Americans have better things to do. (If there were benches, vagrants and homeless people would sit on them, and smokers, driven from smoking indoors, might smoke comfortably.)

But something else, more personal, linked the two German-speaking cities for me: in both, I visited the collections of paintings from the period 1895–1925: in Munich, the Lenbach Haus, where Kandinsky, Marc and others of the *Blaue Reiter* group are strongly represented; in Vienna, the Belvedere Palace, where you can see the Vienna Secession painters, Klimt and Schiele. This is the "other" modernist movement in painting — the German one — which set in somewhat later than the French one we are more familiar with. Dresden and Berlin were its other centres. Kandinsky is one of the few painters who made abstraction into enduring art. In recent years there is a vogue for Klimt and Schiele reproductions. As much in Germany as in France, it was a benefit to painting, and to all art, that there were still rules to break. Breaking them offered the pleasing variant of "liberation".

Incidentally, the visitor to Vienna who is looking for the "Secession" painters can be confused, as I was, by a building — also an art gallery — which bears that name. All it has of the "Secession" is the style of the building and a frieze by Klimt. When I was there, it also had an exhibition by the Irish installation artist James Coleman, who has been making his career on the Continent. The Dublin actress, Olwen Fouéré figured in several of his installations.

On the train from Munich to Vienna I stopped off for an hour or so to meet Róisín Ní Mheara in the station café of a small town. It was set in a landscape of mountains and meadows near the Austrian border. Róisín caused quite a scandal a few years ago in respectable Irish-language circles when she published *Cé hÍ Sin Amuigh?*, the first half of her autobiography. Born of Irish parents in London, she was adopted in the 1920s into the aristocratic Hamilton family and grew up in their circle of pro-German sympathisers. She spent the war years in Berlin, where she was well acquainted with Francis Stuart, and was firmly convinced that the war had been thrust on the Germans by Churchill. Then, rediscovering her Irish roots, she learned Irish in the Aran Islands. These days she is an apostle of Irish culture in Vienna who has invited Bob Quinn and myself to perform there. A specialist in Irish saints in Central Europe, she has collaborated in research with Cardinal Tomás Ó Fiaich. Some life! We talked. She is a lovely lady. I enquired about house prices, for buying or renting, in that beautiful countryside.

As on a previous visit, I was struck in the Vienna station concourse by a large display of small pornographic magazines — their massed covers not a pleasant sight for a woman arriving in Vienna to see. It links in my mind with the miserable daily newspapers of this great city: Vienna, for some odd reason, lacks a single newspaper of any quality or even size. In Sebastian Haffner's excellent book *The Meaning of Hitler,* which I read recently, the author says that research has found no personal experience of Hitler's in Vienna that might have given rise to his virulent anti-Jewishness.[1] When I was on the town one evening with an *echt* Viennese couple — both of them fans of pop, he "the Mick Jagger of the *Favoriten* district" — they told me that Hitler, as a young painter, had been refused entry to the Academy by a Jewish professor who at the same time had admitted a young Jew. That was what made him anti-Jewish. Is this what is called an urban legend? It is not the only false story about Hitler's years in Vienna which, until recently, appeared in book after book.

Talking of *echt* Viennese, Vienna is the only city which has a cuisine named after it, and Helene told me that she sends parcels of Viennese food to her sister in California because the poor woman, without it — it's the only proper food — is reduced to a diet of tuna and yoghurt!

Prosperous, charming Vienna, amid the stage-set of its imperial past, has become trivialised in mentality to a sort of "Swiss" city — something like Zurich. The difference is — you can see it in the bookshops and picture-postcards, hear it in people's talk — that Vienna dwells nostalgically on the great imperial personalities of the past, particularly the empresses Maria Teresia and Elisabeth and the last emperor, Franz Joseph. And concerts of

---

[1] This is confirmed with much detail — including Hitler's friendships with Viennese Jews — in Brigitte Hamann's fascinating *Hitler's Vienna: A Dictator's Apprenticeship,* trans. Thomas Thornton, Oxford University Press, 1999.

Viennese music — all the greats — are advertised everywhere as tourist attractions.

Vienna was a Roman foundation, Vindobona, but as a base for the Tenth Legion, not a city. The local Roman city, distinguished by the death there of the emperor Marcus Aurelius, was Carnuntum, forty kilometres away. The military base was close to the Danube and was built over by Old Vienna. But you can see some unearthed ruins by passing through a sushi shop and descending stairs. They are the remains of two staff officers' quarters, with the heating-system beneath the floor and in the cavity walls well preserved. Evidently the camp had its own tile-works; in the glass display cases it is moving to see tiles stamped LEG X (Tenth Legion) as clearly as if the stamp had been applied yesterday.

Eric Hobsbawm, the British Marxist historian, was originally a Hobsbaum in Vienna. RTÉ recently showed a documentary he made on and around *"die Pressburger Bahn"*, "the Pressburg train". In the good old days, that was the train, an hour's journey, from Vienna to the city the Slavs call Bratislava — just across the border of Slovakia. Bratislavans, said Hobsbawm, used to take it to the theatre in Vienna, returning home the same night. While Czechoslovakia was Communist it ceased to function, but it is now running again and I took it (actually my particular train was going on to Kiev and Moscow).

Suddenly, when you arrive in Bratislava — and it has only been an hour — you are in a quite different, Slav world: only Slovak to be heard around you or seen in public signs, and, surprisingly, speakers of German as thin on the ground as speakers of English. It was an odd experience because, with Germany becoming almost as multi-ethnic as Austria always was, between Mannheim and Vienna I had spoken German with Brazilians, Kurds, Serbs, Albanians, Turks and black Africans.

Another part of the difference when you enter Bratislava is that you have visibly left affluent Europe. Buildings, people's faces and women's clothes retain that poor and worn look that went with the "socialist East". But the old centre is being restored and painted, and is showing a handsome, *Mitteleuropa* face. Fortunately, for my day's visit, I had a Dublin friend, John Minahane, who is teaching English there, to explain the intricacies of Slovak life and politics: among other things, how Slovakia deals with its Hungarian minority and how it is divided, politically, between eastward- and westward-leaning factions.

In the café where I waited for him, there was a press conference about a French-sponsored "festival" of TV advertisements. The young organisers of the conference about this "glamour" event, and the journalists who attended, reminded me of Dublin in the Sixties. How we were thrilled by the Chianti and Mateus Rosé bottles and the espresso coffee-bars, as the great exotic world out there arrived!

On the overnight train to Rome I took a couchette, and part of the deal was that the attendant brought breakfast in the morning. I suspect this is a way of ensuring that everyone gets up early — it happened around Florence — and has restored the compartment to some order before time comes for getting off. But it reminds me of something I noticed about all the trains I travelled on from Cologne right around to France and the Tunnel. The carriages devoted to eating and drinking were furnished, imaginatively, to look like their equivalents on "dry land". Bars had a variety of high-stool and chair arrangements, and the restaurant parts looked like, well, restaurants. A number of the trains also had a play-room for children, complete with rocking-horses *et al*.

Rome was to be a one-day stop to visit a countess in Anguillara before proceeding to Bari to see a poetess. But various telephone calls to Bari from a bar in Rome failed to locate her or her husband. The Anguillara part, however, went ahead. That is an old town on a promontory jutting into a big lake, about a half-hour by train north of Rome. I first met the countess a few years ago, when her villa was providing an occasional base for the itinerant poet Desmond O'Grady. Enquiring now at the café where she read *La*

Repubblica every morning, I learned that she had sold the villa and
was living in a hotel near the station. It turned out that she now
made do with a single room. When I asked her about renting or
buying in Anguillara, she phoned a Russian woman who had a flat
for rent and who duly showed it to me the following day.

Marcella, the *contessa*, told me that Desmond O'Grady was
once again in the vicinity, staying this time with Luigi Attardi in
Rome. So there was a night at a restaurant on Campo dei Fiori
with Desmond, Luigi and his girlfriend, Caterina, and we drank
to the publication of Desmond's collected translations and
collected poems by the University of Salzburg Press. Luigi gave
me his own first ventures into poetry to read on the train to
Montpélier the next day.

I was surprised by how seriously the Italian papers were taking
the separatist movements in Venice and the North. But when I read
detailed reports of public meetings in those parts, and saw pictures
of them, I understood a little better. The rhetoric at the meetings
was both anti-Roman and anti-Italian. The Venetian movement was
harking back to the Venetian Republic. One of the activist groups
was called "Michael Collins Commando". Both the Venetian, and
the broader "Padanian" movement, were carrying banners that
displayed the "Celtic sun" — obviously a recall of those ancient
Roman days when Italy ended at the Rubicon and the land to the
north, "Cisalpine Gaul", was mainly occupied by Celts.

Trust the French railway-workers to provide a strike to disrupt
my progress! Officially, the train from Rome was to terminate in
Narbonne, but at ten o'clock on the Sunday night we were
dumped at the border-post, Ventimiglia, with the choice of staying there for the night or taking a local train to Nice. At the reception desk of the hotel in Nice where some of us sought refuge for
the night, the man, referring to the railway-workers, exclaimed
wearily, *"Les imbéciles!"*.

Fortunately, the strike was for Whit weekend only, so I
reached Montpélier before the following noon. I was there

because Redmond O'Hanlon, who has been promoting Languedoc wines in Ireland, had insisted that a life that leaves out
Languedoc is a life not worth living. So I hired a car, and because
that was an infidelity to trains I was punished for it. Two hours
later, parking at a fence, and not yet fully adjusted to the width of
the vehicle as measured from its left-hand drive, I grazed its right
wing. That discoloured inch and a half cost me more, when it
came to the reckoning, than the hire for two days.

But it is true, the villages and small towns of Languedoc — or
such of them as I saw — are pretty, sometimes beautiful, especially
Péznas, and some of the wines are very good. The cooking is
splendid. To sit in the sun at the harbour in Mèze, eating oysters,
mussels and prawns, comes near to heaven. In Péznas, which
prides itself on its doors — it has a "Doors of Péznas" tourist
poster! — I stayed in the Hotel Molière because Molière spent
seven years in the town. But both there and in a couple of other
towns, I was saddened to notice the underlying depopulation being
partially replaced by "art workshops" of "art for tourists", and by
North Europeans who have retired or bought houses for holidays.

The Third Republic, from the 1880s on, really hammered the
ideology of the Republic — and the "national culture" as defined
by Paris — into people's minds. I know it is the same all over
France, but it hadn't struck me so forcibly before as in this region
remote from Paris and much nearer Spain. Not only has every
town its *"Rue de la République"*: it has streets or parking-lots of the
"14 July" or of "Voltaire" (or Victor Hugo or Montaigne), a *"Café
du Progrés"* and a female statue of the Rights of Man. Those names
of long-dead Parisian politicians, Gambetta, Briand, Clémenceau,
Jaurès, become a bore. A church had *"Liberté, Égalité, Fraternité"*
engraved over its main door.

The journey home was straight to Paris and through the Tunnel, with only a stop and a night in Lyons to visit its Gallo-Roman
museum. It is on a hill which you reach by a funicular and from
which you have fine views of this handsome city at the meeting of

the Rhône with the Saône. (Actually, most visitors take the funicular to reach the great Cathedral at the top.) Apart from the museum being a fine modern building that takes you through its exhibits on a continuously sloping, circling floor, the point in visiting it is that Lyons was the capital of Roman Gaul. The river-harbour traded with northern Europe and the Orient. The Gaulish chiefs assembled in Lugdunum annually, to be bedazzled by Roman urban splendour.

The Sunday morning train from London to Holyhead left me with a few hours to wait for the boat. Holyhead has "cafés" where you can have meals. When the man placed the "meal" in front of me, I looked at it with fascination, and felt really "abroad". After my three weeks' experience of Continental eating, I was spoiled.

A Provincial Passion:
Cleansing Irish Literature of Irishness

InCognito *(Dublin), Vol. 2, 1997. Based on a paper, "A Puritan Passion: Cleansing Irish Literature of Irishness", read at the Kerry International Festival of Living Irish Authors, Tralee, 8 August 1997 (the Festival theme was "Love and Passion in Irish Literature"). Also published in* Éire-Ireland *(Morristown, New Jersey), Samhradh/Fomhar, 1997.*

I

In the Tralee literary journal *Asylum* (Winter 1997), a French-woman, Maggie Pernot wrote about the short stories of Neil Jordan in the late 1970s. The best known of these is "Night in Tunisia". Madame Pernot's particular interest lay in exploring a programmatic decision of Jordan's as reflected in these stories. I quote from her second paragraph:

> From the outset Neil Jordan had chosen to move away from tradition and to write about aspects of everyday life that would not immediately be identified as Irish. The smell of boiled cabbage is conspicuously absent from his stories as are the whitewashed cottages, the rain-drenched winding lanes or the Dublin pubs with their roaring drunkards, to give just a few examples. In the same way, references to the past, or to Irish war, are either non-existent or alluded to briefly and then, only as memories rather than experience.

Madame Pernot explains this decision partly by the fact that Jordan was born in 1950 and had no experience of the major historical events in Ireland in the early part of the century. But there was more to it than that. Jordan had told her that in his stories he was consciously "not referring to ideas of national identity" but "expressing another reality, everyday facts, ordinary facts . . . something mundane, contemporary . . ."

So, recent Irish history and ideas of national identity were out. One of his stories made clear that the "recent Irish history" which was not relevant included even mid-century De Valera and what he stood for. Moreover, Maggie Pernot, quoting further — this time from an interview with Jordan by Richard Kearney — shows that the great works of English Irish literature were also out. Jordan told Kearney:

> When I started writing I felt very pressured by the ques-
> tion: how do I cope with the notion of Irishness? It meant
> almost nothing to me. I was, of course, profoundly moved
> by the Irish literature I encountered as a student — Yeats
> and Joyce. But how was I to write about the experience I
> knew, as someone born in Sligo and growing up in the
> suburban streets of Dublin in the sixties? The great books of
> Anglo-Irish literature had very little to do with this, they
> had no real resonance at this level. My most acute dilemma
> was — how to write stories about contemporary urban life
> in Ireland without being swamped in the language and
> mythology of Joyce. . . . . The only identity, at a cultural
> level, that I could forge was one that came from the worlds
> of television, popular music and cinema which I was
> experiencing daily.

Note, in passing, that these "worlds", and the East Coast urban teenagers who dwelt in them and who figured centrally in Jordan's stories, were actually part of contemporary Irishness: a non-distinctive, largely British and American part of it. So it could be said that Jordan, as compared with most of his predecessors, was simply shifting the focus within Irish life. He was directing it to a previously neglected class of characters — suburban, middle-class Dublin teenagers — and to aspects of Irishness which, in addition to language, were shared with Britain and America. But that is not what he said or what he conceived himself to be doing. Under-

standing Irishness to mean the distinctively native, whether historical, literary or lived, he wanted his writing not to reflect that,
but rather, the contemporary human condition, whether located
in Ireland or elsewhere.

Madame Pernot then proceeds to check out the stories in detail
to see whether Jordan has indeed fulfilled his intention of writing
"un-Irish" literature, which she takes to mean, reasonably enough,
literature that is "simply human". That can mean having human
significance of a contemporary kind or, more broadly, of a perennial nature; here it is a matter of "contemporarily human". As the
checking-out proceeds, item by item, it becomes unintentionally
amusing. The teenagers of many of the stories are into pop culture: there is nothing distinctively Irish about that. The same goes
for their interest in girls and sex; that is how boys are today anywhere. True, the placenames and some other details suggest an
Irish setting, but "that in itself would not be enough to prove their
specific Irishness, especially as the seaside resorts of the east coast
of Ireland, with their beaches, amusement arcades and tennis
courts, could just as well be situated on the other side of the Irish
Sea . . . and the two Dublin street names [that occur] are to be
found in many British towns".

No, where Jordan's stories, in Pernot's judgement, do back-
slide into betraying their Irishness is not so much "in the geographical landscape, as in the spiritual landscape". There are
many indications that the setting is a Catholic country. Moreover,
in the treatment of the adult characters there are clear signs that
they are people who have absorbed not only Catholicism, but the
general Christian and religious scheme of things. That, I would
comment in passing, does not seem a very convincing indication
that the stories are specifically Irish. Rather is it an indication that
they are not British or American; or simply, that they are situated
in a Catholic and religious country. At all events, Madame Pernot
meticulously lists the references and phrases that indicate a
Catholic and generally religious ambience.

As I remarked, this meticulous checking-out becomes amusing. But there is also, on the face of it, something amusing in the reported endeavour of an author of fiction to eradicate any trace of his national milieu from his stories. Clearly, a passion was at work here, a passion as distinct from a reasonable purpose, and it was a strange passion. The distinctively native thing, which is present one way or another in most of the world's literature, was felt to be something that would thwart, sully or diminish the art. To keep it out as much as possible would result in a cleaner, purer, more genuinely human art; an art that would reflect the contemporary human condition in Ireland or wherever.

As we focus in, in this manner, on the passion, it ceases to be amusing and becomes familiarly sad. It is recognisable as an instance of the psychological dermatitis that afflicts deeply colonised people in successive bouts. Literally or metaphorically, they sense that the skin they were born with and grew up in, and which distinguishes them, comes between them and being real persons living a real human life in the world. So, afflicted with angst about their condition in the world and hoping to right it, they try to get rid of their skin, or rather, to change it, literally or metaphorically. In a succession of efforts, and with the dermatitis always recurring to spur them on, they change their faces as much as they can, abandon their distinctive dress or food, their laws and customs, their language, their literary modes; finally, with great difficulty, their religion.[1] And the norm of humanity that they pursue in all this, and that they strive to adopt, is that of the imperial power — singular or hybrid — that is colonising them. As everyone knows, a fresh bout of this psychological dermatitis hit the Irish of the Republic in the 1960s and intensified in the 1970s. The norm of proper humanity to which it aspired was not — as in similar instances it never is — actually the norm of humanity, but rather, the package of new norms proclaimed in those years by New York–

---

[1] See "Engaging Modernity in a Hi-tech Centre", pp. 255–8.

London. So it is not really surprising to find this unease with the native, and desire to abandon it for the dominant contemporary, reflected in the Irish literary sphere in English in the late 1970s.

Jordan was not alone in his endeavour. In Irish literary circles it was in the air. The year after his collection *Night in Tunisia* was published, an American, William Vorm, who had noticed a change in Irish fiction, especially among the young writers, published a collection of new Irish short stories called *Paddy No More*.[2] A more programmatic title would be difficult to imagine. The book included, besides two stories by Jordan, stories by Dermot Healy, Lucile Redmond, John Montague, Desmond Hogan and Juanita Casey. In fact, however, the belief that giving Irish fiction, and Irish writing generally, a non-Irish content was a good thing had surfaced earlier, if in a somewhat different form.

Besides writing stories, set in Ireland, which avoided a distinctively Irish flavour, another way for Irish authors to achieve "non-Irishness" in their work was to set the stories in foreign milieus. Although this is a commonplace in Gaelic Irish fiction since *The Voyage of Maeldún*, it had rarely been done in Irish fiction in English before Aidan Higgins published his collection of stories *Felo de Se* in 1960. The foreign-language title, the fact that Berlin and other European parts figured in a few of the stories, and the sprinkling of foreign languages and names — all this caused pleasurable excitement in Dublin. A sign of the times, this "Continental" quality had a significance not evoked by the few previous forays abroad of English Irish fiction after Joyce (for example, Kate O'Brien to Spain or Francis Stuart to Germany). However, in the early 1960s, the feeling was not so much that Higgins had largely excluded Irishness — some of his stories were recognisably set in Ireland — as that Irish writing was breaking out, conquering new terrain. Higgins had, after all, been actually living on the Continent. I am unaware whether, apart from that, he had any

---

[2] New York, Longship Press, 1978.

programmatic intention, even when — still living mainly abroad
— he followed up with a travel book *Images of Africa* (1971) and a
novel *Balcony of Europe* (1972). But it looked like it. Moreover,
Higgins's "breakout" to distant places in the early sixties was not
unique. The Limerick poet Desmond O'Grady had been in Rome
since 1957, sending poems back to Ireland (on Irish and non-Irish
themes) and editing the international literary journal *The Transatlantic Review*. Another poet, Sean Ó Criadáin, also in Rome, was
editor for a time of the journal *Botteghe Oscure*.[3]

The Paddy No More movement was a passage from the belief
that the expansion of non-Irish content in Irish writing was a good
thing to the belief that reflection of the distinctively native was a
hindrance to portrayal of the contemporary human. John Banville
may well have led this change. Certainly, as early as 1971, when he
published *Nightspawn*, set in Greece, he had the intention of breaking with recognisably Irish writing. In *Birchwood* (1973), even
though it was set in Ireland, he was explicit on the subject, even if
in figurative terms. In an interview published this year in the *European English Messenger* (Spring 1997, Vol. VI/1), he says as follows:

> The only direct statement I've ever made in any book that I
> have written is at the end of *Birchwood* where the protago-
> nist says: "I'll stay in this house and I'll live a life different
> from any the house has known" (p. 174). And that is my
> statement. I stay in this country but I'm not going to be an
> Irish writer. I'm not going to do the Irish thing.

In that, Banville was speaking not only for himself, but for quite a
number of the younger Irish writers of his generation.

---

[3] As it happened, in 1959, the present writer published a travel book *Mainly in
Wonder*, which covered ground from Vienna to the countries of the Far East. As
its Foreword all too embarrassingly shows, this was a self-consciously new
venture in "native Irish" writing — as distinct from what some Anglo-Irish
might have written in the service of the Empire or in other capacities. A glance at
the names just mentioned above illustrates the force of this.

Be it said, in passing, that in the matter of an Irish author excising Irishness from his writing, the great forerunner was, of course, Samuel Beckett. But Beckett had done it spontaneously, without any programmatic intention, simply as part of the process of his developing art. Beginning in the 1930s, his fiction moved from Irish settings and characters to English settings with some vaguely Irish characters, to a merely nominal Irish character (Molloy, Malone) in an undefined environment. Then, in his plays, from *Waiting for Godot* onwards, he proceeded to achieve a virtual eradication of Irishness. True, for those in the know, memories of Irish circumstances, and the occasional Irish turn of phrase, could still be detected; but that was inevitable. It took nothing from the abstract purity of the works for his international public, and even for most Irish people, who were unacquainted with his biographical details.

II

Let us turn now to the situation today, twenty years after *Paddy No More*, and examine what has been the net effect on English Irish[4] fiction of the Paddy No More movement. Has there been a movement away from the distinctively native? Even in the newest fiction the old themes still predominate. In the Dublin *Sunday Tribune*, of 20 July 1997, a new collection of short stories, *Phoenix Irish Short Stories 1997*, edited by David Marcus, was reviewed.[5] The reviewer, Colin Lacy, writes as follows:

> Assuming that "Ireland" is the subject of this collection [note this continuing assumption], one wonders what a reader coming to this nation's literature for the first time

---

[4] See note p. 18.

[5] Dublin, Phoenix House, 1997. At this point the subject of this paper becomes in fact "Trouble with the Contemporary in English Irish Fiction", and but for the "passion" theme in the Tralee festival I might have chosen that title.

since, say, the 1960s would make of us. Emigration looms
large. Over the 16 stories included here, so does the Catholic Church, sex, alcohol and various forms of physical and
cultural displacement — hardy perennials all. Shaping up
as an annual state of the nation report on Irish short fiction,
David Marcus's second Phoenix collection suggests that the
themes that have teased Irish writers since the days when
the Celtic Tiger was a malnourished cub are still the themes
that bind.

Where the reviewer calls "emigration, the Catholic Church, sex,
alcohol and various forms of physical and cultural displacement",
"perennials all", I think we can fairly take it that he is not referring to those themes individually — for individually they can be
found in many national literatures — but to their conjunction and
joint recurrence in an Irish setting and with a fairly predictable
treatment. So not only is the subject-matter distinctively Irish: it is
stereotypically so.

Has Irish prose fiction contributed notably to the depiction of
the contemporary human condition? By "notably", I mean has it
created fictional worlds or characters which have become representative icons of the contemporary in — at least — the English-
speaking world? Joyce created such a world in *Dubliners* and
Ulysses, and such characters in Leopold Bloom and Stephen Deda-
lus. (His Molly Bloom went beyond the merely contemporary to
become an icon of perennial woman.) But — leaving abruptly
aside the question of the last thirty years — the fact is that, since
Joyce, no Irish writer of prose fiction has done either. Beckett,
alone among Irish writers, contributed icons of the contemporary,
not in his prose fiction, but in his plays of the 1950s and '60s. All
the other fictional worlds and characters that have lodged, as
icons, in the consciousness of literate, English-speaking people,
ourselves included, have come from English or American fiction.
For example, and in no particular order: the "Greene world" of
Graham Greene and the characters of Pinkie, Scobie, the Mexican

whisky-priest, and the "Quiet American"; George Orwell's *Nineteen-Eighty-Four* and *Animal Farm* and the character, Big Brother; John Updike's contemporary everyman, Rabbit, the car salesman; Aldous Huxley's *Brave New World*; Evelyn Waugh's *Brideshead Revisited* and the character, Sebastian Flyte; Raymond Chandler's world, the character, Philip Marlowe, and the image of "the mean streets"; the worlds and principal characters of Hemingway and Scott Fitzgerald; Saul Bellow's *Herzog;* the world of John Le Carré's novels, the title and images of *The Spy Who Came in from the Cold,* and the character, Smiley; J.P. Donleavy's *The Ginger Man*; the Agatha Christie world; Kingsley Amis's Lucky Jim; the woman's world of Doris Lessing's *The Golden Notebook*. As you will have noticed, quite a number of those titles, worlds and characters have passed into everyday language.[6]

Let us be clear. Quite a number of good Irish prose writers since Joyce have created fiction with a modest contemporary dimension. Some have attained, if again modestly, the perennially human. The work of others has exuded no significant human radiance of either kind. And all this has occurred regardless of whether the work in question has or has not exhibited recognisable Irishness. John Broderick, setting his novels in a recognisably Irish town (Athlone), and in a middle-class milieu, achieved some general human dimension. In the unmistakably Irish tales of Seamus O'Kelly, Mary Lavin, Kate O'Brien, and Sean O'Faolain at his best, the perennially human is present. In John Banville's novels, because a voice rather than a person is central and the brilliances are mainly verbal and intellectual, little of human significance is exuded, regardless of whether the settings are non-Irish or Irish. Maeve Binchy's stories, set in Ireland and with a casual, unstereo-

---

[6] Alone in Irish prose fiction since World War II, Francis Stuart's novels *Pillar of Cloud* and *Redemption* had the makings of contemporary iconic status. However, Stuart's critical eclipse because of his presence and activities in Nazi Germany precluded this potential from being realised.

typed Irish ambience, have contemporary meaning for the English-speaking world and beyond. Valerie Mulkerns's novel *Very Like a Whale*, situated in contemporary, middle-class Dublin, Brian Friel's *The Faith Healer* set in England, or a Hugo Hamilton novel moving through present-day Berlin, all these have a contemporary edge and, in Friel's play, perennial meaning also.

That much clarified, the point I am making is that no Irish prose fiction since Joyce has supplied a notable (i.e. iconic) depiction of the contemporary human condition. And more: inasmuch as Joyce pre-eminently, and others since him, have achieved a greater or lesser degree of human dimension with fiction marked by recognisable Irishness, the latter cannot be the impeding factor. In assuming that it was, the Paddy No More movement was wrong. The notion that there was an opposition between Irishness and the contemporary, and that the way to depict the "contemporarily human" successfully was to avoid the distinctively native, was a delusion. No such literary rule exists. But the Paddy No More movement did correctly intuit a continuing weakness in English Irish fiction; did sense that there is something about it which prevents it dealing notably with contemporary life.

III

Consider that random list of "icons of the contemporary" which I gave above. It seems to me that, apart from notable representational skill and subtle insight, what qualifies fictional writing to be notably contemporary, by the measure I am using, is its contemporary adult theme. By that I mean, roughly, *a recognisably contemporary adult person (or persons) involved in typically contemporary preoccupations and activities.* Given that most English-speakers, in Ireland as elsewhere, are such people, this is a theme-category central to the consciousness and interest of our times. (True, I am using the word "adult" to refer to something more than mere age, without troubling to define exactly what more. But it is interesting to note that Neil Jordan's attempt at the contemporary focused on teenagers.)

What Irish writing continues to be notable for, and most valued for, both abroad and in Ireland, is its occasional, strong depiction of life that is sub-adult, sub-literate, offbeat, weird, poor, and possessed of a naïve, occasionally hilarious, charm. Life, in short, which is an *attractive marginal oddity*. This is, of course, an age-old stereotype of Irishness in the English-speaking world.

I am thinking, most immediately, of the recent, simultaneous success abroad — and by derivation in Ireland — of the novelist Roddy Doyle, the memoirist Frank McCourt and the playwright Martin McDonagh. Frank McCourt, whose remembered depiction of life in Limerick slums, and of those awful Catholic priests and nuns, was extracted, prior to publication, in the *New Yorker*, went on to win the Pulitzer Prize, and is being advertised in London — I saw the posters — with this quote from a review: "Out Roddy Doyles Roddy Doyle . . . It is amazing". London Irishman Martin McDonagh, launched by the Druid Theatre in Galway with his play *The Beauty Queen of Leenane*, went on to scale the heights in London, and will soon be big in New York, with plays entitled *A Skull in Connemara, The Lonesome West, The Cripple from Inishmaan*. The titles adequately reflect the content. But I am also thinking — in terms of theme only, let me stress — of the other Irish novels and plays that have drawn most hype and acclaim in recent years in Britain, or in Britain and America, and therefore, of course, in Ireland. Dermot Healy's *A Goat's Song,* with its trumpeted bucolic title and mainly West of Ireland setting, where the narrator's central concerns — when lonesome without his woman or despairing in her company — are whether something alcoholic is left over from the night before, and which pub is the best one to begin the day's drinking in. Patrick McCabe's *The Butcher Boy,* about a curious, violent, idiot-boy, seeing visions of the Virgin, begorrah, and other marvels in a moronic Border town. John McGahern's *Amongst Women*, about the dour peasant, Moran, patriarching his womenfolk in a timewarp Irish rural scene, set in timeless Irish amber; fascinating book-at-bedtime reading — "Really quite remarkable people, the Irish, and what beautiful writing!"— for the folk, jaded with contemporaneity, who heard it "at bedtime" on BBC 4. And for good measure, Brian Friel, with his tales of Ballybeg peasants, and above all his greatest international success, *Dancing at Lughnasa,* where those Donegal wenches get up and jig like mad on the kitchen table and chairs to the music from the old steam radio.

These are the sort of fictional works for which Ireland remains notable. All of them are valued by the contemporary English-speaking world as icons of Irishness, which define by their contrast the adult normality of that world. This valuation translates into a demand for such works. Partly in response to it, partly because of the happy chance that many Irish writers like depicting such "Irishness", the representation of it has been, and remains, the dominant tendency of Irish fictive writing. As a result, an Irish fiction writer who wants to represent the "contemporary human" must go against the grain of the writing profession in Ireland; must *snámh in aghaidh an easa.* This has been and remains the main impediment to notable Irish success in this respect.

If, occasionally, to make a point, I have referred to plays as well as prose fiction, that is because, in the matter of the weakness I am discussing, there is no meaningful boundary between one kind of fictive creation and another. It is not simply a question of failing "to deal notably" with the contemporary. That is merely a handy yardstick for measuring and identifying a general difficulty with the contemporary in Irish fictive writing of all kinds. With the Paddy No More movement now a distant memory, our highly productive and self-proud literary industry no longer adverts to this weakness, let alone explores it. It is not, of course, a national tragedy nor even necessarily a literary defect; but it is a significant feature of our cultural life which, given the inattention to it, is likely to continue.

It is reflected on the level of television soaps. Although Irish television is centrally situated in the English-speaking world, it has failed in its thirty-five-year history to make TV soaps which other countries want. The only serial drama it has exported outside the domestic or ethnic-Irish markets is *Glenroe*, which has been shown on Australian television. An excellent drama series, *Glenroe* is set in a recognisably contemporary Irish rural village, and mingles serious human matters with the charm of the simple life. By contrast, Australian television, which is hardly advantaged over Ireland by its situation in the English-speaking world, sends a flow of TV dramas around the world, including Ireland. These include, to mention two we have seen on our screens, soaps with such contemporary adult themes as Australian harbour police going about their duties (*Water Rats*) and doctors using planes to bring medical services to remote rural communities (*Flying Doctors*). Irish television has never, as it happens, made a soap with such typically contemporary, adult themes.

Again, the weakness of Irish fiction with regard to the contemporary is reflected in the reading habits of the representatively contemporary people who inhabit Ireland. True, in the last ten years, Maeve Binchy, Patricia Scanlan and Deirdre Purcell have successfully supplied mainly female readers with an Irish near-equivalent of contemporary popular fiction elsewhere. But men who require popular fiction with a contemporary edge, and all sophisticated readers of both sexes, look mainly to British and American writers to supply novels which reflect their lives: mentally, emotionally, occupationally; in a word, circumstantially. And this is small wonder when, to mention only the most obvious, there is almost no notable Irish fiction reflecting the life and work of representative Dubliners in recent decades — the dramas of money, power and rivalry, of sex, politics, morality and the spirit, which they know from their daily lives: their gyms, health-food shops, dress designers, call girls, and tribunals of public enquiry. On the evidence presented by Irish fiction, one would not know or believe that Dublin, a few years ago, liked to think of itself as "the night-club capital of Europe" or has lately been priding itself as the powerhouse of the "Celtic Tiger" economy. (One could also instance the lack of an outstanding novel by an Irish novelist on the Northern Ireland conflict and its international ramifications.)

Abroad, this weakness of Irish literary fiction has had two extra-literary effects. The typically contemporary nature of Irish life has not entered the consciousness of literate, sophisticated people in other countries of the western world. Over the past thirty years, the Dublin liberal bourgeoisie and their allies throughout the Republic have expended great and largely successful efforts to make their lives and Irish life resemble lives and life in the West's metropolitan centres. They expected to be recognised for this abroad, approvingly. But because Irish fiction, from novels and plays to television drama and films, has failed to image the success of their efforts, it has largely passed unnoticed.

Second, and arising from this, there has been nothing to counteract, effectively, the favoured literary image of Ireland in the literate English-speaking world and beyond as a poverty-stricken, sub-adult, non-contemporary marginal oddity that produces good writers. This image has remained predominant, with the cause and effect identifiable. Because, however, the Irish literary industry is unaware of this cause and effect, a very funny thing occurred at the Frankfurt Book Fair in 1996. The theme of the year was "Ireland". The Irish literary and cultural functionaries who attended in force — very contemporary types all of them — were taken aback and a bit miffed to find that the images which the German organisers had chosen to represent *Irland* were of the thatched-cottage, round tower and Aran fisherman variety. How boring! The German organisers seemed to be unaware of the real Ireland, the with-it, Celtic Tiger Ireland, which the literary and cultural functionaries lived in. How could this be?

This anecdote neatly illustrates that, twenty years after *Paddy No More*, contemporary Irish life and its literary fictions are still at odds with each other, but that now, in contrast to then, there is no articulated awareness of this. I hope that these brief observations will at least make the matter a subject of discussion and curious enquiry.

Postscript: A few months after I had written this essay, an American woman to whom I showed it questioned my statement that no Irish prose fiction since Joyce had become a "representative icon" of contemporary adult experience. The fictional world of Edna O'Brien had attained this status. I accept that — it slipped my mind. It is true of that part of O'Brien's fiction that has non-Irish settings. But this exception doesn't affect the general rule that Irish fiction specialises — with success — in the "sub-adult, sub-literate, weird and charmingly primitive". The examples multiply. In a recent interview with Thomas Kilroy in the magazine InCognito, *Kilroy tells us that his forthcoming novel is about "an innocuous little man in a small Irish town who starts to have visions". In Rome, where I'm living, the two latest Irish books to appear in translation are* Angela's Ashes *and Seamus Deane's prize-winning novel* Reading in the Dark. *On the cover of the former is a little girl, on that of the latter a little boy. The rule running through current Irish fiction — including the fictional memoir and drama — seems to be a central character, or characters, that are "less" in age, physical stature or mental/moral development (or all three) than the author and the people he associates with; contemporary grown-ups, in every sense.*

Autumn Day

Translation of Herbsttag *by Rainer Maria Rilke, published in* The Irish Times, *18 October 1997, Saturday book pages*

Lord, it is time. The summer was immense.
Lay your shadow on the sun-dials
and on the plains release the winds.

Command the last fruits to fill themselves;
Grant them two more temperate days,
urge them to completeness and chase
the last sweetness into the heavy wine.

Who now is homeless builds himself no house.
Who is alone now will long remain so,
will stay awake, and read, and write long letters,
and in the avenues, when the leaves are drifting,
wander anxiously.

1998

The Fernando Stripe

Written October 1998, in memory of a new friend suddenly lost

I stood back from the long, horizontal strip of new plaster I had finished painting yellow-ochre. "That will be 'the Fernando stripe'," I said aloud. Sixteen centimetres wide, it ran in a straight line below the black and white railing that enclosed the veranda. It was the same colour as the house, or rather, the façade, which I had painted the week before. Beneath it, descending to the cobbled street, was solid stonework, grey and beige. That the strip was the same colour as the façade was the point. Optically, it referred back and upwards to it, so as to enclose the black and white railing in an ochre frame, making house-front, railing and supporting stone wall a connected whole. That was why Fernando suggested it, as we viewed the bleak, grey house together and discussed what should be done.

The house faces across the street to a high stone wall, and above that, houses rise. Fernando lived in one of them. They belong to the same street; it rises and curves sharply to get to them. The town is that sort of higgledy-piggledy, up-steps-and-down-steps old town, built on a hill which is also a headland, jutting out into a lake. Before I bought the house, I had been living in a rented apartment near the top of the hill. Since the furniture was not mine, and I had no car, "moving" was a matter of carrying suitcases; laden on the downward journey, empty on the climb back. It was early summer, and the labour was lightened on the way down by the recurring appearances of the sunlit lake, sometimes wide from shore to shore, other times glimpsed at the end of a narrow alley or a flight of steps. Where the street surface was smooth enough to use them, the wheels on the suitcases also helped. I didn't push myself. Operation *trasloco*, as the Italians call a house move, took perhaps a fortnight. My route took me past an old woman whose occupation was to sit outside her house, observing. The suitcases were large and black, the tall, studious-looking man with greying hair had a purposeful air. One after-noon she addressed me. "*Signore*, excuse me, you pass every day. What are you carrying in the suitcases?" When I explained that I was doing a *trasloco*, she nodded dismissively. It was a let-down. She had heard of that before.

It was about the third day that Fernando first addressed me. I had left down my suitcases and was struggling with the key to the front door, or rather, with the recalcitrant lock which needed subtle manoeuvring. His voice came from up above; he was standing in front of one of the houses above the wall. Good after-noon, was I the new occupant? When I was returning, would I like to come in for a cup of tea? "Yes," I said, "thanks." He was about twenty-eight, tall, slender, with an exuberance of yellow-blonde hair framing a lean, smiling face. The hair, probably with the sun on it, connected in my mind with images of Apollo. I was surprised. Italians are not usually so forthcoming with strangers. Not merely bidding me welcome to the neighbourhood with that broad smile, but inviting me to a cup of tea in his house — and tea, not coffee. I sensed a free, self-possessed, unusual person.

When I had finished in the house and locked up, I mounted the steep curve, and through the open door saw him seated at a table, peering at a model of a building. He came towards me with that same smile, seated me on a sofa near the door, and asked would I like tea or a beer. When I said tea, he said, "I hoped you'd take tea. I collect teas."

"Well, I'm Irish," I said, "we know something about tea."

He went into the back part of the room to put water on, and came forward again with a small trayful of teas in packages and labelled jars. I was to choose, and to help me he pointed to each in turn, telling me where it came from. He had graceful hands, long slender fingers. Some of the teas were perfumed. I chose a plain Ceylon.

When he handed me the cup and saucer, he said, "You, sit there and relax. I study architecture in Rome" — Rome is an hour away by bus — "and I have to have this model ready for the professor tomorrow." He returned to the table, and I sat and relaxed. There was low music, maybe Haydn. After a while I said, "I thought an Englishwoman, a journalist, lived in this house. Someone told me that, or is it the next house?"

"It's this house," he said, "her name is Jane. But she isn't a journalist, she manages the Tre Piccioni restaurant on Piazza del Molo. She's away in England. Have you bought that house where you're bringing the stuff?"

I said I had, and shortly afterwards I told him the tea was good, many thanks, and I'd be on my way. I rose and took my cases. "Call in any time you like," he said, "when you're finished in the house. For tea or a beer. And we can talk."

Some days he was not at home when I came down with my bags. I knew this because his door was closed and the black bicycle that he kept locked to a drainpipe gone. But when I saw the door was open, I called in. I brought him a packet of Irish Breakfast Tea. On days when he was not working, he sat on the edge of a chair near me, his eyes keen in his beaked face, and that great loose mass of Apollo hair framing it. He talked fluently and expressively, sipping tea. He said that when he had qualified in Rome, he would go to Paris. Nothing interesting, architecturally, had been done in Rome since Mussolini built that new quarter, EUR, for the world exhibition. We discussed the pros and cons of Mussolini's demolishing bits of medieval and early-modern Rome to make fine vistas, or to give easy access to the remains of ancient Rome. I asked him, since he had access to specialist libraries, did he know of any book about the organisation of building work in ancient Rome; that large class of architects, engineers and, I assumed, contractors, who are hardly ever mentioned in history, but who got it all to happen. He said there was a detailed study of the building of the Baths of Caracalla by an American woman; he'd try to borrow it for me.

One day he said, "Let me show you a view." Jane's landlord owned the house next door, but he was seldom there and had left a key with Fernando. Taking the key with him, he led the way into the house and brought me to the first floor and out onto the balcony. It was the most beautiful view of the lake that I had seen. It wasn't only that it was blue and sparkling, and that you could see it widely to right and left, and across to the hills and town on the far side. In the foreground, forming the approach to it, was a descending array of red-tiled roofs, so that the works of man and of nature were combined, and you saw the lake, not abstractly as mere "nature", but in its true, domesticated setting.

Another day — I mention this because, later, my groping mind went back to it — Fernando asked me what did I think of the Americans threatening to bomb Iraq. The news bulletins, like a stuck record, had again been carrying reports of "US planes and aircraft carriers being moved to the Gulf". "It's an obsession," I said, "a sick obsession."

"What I hate," he said, "is how the newspapers and television go on about a 'threat of war'. 'War again with Iraq' and so on. It's not war. It's an attack by the most powerful country in the world on a country that is practically defenceless. If they want to bomb people — and they seem to like bombing people — can't they find their match? It makes you wish to have the Soviet Union back again."

It was the only time he mentioned politics. He talked a lot about the predawn of history: dinosaurs and Neanderthals, and little African Eve making a point of walking erect across the Kenyan prairies. Why do I think he waved his arms a lot? Perhaps he did. In my mind's eye, I see a flailing, smiling Icarus.

Twice he came down to my house. The first time was when I invited him to give me his "professional" advice. I was thinking of colouring the dull grey front with yellow-ochre emulsion and putting in a window. Beneath the rusted railing that enclosed the veranda, crumbling plaster hid the supporting stone wall. I wanted to strip off the plaster and leave the stone bare. It was then, with a horizontal movement of his hand, that Fernando suggested the ochre strip beneath the railing. Another day, when I had failed utterly to open the lock on the front door, I called him to my rescue. He came down, held the key in the lock, applied tentative pressures with his shoulder and his other hand, and the door opened. He said that, in the matter of opening them, old doors could develop very distinctive personalities. You had to know the special trick. I got him to repeat the easy-opening procedure and imitated him successfully.

I was delighted to have made this friend. It was great to know that in another week or so, when I moved into the house, I already had someone in this strange neighbourhood whom I could talk to, invite to tea. I was quietly amazed by the simplicity of his introduction into my life, from that first day when he had "hailed" me from on high. It had been as if a conversation were being resumed. None of the tedious questions about why I was in Italy, or for how long, nor predictable remarks about how beautiful Ireland must be, and how he would love to visit it.

I moved in, Jane came back. I gathered it was she when I saw a small, fortyish woman watering the plants outside the door up above. Passing one night, I heard them inside talking loudly in Italian. It sounded like an intense discussion. Naturally, I wondered about their relationship. Fernando had said nothing and I never asked him. I got used to seeing her passing in front of my house twice daily, going to and from the restaurant, accompanied by a large dog. I introduced myself, told her I had got to know Fernando and had heard about her. She had a North of England accent. She had been living in the town, she said, for the past eight years.

I was puzzled that Fernando's bicycle was there, but that I hadn't seen him for several days, perhaps a week. Knowing that Jane passed about 4.30 in the afternoon, I walked up and down the veranda waiting for her. She came, leading the big dog, her head thrust forward and down. My "Hello Jane" caught her attention, but as I continued with "Where's Fernando? I haven't seen him for several days," her face became a grimace, snarling, "He went and killed himself." The dog began to bark at me very loudly. "What?" I spluttered. Shouting in competition with the barking dog, she said, "Sorry for being so harsh about it. He was found in a car last Monday, he had taken pills. He seemed to have it well planned. Oh, the world was too cruel and nasty for him." I brought out a slow "Oh my God!" and then, "I won't try to talk to you now." She was shouting at the dog to be quiet. "I'll talk to you about it another time," she said. She moved on.

I stood for a long time, stock still, my mind groping for a hold. "The world too cruel and nasty for him". What did she mean? For me he was sunlight. "Well planned." What did I not know? Iraq? It would be ridiculous to kill yourself for Iraq. Had that intense discussion I had overheard got anything to do with it? Fernando has killed himself. And so on, trying for a hold.

Because one way or another Jane had been so close to him, I delayed approaching her to hear more. There were still a few bits and pieces to be brought down the hill, and next day, as I came to the steps that brought me towards Fernando's door, I talked aloud to him. I asked him why. And where was he now? Why had he not told me he had this plan? "Fernando, you were to bring me that book. And you were to go to Paris. Fernando, you can't be serious, no 'tea or beer' or chat, for ever, ever more?" Not just that day, but the next day, too, as I came down the same steps, and passed the door and the black bicycle, I said those things to him.

One afternoon, looking up from below, I saw a beautiful young woman, a redhead, emerging from Jane's house, carrying bags. When I met Jane, briefly, in passing, she said that

Fernando's sister had come to collect his things. About a week later I visited her and asked her to tell me the story.

I can only summarise what Jane said, without pretending that it makes sense. Somehow, though he was from Rome, he had a job in her restaurant. Six months previously, she had suggested he stay at her place. On the weekend in question he had been in Rome, and on the Monday did not turn up for work. That afternoon, when Jane was at home, his sister phoned from Rome. The police had found him in a car parked in the hills above the lake. The spot was obviously chosen with care: it had a fine view of the lake. His sister phoned his girlfriend in Rome and gave her the shocking news. The girlfriend was a most destructive woman who had caused him a lot of suffering. On the following day she left a message on Jane's answering-machine. *"Ciao, Fernando."* What a thing to do, imagine. No, he had left no note, and nothing particular had happened in the previous days that would point to why he did it. But several things had gone wrong for him recently, and he was a very sensitive fellow. He was not really made for this harsh world. Nasty things distressed him greatly. Yes, he might well have seemed in good form in the past few weeks. But people who have decided to commit suicide often are that way: once they have made the decision, they have a sort of peace. They give no hint of their intention to those around them.

I did not press Jane beyond that blur. Not only had I moved into a new neighbourhood; I had bumped against an intricate set of relationships where my place was that of total outsider. One afternoon, looking up, I saw a middle-aged woman, with a young man who might have been her son, in the doorway of Jane's house. They were leaving, but the woman stayed in the doorway a long time, talking intensely to Jane, and Jane, whose face I could see, was replying in a controlled way. I knew it must be Fernando's mother. Later, when I bumped into Jane, I said, "I saw you the other day having a hard time." "Yes," she said, and I left it at that.

In the matter of naming something after him, the ochre strip had no real competition. For a while there was the front-door. When I leant my shoulder against it, and did the opening trick, I thought of him of course. But I got a new door that opened easily. Near the fridge there is a power-point which had lost its plastic cover before I arrived, and I have still not replaced it. Early on, in the suitcase days, when I tried inserting the two-pronged plug directly into the exposed innards, the sparks intimidated me, and Fernando, with one bold movement, showed me how. Still today, when I unplug the fridge to defrost it, and later, plug it in again, I think of him. But the ochre-coloured strip of plaster has the advantage of being his idea, and utterly new, and paid for by me and painted by me. I know that it is not a "stripe", but a strip — of painted plaster laid on a stone surface. But as a name, "the Fernando stripe" sounds better.

When I stood back and said it, "the Fernando stripe", I sensed him up above there, grinning. And I must say I grinned too, because I knew that his grin meant "the absurdity of it all — and the beauty".

The Recent Birth and Chequered Career of "Rural Ireland"

InCognito *(Dublin), Vol. 4, Autumn 1998. Final revision of a paper read at the William Carleton Summer School, 1996, which appeared as an article in* New Hibernia Review *(St Paul, Minnesota), Winter 1997.*

As a concept and a combination of words, "rural Ireland" is only about a century old. Throughout the millennia of Irish life before that, to think "Éire/Ireland" was to think rurality; to say "rural Ireland" would have been tautologous. Gaelic Ireland was so absolutely a rural civilisation that no one within it thought of adverting to the fact. But also, through the eighteenth century and most of the nineteenth, bilingual Ireland continued to be, and to be seen as, an essentially rural society of landlords and peasants. Indeed, as the Industrial Revolution in Britain moved manufacturing and national wealth preponderantly to urban settings and people followed, the rural character of Ireland was emphasised by contrast. The typical Irishman was, and was seen as being, a countryman. Irish town-dwellers conceived of themselves as belonging to an essentially rural society. Depictions of life in the Irish countryside were intended as, and taken to be, representative depictions of Irish life.

William Carleton's preface to his first collection of *Traits and Stories of the Irish Peasantry* illustrates this. He writes that "the Author can with confidence assure [the public] that what he offers is, both in manufacture and material, genuine Irish; yes, genuine Irish as to character . . ." His stories are particularly reliable with regard to "the Northern Irish". The author's "desire is neither to distort his countrymen into demons, nor to enshrine them as suffering innocents and saints, but to exhibit them as they really are". The stories "contain probably a greater number of facts than any other book ever published on Irish life".

Moreover, it wasn't only that Irish rural life, even a Northern part of it, was "Irish life". Carleton was writing specifically about the Irish Catholic peasantry: *their* life was "Irish life". And again, for Carleton personally it was not just "Irish" life. In a passage quoted in the Carleton Summer School brochure, Anthony Cronin comes close to the truth when he says that Carleton delighted "in the recreation of a world which to him, after all, was really the ordinary one". It would be a shade more accurate to say "had been" the ordinary one. Carleton, in his new-found existence as a Protestant evangelical living in Dublin and writing in English, had acquired some mental distance from that previously "ordinary life" — in which towns and Protestants were extraneous to the normal.

For "rural Ireland", meaning a distinct kind of Irish life, to become a phrase and a concept, it was necessary for a consciousness of urban life as a distinct form of Irish life to take shape. That had to wait until the end of the nineteenth century and the beginning of the present one. This was the period when the urban population, as reckoned by the Census, was approaching or passing 30 per cent. In 1901, it was 28 per cent. More to the point, it was the period when the population of Dublin, the chief location where consciousness of an Irish urban condition formed, was approaching or rising beyond 300,000, while that of Dublin city and county was nearing and exceeding 450,000. In these years, the term "rural Ireland" appears, for example, in writings connected with the (rural) co-operative movement. The emergence of this divided consciousness[1] did not mean that Irish people and others ceased to regard Ireland as an essentially rural country; it meant that thenceforth that way of regarding Ireland was competing with a

---

[1] At a local level there had always been a sense of town/country divide. The new thing was the emergence of that consciousness at a national level.

view of it as divided between rural and non-rural or urban "states of being". However, this view remained located mainly in Dublin; a comprehensive notion of "urban Ireland" did not take hold.

Additional reasons might be found, but these historical circumstances suffice to explain why "pastoral" and "anti-pastoral" — the celebration or denigration of rural life, especially as opposed to city life — are absent from Irish literature in both languages before the present century. That said, Goldsmith's "Deserted Village" springs to mind and requires to be disposed of. It is a distinctly pastoral presentation of a lost rural past, contrasted with the human desolation of the present, after land clearances. Here are the well-known opening lines:

> Sweet Auburn! loveliest village of the plain
> Where wealth and plenty cheered the labouring swain
> Where smiling spring its earliest visit paid,
> And parting summer's lingering blooms delayed.
> Dear lovely bowers of innocence and ease
> Seats of my youth, when every sport could please.
> How often have I paused on every charm,
> The sheltered cot, the cultivated farm,
> The never-failing brook, the busy mill,
> The decent church that topt the neighbouring hill,
> The hawthorn bush, with seats beneath the shade,
> For talking age and whispering lovers made.

That is certainly an example of "pastoral", and it is associated, ambiguously, with Goldsmith's home village in County Longford. Ambiguously, because while idealised memories of that rural life doubtless enter into it, it is not specifically about that slice, or any slice, of rural Ireland. Written in London, it participates in an already established English tradition of the pastoral poem which exalts the rural, and specifically the lost rural, as a way of life morally and otherwise superior not only to the present rural condition, but to contemporary English city life, especially in London. This combination of circumstances disqualifies the poem as "Irish pastoral". But its oddity, coming from an Irish writer, does point up the kind of express and loaded treatment of the rural which was absent from Irish literature and ideology virtually until the present century.

II

I have widened the argument by saying "absent from Irish ideology" as well as literature. It is not only imaginative literature that occasionally idealises or denigrates rural life; political ideology may also do so. For example, hostile depiction of Paddy the Irishman by English nineteenth-century propaganda was not only anti-Irish in intent; it also conveyed an English urban contempt for rural life — Paddy was rural life — seen as dirty, backward and ignorant. Add the fact that most imaginative literature takes no position on the matter: being primarily interested in the human drama, it regards rurality not as a theme, but as an incidental condition or location. In effect, then, once "rural life" has been isolated as a distinct idea, it gets caught up in a tangle of varying representations. While continuing to figure in literature simply as one environment of human action, it is also represented, by literature and ideology, as a good and superior or bad and inferior condition of being. The "chequered career" of "rural Ireland" in this century has taken place in this three-threaded tangle. Before commenting on that career directly, I want to sort out what is at work, and what is really being indicated, when these various representations of rurality occur.

In the first place, what is at work has nothing really to do with rurality as such, meaning a life characterised by fields and villages and engaged to a greater or lesser degree in agriculture. City life, for example, is subject to the same assortment of neutral, positive and negative representations. There is a "pastoral" and "anti-pastoral" of the city as well as of the country. On the first page of his book *The Country and the City* Raymond Williams makes this clear. He is writing about urban and rural "settlements" in the course of history:

> On the actual settlements, which in the real history have been astonishingly varied, powerful feelings have gathered and have been generalised. On the country has gathered the idea of a natural way of life: of peace, innocence, and simple virtue. On the city has gathered the idea of an achieved centre: of learning, communication, light. Powerful hostile associations have also developed: on the city as a place of noise, worldliness and ambition; on the country as a place of backwardness, ignorance, limitation. A contrast between country and city, as fundamental ways of life, reaches back into classical times.

Williams is not saying that literature and political ideology always represent city or country in idealising or denigrating ways. Just as most literature is not concerned with "the country" as a theme, it is not concerned with "the city". When it uses city or country, or a combination of them, as settings, it usually depicts them as "ordinary life", with life's ordinary variety of light and shade, good and evil, fulfilment and non-fulfilment, embodied in character and action. Williams is saying that (additionally) imaginative literature, as well as public opinion and political ideology, have often deliberately depicted both city life and country life as conditions that are bad or good for human beings.

What is emerging, then, is qualitative life-images that remain constant, while the realities they apply to vary. What literature and ideology have done with rural and city life, they have also done with other kinds of collective life: working-class life or Big House life, Communist or Red Indian life, the warrior life. In sum, ideology for its political ends, and literature for all sorts of ends from politics to entertainment, project a standard set of qualitative images on one or other human collective life in order to indicate that the life in question is desirable or undesirable, good or bad, or a life like any life. Thus the images and the applying of them are the constant, the lives which they are projected onto — rural, urban, working-class, Jewish or clerical — incidental, a matter of circumstance.

The images are essentially four. A collective life is represented as *ordinary* human being, or as *full* being, or as *defective* being or as *non-being*. The literary art projects all four of these images, politics only the last three. The most common of them, "ordinary being", is the least noticed because it is unsensational. It is the human stuff in which literature usually takes shape. "Ordinary being" is Earthly Life, as distinct from the unearthly conditions of Paradise, Hell, Hades or Purgatory. It is life, simply, as most people know it, or imagine it, most of the time. The abundant literary images of it, and of movement within it, serve the human need for contemplation and wonder. When they are well wrought, they refine the sensibility and understanding of those who contemplate them, and in so doing give pleasure and catharsis.

Images of full being, and of defective or non-being, do not invite such disinterested contemplation. They express and cater to human desires, fears and emotional needs. They exert attraction, elicit aversion, and promote positive or negative feelings of selfhood in the social, ethnic or political groups involved.

"Full being" is Heaven or Paradise. It is the life of realised human presence and moral integrity; of freedom; or of fruitfulness, material wellbeing and ease. It is union with nature; or enlightenment and brightness; or a life characterised by that charming primitiveness which is simplicity and moral innocence. It is the rural life of pastoral poetry; or the all-Ireland Republic and "nation once again" of Irish nationalism. It is Paris, projected as *ville lumière*, "city of light", to serve the purposes of the French Revolution and French nationalism, and the centralisation of the French state.

Or again, it is the communist society of Marxist imagery, created by the redemptive action of the urban industrial workers. When Mao Tse-tung retained that promise of full being but changed its agents, Marxism made its contribution to the age-old symbolic war of "country" and "city". Not, said Mao, the urban industrial workers, but the peasants, rural China, were the morally sound force that, by overcoming the corrupt cities, would produce the full human being of a communist society. Many of the leading spirits of the Irish Revolution, from Yeats and Hyde to Collins and de Valera, said *mutatis mutandis* much the same.

The images of "non-being" and "defective being" are Hell or Hades. Or they can be Purgatory in the sense of a suffering or degraded state from which liberation is assured. The images hover on an unstable scale that ascends from human absence or barrenness, or mental and moral darkness, to degrees of oppression or paralysis; primitiveness in its uncouth sense; or clownishness. All of these are modes of not being — at all or properly or fully — human.

The Hell that is imaged is not that of flames, but the more philosophical hell of darkness, despair, desolation, absence from self. A "priest-ridden people" dwells in its darkness, the "proletariat" of Marxist doctrine in its absence from self. In his *Thesis on Feuerbach*[2] Marx describes the proletariat as "the complete loss of man", which "can win itself only through the complete rewinning of man", in the full humanity of communism. "The complete loss of man": human absence, emptiness. There are correspondences there not only with Goldsmith's "deserted village", but with George Moore's title for his collection of stories. *The Untilled Field*, and Seamus O'Kelly's image of South Galway, denuded by emigration, in his programmatic story "The Land of Loneliness". Echoes, too, of *The Waste Land*, and of Beckett's barren stage-sets.

Hades, precursor of the Christian limbo, is a realm of half-light and gibbering shades. It is imaged by the Dublin of *Ulysses*, and by those lines with which Yeats opens "Easter 1916":

[2] Karl Marx, Friedrich Engels, *Collected Works*, Vol. 3, London, 1975, p. 186.

> I have met them at close of day
> Coming with vivid faces
> From counter or desk among grey
> Eighteenth century houses.

And so on with "a nod of the head", "polite meaningless words," more "polite meaningless words", in "a place where motley is worn". Both Wolfe Tone and James Joyce found in "paralysis" — a state of semi-being — an image of Ireland. Like "Ireland a province" it is a Hades image; but the Irish nationalist promise made it Purgatory.

Horace Plunkett, and George Russell in his role of organiser of co-operatives, held out a similar hope to the meagre semi-being of rural Ireland: co-operativism could transform it into the full being of the "co-operative commonwealth" And again, the frustrated, subhuman lives of Kavanagh's small farmers are not Hell, but Purgatory. Through them, even through the life of Pat Maguire, God shines, and redemption into full being awaits them, posthumously.

III

That is the full context of the chequered career of "rural Ireland" over the past hundred years. The actuality of rural Ireland — all those fields and people and activities from Malin Head to Carnsore Point and from Antrim to Kerry — has been one thing, the tangle of images that ostensibly relates to them quite another. Many of the images, literary ones, have expressed, and catered to, the human need for contemplation and wonder. Others, literary and political, have expressed, or catered to, longings, abhorrences, needs to feel good or secure, or needs to triumph or subject. Many of this latter kind have served, incidentally or by design, two distinct political enterprises: the construction and maintenance of the new Irish state, and the rise to power, from the 1960s onwards in Dublin, of a counter-revolutionary ascendancy.

We know the general story as it is conventionally related. In the early decades of the century, the revolutionary enterprise, directed at the establishment of an independent Ireland, projected to the people images of themselves as a nationalist, anti-imperialist, essentially Catholic and rural people, and in so doing idealised the rural as a superior way of life. Apart from the enterprise of state-building, it was logical as democratic politics. In 1946, "rural" still described the life of over 60 per cent of the population.[3] Some literary and journalistic voices dissented from that idealisation of the rural; but it was only from the mid-60s onwards that this kind of voice gradually ceased to express dissent, and became a confidently ascendant denigration of "rural Ireland".

The vehicle for this turnabout was the ideology called Dublin-liberal, Dublin-4, or revisionist. Broadcast powerfully by the Dublin media, it projected political images of "rural Ireland" as darkness, repression and backwardness. Increasingly, in the 1970s, these were merged with similar images of Catholic and nationalist Ireland; so that, overall, a copybook reaction to the previously ascendant ideology emerged. Its thrust was to justify and buttress a new elite of businessmen, journalists, politicians, civil servants and academics who aimed to derive self-esteem and power, not from association with a remade Irish nation, but from association with external powers which would finance the national economy in exchange for an outwardly conforming mentality.

As an adjunct to the new line, ostensibly "anti-rural" literary images from the previous period — such as Brinsley Macnamara's *Valley of the Squinting Windows,* Eric Cross's *The Tailor and Ansty,* Flann O'Brien's *An Béal Bocht* or Patrick Kavanagh's *The Great Hunger* — were put to use. The literary images were not necessarily "anti-rural" in intent: they may have been simply images of non-being or semi-being such as literature has often produced, along with images of full being, for contemplation and to display its skill.

---

[3] In the Census, "rural" includes towns with less than 1,500 population.

But literature has no say in what politics does with its images; politics always has the last, interpretative word. As imaginative literature supplied new, similarly serviceable images, they were given prominence and utilised. An early instance was John McGahern's novel *The Dark*, which was almost programmatic in its title and date (1965), and in its blurb which reads:

> The scene is set in rural Ireland and the central theme is adolescence, impelled forward by ambition and sexuality, guilty and uncontrollable, contorted and twisted by a puritanical and passionate religion, and above all by a strange, powerful, ambiguous relationship between son and widowed father.

McGahern's novel yielded a further, extraneous harvest for the new myth-making when it led to the author's losing his teaching job in a Dublin Catholic school at the behest of the city's Catholic archbishop!

Once again, in terms of democratic politics, there was an underlying logic. In the census of 1966, for the first time, the urban population of the Republic exceeded the rural. From then on, the rural population went into steep relative decline, and the meagre remains of autonomous rural culture gave way to the spreading consumerist ethos of the towns. For simplicity's sake, I have depicted the counter-revolutionary ideology and its verbal usage in their pure or "headquarters" formulations. From the 1970s onwards, the ideology, with necessary verbal modifications, became active throughout the Republic.

That is the rough story of "rural Ireland's chequered career" as it is conventionally told and understood. It can be summed up, semi-humorously, by contrasting verses from AE and Michael Hartnett. In 1925 George Russell wrote of the poor small farmers of the West of Ireland:

> They huddle at night within low, clay-built cabins;
> And to themselves unknown,
> They carry with them diadem and sceptre
> And move from throne to throne.[4]

And in 1985, Michael Hartnett, in a poem called "A Small Farm", wrote:

> All the perversions of the soul
> I learned on a small farm.
> How to do the neighbours harm
> By magic, how to hate.[5]

However, because what I have just related is the rough, conventional story of "rural Ireland's" chequered career, it is a story which must be modified in important respects to approach the truth of the matter.

IV

The only people who have really addressed themselves to rural Ireland, and meant rural Ireland when they said it, were the leaders of the co-operative movement at the beginning of the century; the revolutionaries, such as Collins and de Valera, who dreamed of a re-industrialised countryside; the leaders of farmers' organisations; and those civil servants, economists and others whose professional concern was Irish agriculture. The fictional writers in prose, verse or play who have used rural settings have not addressed themselves to rural Ireland, but rather, as imaginative writers generally do, to particular, imagined instances of Irish rural life. When one such work, or the *oeuvre* of one such writer, is represented as being about "rural Ireland", this is as sensible as saying that a novel by Roddy Doyle or John Broderick, or the *oeuvre* of either of them — the for-

---

[4] *Collected Poems*, London, 1926, p. 304.

[5] *The Penguin Book of Contemporary Irish Poetry*, eds. Peter Fallon and Derek Mahon, London, 1990, p. 209.

mer set in a poor North Dublin suburb, the latter in middle-class Athlone — is "about urban Ireland". Even McGahern's *The Dark* is not, despite the myth-making title and blurb, set in "rural Ireland"; it is set in a family and a place in rural County Roscommon.

Again, when the body of twentieth-century Irish literature with rural settings is regarded as a whole, it is seen not to be "about rural Ireland", but obsessively about a particular kind of Irish rural life, and only marginally about any other kind. It is predominantly concerned with the lives of small-farming communities, situated mainly in the West of Ireland and its islands, but occasionally elsewhere. Often Gaelic speech and custom, and almost always poverty, absolute or relative, have characterised the lives in question. In particular, both the idealising and the negative treatments of rural lives have been located, overwhelmingly, in poor, often Gaelic or recently Gaelic, communities. It was the pervasive idealisation of remembered poverty in the works of such popular Gaeltacht writers as Séamus Ó Grianna, Padraig Óg Ó Conaire, Nioclás Tóibín and Tomás Ó Criomhthain that led Flann O'Brien to satirise this aspect of such writing, specifically, in *An Béal Bocht*. The Ireland of big farms and fat land in Leinster and Munster, and in parts of Connacht and Ulster, is markedly under-represented in Irish literature in this century. More to the point, it has not figured for idealising, and only slightly for satirising treatment.

This literary concentration on a certain kind of Irish rural life was powerfully reinforced by a concentration of painting and film on the same kind of life. As a result, there emerged an image of "rural Ireland" as a small-farming, poor, usually western, devotedly Catholic life that was often Gaelic-speaking and occasionally, savagely, pagan. This mythical image of "rural Ireland" has become a fixed property of journalism and of Irish Studies courses throughout the world.[6] It was also of service to the ideological turnabout from the 1960s onwards.

---

[6] See in "Irish Studies in the United States", pp. 17–27.

In their rebellion against all that Ireland had signified during the revolutionary decades, the ideologues and journalists of Dublin 4 applied this ready-made image of "rural Ireland", not to rural Ireland, but to the provincial or non-Dublin parts of the Republic, including substantial cities and towns. This was most obvious when they were talking about voting figures in the context of an election or a referendum, and were seeking to make a point about progress and backwardness. In other words, they used "rural Ireland" with a connotation similar to that of *la province* in traditional Parisian usage. But of course, *la province*, besides connoting a sluggish mental condition, also denotes, literally, what it says: the non-Parisian parts, urban and rural, of all of France.

This Dublin-liberal merging of the concepts "rural" and "provincial" was reflected, jocularly, in the 1970s, when there was a daily programme on national television dealing, professedly, with "provincial news". The journalists working on the programme referred to it in private as "Redneck Roundup". The double Americanism is indicative of the new mentality. Of course, Dublin-liberal usage can occasionally include even North Dublin, across the Liffey, in a "rural Ireland" which stands, in effect, for "benighted 26-county Ireland outside our enlightened Southside Pale, where the suns of London, New York and 'Europe' illuminate us". On the other hand, and in line with the underlying image, when this power-game wishes to designate darkest, non-consumerist, rural-Ireland night, it says "West of Ireland farmer" — imagining a poor man, possibly of Gaelic speech and probably a bachelor, tending his cattle and potatoes amid rushes and rocks.[7]

---

[7] As I revise this paper a day after the end of the Carleton Summer School, I read, in a review of a new novel in *The Irish Times* (9 August 1996) the following: "This novel is at best a display by the author of her liberal credentials. Rural life, Catholic morality, and Ireland in general are imbued with negative qualities in a display of cultural snobbery that is as simple-minded as it is irritating." The context in which contempt for the "rural" is displayed here is noteworthy.

To return to the literature in the light of the foregoing: in Irish imaginative literature in this century there has been no idealisation of rural life as such. The absence of "pastoral" has continued. True, in Liam O'Flaherty and Seamus O'Kelly, there was some idealisation of "life in union with nature". But that is a metaphysics and a programme which, as contemporary evidence from California to Stockholm shows, can be practised by people living in cities.

The great mass of literature in the first half of this century which — with no concern for "union with nature" — idealises the lives of mainly Gaelic-speaking, sometimes English-speaking, Irish Catholic rural poor, is not addressing itself to *rural life as such*, let alone idealising it. Poverty was not, in the first half of this century, a characteristic of Irish rural life as distinct from Irish urban life. Moreover, much rural life was not a life of poor small-farmers, and very little of it was Gaelic-speaking.

What we have here in fact is a literature that is anti-colonial, and partly "socialist", in inspiration and intent. In the reigning, colonial perspective, rurality, poverty, Catholicism and Gaelic culture had long figured both as typical of Ireland and as anti-values. To convert them into values, and to celebrate them all together, was, intelligibly, an anti-colonial strategy. It provided a literary wing to the Irish anti-colonial revolution.

As for the "socialist" inspiration, I use the term more loosely, with one salient feature of socialism in mind: its romanticisation of the urban poor, in the guise of the working class or proletariat. When the rural poor figure in our literature as a focus of virtuous and noble living, this is a participation in that contemporary socialist sentiment. In an Ireland where rural life was still the norm and most of the poor were rural, the contemporary socialist romanticisation of the poor took, as in China, a rural form.

Something similar applies, in reverse, to the Dublin media propaganda and, occasionally, literature, of recent decades which, because of its verbal hostility to the "rural", might seem to be denigrating rural life. From the factual account of it that I have given, it must be obvious to the reader that it has had little to do with fields and agriculture. Its "rural Ireland" is an aggressive representation of traditional, non-consumerist, Catholic, nationalist Ireland as "a malevolent absence of humanity, a desert of non-being, Hell". "Rural Ireland" is its code for this.

I have been talking about modifications which must be made, for the sake of accuracy and truth, in the conventional story of how rural Ireland has been represented in Ireland in this century. I conclude with the chief of these, namely, that a great deal, and perhaps most, of the literary representation of life in rural Ireland has neither idealised nor pilloried. It has not even had rurality as a notable theme. Rather has it been a representation of "ordinary human being" in an Irish rural setting.

Take even Synge, whom some might see as a leader of the so-called ruralist literary movement. His main interest is clearly the relation between men and women. If he went along with the vogue for western settings, and for marginal rural people generally, this was because he found that the untamed nature of such settings allowed him to explore his intersexual theme with a freedom he would not have had in other milieus. Synge has precious little to do with agriculture! One could also instance as "ordinary human being in a rural setting" much of Frank O'Connor, most of Seán O'Faolain, most of Seamus O'Kelly, Brian Friel's "rural" plays *Translations* and *Aristocrats* or Sebastian Barry's *Prayers of Sherkin*. And that is only some of the prose without touching on the poetry.

Incidentally, if I were to touch on the poetry, I would argue that people who regard Seamus Heaney's rural poems as "pastoral" are investing these "still lifes" of rural scenes with a quality they do not have. Apart from the fact that the poems do not, in fact, idealise rural life, they are not, in the first instance, really about it. In the first instance, they are about themselves. They are delicately chiselled verbal icons, having a tangential relation with incidents and individuals from a remembered rural life, but designed to exist apart from that life and from all life.

But to return to the point I was making and to conclude, I will illustrate the kind of mainstream Irish writing I am talking about by the example of Mary Lavin, who is inseparably associated with the eastern fatlands of Meath. I quote from what Lord Dunsany said about her in his introduction to her first collection of stories, *Tales from Bective Bridge*.[8] He wrote: "I have pleasure in introducing another fine writer, Miss Mary Lavin: very different from Francis Ledwidge, except for the same piercing eye, which to Ledwidge revealed the minutest details of Irish hedgerows, with all their flowers and buds, and to Mary Lavin the hearts of women and children and men." Further on, he refers to "her searching insight into the human heart and vivid appreciation of the beauty of the fields", and he adds: "She tells stories of quite ordinary lives, the stories of people who many might suppose have no story in all their experience . . ." That is what I mean by the depiction of human life in a rural setting. There, not only is the theme not "rural Ireland"; it is not even, despite the setting, rural life.

Epilogue

"Rural Ireland" exists as much as "urban Ireland". To ascertain the nature and degree of existence in question, the reader might try describing "urban Ireland".

---

[8] London, Michael Joseph, 1943.

1999

The European Dialect of Lingua Humana

Paper read at Second International Symposium of Eurolinguistics, in Pushkin, Russia, 10–16 September 1999 and published in Studies in Eurolinguistics, *Vol. 1, ed. P. Sture Ureland, Berlin, Logos Verlag, 2003*

1. The search for an "essential human idiom"

I am not, as are most of you, a professional linguist. I am a writer who occupies himself, professionally, with language, and my education was mainly in history. It's from this background that I want to offer you some thoughts on the common human language and its European dialect. One of the main themes of the conference is language contact[1] in Europe. I shall be dealing with that phenomenon, as it has occurred mainly in Western Europe in the formation and development of European civilisation.

My first book, *Mainly in Wonder*, published in London in 1960, was a young Irishman's account of a year's travel extending from Vienna and Yugoslavia to India, Pakistan, Burma, Thailand, Japan, and two Chinese cities. My reading, and my experience of living in several European countries, had given me an idea of the human condition as exemplified, historically, in Europe. In my journey to the Far East, I was hoping to learn what Asia could teach me on that subject. In particular, I wanted to find what both presentations had in common. In the Preface to my account of that journey, I wrote as follows:

> As [this] book was taking shape, it became a personal quest. While trying merely to tell well, I found myself wrestling with the very means of telling. I found myself seeking

---

[1] A branch of linguistics which studies the interaction of (usually) adjacent languages.

a common language of dialogue and common terms of reference for all the different peoples. Surely only such a language can truly be called valid. I believe there must needs exist an essential human idiom, though barriers of religion, ideology, race and formal language have kept us from learning it. I should like my book to help in finding it.

On the book's second-last page, I wrote as follows:[2]

The East really taught me man, put him on a blackboard with chalk and diagrams, spelled him to me in block letters. I learned there that the first and greatest *good of man* on this *earth* is to *exist* and *grow*. In other words, the first imperative purpose of any society — of all its wisdom, morality and jurisprudence — must be to *ensure* that the *children* shall have *rice* or *bread*.

This task requires the building of an edifice of *trust*. . . . It rests partly on the *sacredness* of *blood bonds*, partly on the *sacramentality* of *words spoken, promises given, hands pressed, gifts exchanged*. This edifice of trust permits each man to exist and begin to grow.

Loyalty and *truth*, then, are the primary *virtues* [because they are the things most needed for trust.] But for trust, loyalty and truth to exist, *belief* is also needed. . . .

I did not write, but I implied, that people also feel the need to *name* all those elementary things and concepts, and that they have a desire and a capacity to do so. Every human need implies a corresponding desire and capacity. What I wrote there, at the end of the book, was simply a sketchy attempt at an answer to the search I had referred to in the Preface: my search for the essential human idiom, for the *lingua humana*.

---

[2] Key words are italicised and were vocally emphasised at the presentation of this paper.

Later, I thought the matter through more systematically. I arrived at conclusions which remain sketchy, but which can serve, I suggest, as a working model, while remaining open to contestation.

2. The basic human vocabulary — primitive culture

There is a basic human vocabulary which can be found throughout history and throughout the world. It has been expressed in countless tongues. It consists of names of persons, things, concepts and actions, and of qualifiers of those names. These words, which number several hundred, form the basic human vocabulary.

There is also a composite system — partly inflection, partly auxiliary words, partly syntax — for combining groups of the names and qualifiers into intelligible patterns. This, too, has taken different forms in countless tongues. Together, the basic vocabulary and the combination system, constitute a language — the basic *lingua humana*. The entire package, consisting of less than a thousand words, has been reproduced in countless versions. Here I will concern myself only with that part of the package which can be called "vocabulary": the names of persons, things, concepts and actions, and the qualifiers of those names.

This basic human language is created, initially, by groups of people living in face-to-face contact: they all know each other, more or less. They may be stationary or they may be nomadic within a defined area. Their language reflects needs of their human nature — including the need to name and speak — as well as the elementary desires and capacities which correspond to these needs. Put differently, the basic human language reflects the experience of people satisfying man's natural needs, and fulfilling that minimal part of his desires and capacities which correspond to these needs. That experience is the experience of "primitive culture". The basic *lingua humana* is therefore the language of primitive culture.

Primitive cultures have many different physical circumstances and mental inclinations. As a consequence, in each of them, respectively, certain elements of the physical world and certain concepts receive special, concentrated attention. The vocabulary naming these things and concepts reflects this special attention by its highly developed differentiation. For example, the name for snow in Inuit has been developed into twenty names for different kinds or conditions of snow. Bedouins have many names for different kinds of desert. A people who have much to do with horses will develop an extensive equine vocabulary. A people with a strong attraction to ethics will develop to a high degree the terminology dealing with right behaviour. But if this development of distinctions, this differentiation, occurs only in relation to a few words in the basic vocabulary, and not in relation to that vocabulary in general, the language remains basic *lingua humana*, and the culture a primitive culture.

3. Developed human vocabulary — civilisation

When, however, the development of verbal distinctions occurs throughout the entire vocabulary — when it affects the entire vocabulary of the basic language — the language becomes a language of "high culture" or "civilisation".

This differentiating development of the entire basic vocabulary is caused by two related factors. On the one hand, human desire and capacity increase their fulfilment far beyond the minimal fulfilment that they have in primitive culture. On the other, created needs are added to natural needs. Together, these two factors produce a wide and varied experience. It is this highly developed range of experience that is reflected in the developed, differentiating language of a civilisation.

In other words, people now speak a language which is no longer that of assured existence and survival only, but rather, of that condition combined with facilitating amenities, variety of all kinds, capacity exercised to a high degree, desire offered abundant satisfactions. Food does not mean only boiled rice, seaweed and a few kinds of fish, or bread, two kinds of meat and three vegetables, but hundreds of different kinds of food. Music is not only one or two particular kinds of music, but many kinds played variously by many instruments in many conventional formats — all these kinds, instruments, ways of playing, and formats having names.

The speakers of this "language of civilisation" do not know personally most of the people who speak it. They live and move in a wide area where the rules that govern and measure behaviour have not been worked out, consensually, in a face-to-face community. Instead, these rules are being preached and enforced by a single cohesive group of rulers and ethical preachers throughout the area in question. And they are subscribed to, more or less, by many face-to-face communities, whose previous, autonomously established rules now take second place to them. A "civilisation" is, essentially, a hierarchical set of rules of behaviour subscribed to by rulers and ruled throughout an extensive area for a long time.

3.1. Division into dialects

When the *lingua humana* achieves full development in various parts of the world, and at various times in history, it divides into a variety of languages which function as "dialects" of *lingua humana*. The most important of these are the languages of the great civilisations. These are *lingua humana* because each of them is an advanced, differentiating development of the shared basic vocabulary of *lingua humana*. They are dialects because, in each case, this development — this making of distinctions within the basic vocabulary — follows a different course, in accordance with the particular circumstances and genius of each civilisation. For example, most of the two or three hundred words which named forms or aspects of music in European civilisation were not equivalents of the two or three hundred that did the same in Indian civilisation. Many of the names and qualifiers that developed the idea of *loyalty* and the notion of *going* in Japanese civilisation were not equivalents of the words that did the same in Roman civilisation. And so on. In each great, collective fulfilment of desire and capacity, with its by-product of created needs, the process of verbal differentiation has occurred differently.

3.2. Higginbotham and Chomsky

Last year (1998) I learned that the English linguist James Higginbotham has a theory of language which seems broadly related to what I have been saying here. He gave some lectures in Milan which took their inspiration from a remark by Leibniz that the tongues spoken by human beings "are the best mirror of the human mind". In an article by Higginbotham which I read in an Italian newspaper, he explained his hypothesis as meaning that "all tongues are a series of variations on a single theme"; that "the differences of vocabulary are the only discoverable differences among the human tongues". He described his theory as "the homologue, in the field of semantics", of Chomsky's theory of language as a "perfect" construction; perfect in its relation to the human mind and its needs. I mention these theories of professional linguists only in passing. It is not my purpose now, and I don't possess the requisite knowledge, to go deeper into them. While continuing to use the rough-and-ready scheme of *lingua humana* and its major dialects that I have outlined, I want to discuss the dialect of *lingua humana* that was created, spoken and written by European civilisation.

4. The two-tongued language of Roman civilisation

Whether a given system of verbal communication ranks as a language or as a dialect is, as we know, a by-product of political history. There is no essential difference. So, for simplicity's sake, I shall use the word languages for the dialects of *lingua humana* that have been created by the great civilisations. Sometimes, as in the case of Japan or of ancient Egypt, the language of a civilisation is couched in a single tongue or vernacular; in other instances it uses a plurality of vernaculars. Roman civilisation from an early stage, after it had encountered Greek civilisation in Italy, used two vernaculars: Latin and Greek. More precisely: the language of Roman civilisation was expressed in Latin and in Greek. This became the case on a grand scale when Roman civilisation came to include the entire Mediterranean area.

The common, two-tongued Roman language was achieved through contact between the tongues and verbal transferences. The transferences took either of two forms: adoption or translation. It was adoption when a word from one vernacular was simply adopted by the other, with or without minor phonetic changes. The Greek *stadion* entered Latin as *stadium,* the Latin *porta* entered Greek unchanged. Translation occurred mainly in two ways. An existing word was given an extra meaning: the Greek *hupatos* (highest one) was made to express the Latin *consul;* the Latin *forma* was used to render the Greek philosophic term *eidos.* Or a descriptive equivalent was invented: for the Greek *stoa,* the Latin *porticus.*[3] The net result was that from one end to another of Roman civilisation there was a common Roman language, entirely expressed in two vernaculars.

This result reached its most complete and mature form at the beginning of the fourth century AD. That was just before the Christian adulteration of Roman rules of behaviour, and of Roman language, began to create a new civilisation, from 313 onwards. In other words, it is in the Roman language, in both tongues, in, say, the years 300–310, that we find the collective mind of Roman civilisation mirrored, integrally, in its final, most complete form.

---

[3] I am grateful to Prof. Brian Arkins of NUI Galway for help with these examples.

5. The multi-tongued European language — its culmination in 1920–30

The civilisation which the world calls "European" developed in the western third of the European continent. In the course of its growth, it, too, developed a unique language: a particular way of identifying, analysing and referring to reality. In its first stage, until the fifteenth century, this language was expressed in a single tongue, Latin. After that, it was expressed and developed through contacts and transferences among a number of tongues. This unique, European dialect of *lingua humana*, expressed in a growing number of vernaculars, reached its final and most complete form in the early twentieth century. If we were to name a decade, it might be 1920–30 — though a case could be made for 1905–15 or the 1950s. I choose 1920–30 because after that an adulteration of the European rules of behaviour (civilisation), and of the European language, began.

In Western Europe, which was the core of the civilisation, the adulterating forces were, first of all, to a partial degree and impermanently, Nazism, and then definitively, the New Americanism that has dominated Western Europe since World War II. As we know, the revolutionary New America that emerged after that war has become, for good or ill, the central authority on rules of right and wrong behaviour for the West as a whole. For good or ill, its rulers and ethical preachers, acting in unison, have overthrown the set of rules that characterised European civilisation; in every sphere from the ethics of massacre and abortion to sexual morality, from the norms defining work relations between men and women to those governing relations between parents and children, and between young and old. New America has engaged in this new rule-making as an autonomous entity, no longer taking guidance from Europe, but with its principal external cultural influences coming from Japan and Latin America. In short, under the leadership of this increasingly non-European USA, Europe is launched into a New American civilisation that has replaced the

European one that preceded it on both sides of the Atlantic. And with this new civilisation has come a new language: a non-European way of identifying, analysing and referring to reality.

As a result, when I propose as an object of linguistic study the European dialect of *lingua humana*, I am talking about a many-tongued linguistic entity that has become as historical — as much a thing of the past — as the two-tongued language of Roman civilisation. I have suggested that the last period in which we find this language being spoken and written, and still substantially intact, is, in Western Europe, the decade 1920–30. I will enlarge on that. Those years 1920–30 are the last decade in which we find the substantially unadulterated European language being used, with the support of the rulers and the ethical establishment, throughout the wide area in Europe and elsewhere where it had become present to a greater or lesser degree. For Russia, because of the adulteration of the common European language that was caused by the Bolshevik regime, we would need to pick a somewhat earlier decade, say, 1905–1915, as the last period when the European language was still substantially intact and endorsed by the rulers and ethical preachers.

Addressing ourselves to this language, as it existed in the early twentieth century, we find a unique system of identifying, analysing, and referring to reality that has been developing since around the year 400 AD, that is, for 1600 years. This system uses a single, common vocabulary, expressed in many European vernaculars. We can find this common vocabulary in a dictionary of any developed European vernacular — say, English, Swedish, Czech, Portuguese or Russian — published in the early part of the twentieth century. This indicates that a great deal of contact between tongues, and of transference from one to another, has taken place.

5.1. Study of the European language

As earlier, in the Roman civilisation, between Latin and Greek, these transferences have been either by adoption or by one method or another of translation. Study of the European dialect of *lingua humana* would mean, therefore, in large measure, study of its linguistic formation and development through this network of verbal transferences. How, we would be asking, did those many-tongued dictionaries of a common and distinctively European language come into existence?

6. Development of the European language — a tentative scheme

In conclusion, let me sketch out, very tentatively and subject to correction, the answer that I believe we might find. The shared vocabulary did not come into existence through casual, unordered contacts and transferences among the many European tongues involved. First, in the medieval period, transferences from medieval Latin into the West European vernaculars — including those of Latin origin — provided a basic layer of common vocabulary peculiar to European civilisation. Then, from the sixteenth century to the early twentieth, five tongues were the source of by far the greater part of the expanding and distinctive common vocabulary. Placing them in a tentative order of importance, I would say: Latin, followed by French, Italian, German and Ancient Greek. (Incidentally, the absence of English from this leading category is yet another illustration of the decisive difference between the first and second half of the twentieth century in European linguistic practice.)

Then again, the impact of those five tongues on the common vocabulary was not of the same degree throughout the period. Apart from Latin, which maintained a high degree of impact throughout, the other tongues had successive ascendancies as sources of new common vocabulary. The chronology of these ascendancies was Italian, followed by French, followed by German and Greek on something like a par.

Finally, one must make a modifying remark about the continuing leading role of Latin. It remained the main ultimate, as distinct from direct source of new common vocabulary. It did not, as previously in its medieval form, have a direct and more or less simultaneous impact on all the main vernaculars. This impact now occurred by the mediation of one of the main "driving" vernaculars, principally French. The same is, of course, true of Ancient Greek. Most of the contributions of Greek to the common European vocabulary — words like "orthopaedics" or "biology" — occurred *via* French and German from the mid-eighteenth century onwards.

That, I suggest, was the main linguistic dynamic in the formation of the European dialect of *lingua humana*. Contributions by other tongues than the Famous Five were minor by comparison; but cumulatively, they were many. To name just a few examples, Portuguese supplied *baroque*; Spanish *toreador, castanet, sherry, quixotic, bolero, eldorado;* English, *common sense, understatement, clown, lord, Hamlet, tram, beefsteak, garden party;* Gaelic, *whisky* and *slogan;* Hungarian, *goulash* and *csardas;* Russian, *troika, vodka, pogrom, boyar, ukase, knout, Raskolnikov, Rasputin.*

Three Views of Reality: The Poetry of Higgins, Kavanagh and Heaney

InCognito *(Dublin)*, *Vol. 5, 1999. Based on a paper first aired at the F.R. Higgins Weekend in Foxford, County Mayo, and rewritten for the national meeting of the American Conference for Irish Studies, Omaha, Nebraska, 1994*

Of the three poets whose work I want to discuss, only F.R. Higgins requires a few words of introduction. Frederick Robert Higgins was born in Foxford, County Mayo in 1891 and died in Dublin in 1941. A Protestant, he spent most of his life in Dublin where he worked as a clerk and then as editor for a publisher of magazines. He was closely associated with W.B. Yeats, became a director of the Abbey Theatre in 1935, and later its managing director. Physically rather similar to the younger Yeats, he was regarded by some as Yeats's successor in poetry. He was a close friend of AE, but somewhat more robust. He was a frequent contributor to the *Dublin Magazine*. Higgins' first book of poems *Island Blood* was published in 1925. It was followed by *The Dark Breed* in 1927 and *The Gap of Brightness* in 1940. His books went out of print, but a selection of thirty-nine of his poems, made by Dardis Clarke, son of Austin Clarke, was published in 1992.[1]

Given that Higgins, in his time, was a well-known poet and regarded by some as the successor of Yeats, why has he been virtually eclipsed? At the first F.R. Higgins Weekend in Foxford in 1991, Val Mulkems, the novelist, suggested some general, practical reasons and concluded: "But the particular reason for his eclipse is that shortly after his death a radically different sort of poet began to establish himself as the voice of the real Ireland.

---

[1] R.D. Clarke, ed, *F.R. Higgins — The 39 Poems*, Dublin, The Bridge Press, 1992.

That was Patrick Kavanagh, of course." Note there, "as the voice of the real Ireland". I think it would have been more accurate to say "as the voice of reality in Ireland", or "of reality", quite simply. For the main reason why Higgins's work has been eclipsed is that, from Kavanagh onwards, the image of reality which Higgins's poetry suggests became unacceptable in literary Ireland.

It is common knowledge that the Irish Literary Renaissance included efforts by Irish writers to depict "the real Ireland", as distinct from "unreal", inauthentic or superficial Ireland. But the most serious participants in this project, like all serious literary artists were also, and fundamentally, concerned with representing reality in general: *reality as such*. Zeal for that, and the endeavour to make it manifest as nearly as a given medium can, are the core of artistic motivation. Consequently, the literature of the Irish Renaissance was, among other things, a tacit manifestation of beliefs about the nature of reality. In particular, it was a participation in the age-old debate about the materiality or otherwise of the real. Is the visible — material, fleshly — world real? Or is reality an invisible world of spiritual being and insubstantial habitat, and the visible world illusion? Plato believed this, Hinduism affirms it, Calderón made it the theme of his play *La Vida Es Sueño*. Prospero states it as fact in *The Tempest*, after the pageant of spirits has vanished:

> The cloud-capp'd towers, the gorgeous palaces,
> The solemn temples, the great globe itself,
> Yea, all which it inherit, shall dissolve
> And, like this insubstantial pageant faded,
> Leave not a wrack behind. We are such stuff
> As dreams are made of, and our little life
> Is rounded with a sleep.[2]

Throughout history, three answers to those fundamental questions are repeatedly affirmed: reality is, ultimately, non-material; is matter only; or is a combination of material and immaterial

---

[2] William Shakespeare, *The Tempest*, Act IV, Sc. 1.

being. Poetry contributes its voice to these competing affirma-
tions. It does so either explicitly, by making a statement such as
we have just read, or implicitly, by the way it images — as it must
willy-nilly image — the material world. Of the latter method,
which is the more common, the poetry of Higgins and Kavanagh
offer sharply contrasting instances.

As a rejecter of the mindset of the literary renaissance, Patrick
Kavanagh had no view on the hackneyed question of "the real
Ireland"; he was not interested in playing that game. But he held a
very firm view about the general nature of reality and the artist's
obligation to make it manifest. This view, suggested by his poetry
and stated in his prose criticism, was very different from the view
of reality conveyed by F.R. Higgins's poetry — and, as it happens,
by the poetry and painting of Higgins's friend AE, and the poetry
of the early Yeats. Indeed, the gulf in this respect between
Kavanagh and Higgins was so great, and of such passionate
importance to Kavanagh, that he found the unreality suffusing
Higgins's poetry deeply repellent, and said so in one of the most
virulent attacks ever made by one Irish poet on another. That was
in the magazine *Irish Writing* of November 1947, six years after
Higgins's death.

In the early part of his short essay, Kavanagh describes
Higgins's poetry as insincere dabbling. It is a failed attempt to be
Irish by a Protestant who was troubled about the doubtful Irish-
ness of his Protestantism. Kavanagh then continues:

> It is not very easy to base a critical argument on the work of
> [Higgins] when it is so unreal, so unrelated to any values
> we know.

> What is getting me down as I write these words is the futil-
> ity of all this verse, its meaninglessness. We have reached a
> point where we cannot continue this pleasant dabbling. A
> poet must be going somewhere. He must be vitalising the
> spirit of man in some way. He must have dug deep beneath
> the poverty-stricken crust of our time and uncovered new

veins of — uranium, the uranium of faith and hope, a transcendent purpose.

Now is the time for silent prayer and long fasting. Literature as we have known it has come to the end of its tether. It can be said for Higgins that he wrote before the final disillusionment. In his day it was still possible to believe that pleasant dabbling in verse, word-weaving, white magic, was enough.

By finding ourselves prostrate before God and admitting our dire distress we may be admitted to a new dispensation. The best poets are those who lie prostrate before God. But poets like Higgins keep on pretending that the futile decoration on the walls is enough for the day.

Oh for the kick of Reality.

. . . By a peculiar paradox the pursuit of the Universal and fundamental produces the most exciting local colour. In desiring to be "Irish" a man is pursuing the non-essential local colour. "Seek first the Kingdom of God and its justice and all things will be added."[3]

These passages make it pretty obvious that Kavanagh's quarrel with Higgins's poetry was not that it missed "the real Ireland", but that it didn't represent reality — in Ireland or anywhere else. Kavanagh's belief about the nature of the real clashed with Higgins's. As we shall see, the divergence between them had to do with whether materiality is real or unreal, and with the role of the immaterial in reality. Higgins's poetry suggests one answer to this question, Kavanagh's another.

I will quote a fairly typical poem by each and ask the reader to look for one thing only in them: how is the visible, material world,

---

[3] "The Gallivanting Poet" in Peter Kavanagh, *Sacred Keeper: A Biography of Patrick Kavanagh*, The Curragh, The Goldsmith Press, 1979, pp. 162–5.

including the corporeity of human beings, being represented?
First, "Connemara" by Higgins:

> The soft rain is falling
> Round bushy isles,
> Veiling the waters
> Over wet miles,
> And hushing the grasses
> Where plovers call,
> While soft clouds are falling
> Over all.
>
> I pulled my new curragh
> Through the clear sea
> And left the brown sailings
> Far behind me,
> For who would not hurry
> Down to the isle,
> Where Una has lured me
> With a smile.
> She moves through her sheiling
>
> Under the haws,
> Her movements are softer
> Than kitten's paws;
> And shiny blackberries
> Sweeten the rain,
> Where I haunt her beaded
> Window-pane.
>
> I would she were heeding —
> Keeping my tryst —
> That soft moon of amber
> Blurred in the mist,
> And rising the plovers
> Where salleys fall,
> Till slumbers come hushing
> One and all.

The effect of that verse is to etherealise the material world. "Ethereal" — "of unearthly delicacy of substance, character or appearance". The visible world is presented as "etherealised matter". This conveys scepticism at least, disbelief at most, regarding the reality of matter, and a belief that reality lies in the invisible world. Or, taking that belief as given: the verbal etherealising is a means of suggesting the unreality of the visible world and of bringing it as near as words can bring it to reality. It is a technique *for rendering reality* (as understood by the poet) *as fully as a poem can do this.*

A statement by Higgins in 1939 refers vaguely to the underlying belief, which he regarded as characteristically Irish. In a radio discussion with Louis MacNeice, he said: "Present-day Irish poets are believers — believers in life, nature, revealed religion, the nation . . ." and then, conclusively and most personally, "in a sort of dream that produces a sense of magic".[4] But it appears that Higgins, in his last years, was acquiring a critical distance to this privileging of the invisible. The poet Padraig Fallon reports that Higgins told him in 1940 that he did not want to be regarded as "a mere poet of atmosphere".[5] "Ether" is a fair rendering of "atmosphere".

Now some stanzas from Patrick Kavanagh's "The Long Garden".

> It was the garden of the golden apples
> A long garden between a railway and a road,
> In the sow's rooting where the hen scratches
> We dipped our fingers in the pockets of God.
>
> In the thistly hedge old boots were flying sandals
> By which we travelled through the childhood skies,
> Old buckets rusty-holed with half-hung handles
> Were drums to play when old men married wives.

---

[4] Paul Muldoon, *The Faber Book of Contemporary Irish Poetry*, London, Faber, 1986, pp. 17–18.

[5] *The Dublin Magazine*, July to September 1941.

The pole that lifted the clothes-line in the middle
Was the flag-pole on a prince's palace when
We looked at it through fingers crossed to riddle
In evening sunlight miracles for men. . . .

And when the sun went down into Drumcatton
And the New Moon by its little finger swung
From the telegraph wires, we knew how God had happened
And what the blackbird in the whitethorn sang.

It was the garden of the golden apples,
The half-way house where we had stopped a day
Before we took the west road to Drumcatton
Where the sun was always setting on the play.[6]

Kavanagh's attack on the Higgins kind of poetry contained an implicit statement of his own view of the real and of how it must be represented. While excoriating intangibility, he spoke for transcendence of the visible. Consequently, this poem's presentation of the visible world as "matter transcendent" should not surprise. Reality, this image of it conveys, is both very tangibly material and absolutely non-material, with the matter having its ground and completion in immaterial being. We have seen Kavanagh, from his stance in that conviction, rejecting Higgins's immaterialism. In a short piece of art criticism, we can observe him, from the same stance, equally rejecting pure materialism. His subject was an exhibition of French painting in Dublin. He writes:

> Here is a nude by Renoir. A fat, very seductive female is going to the bath, presenting to us a back view in which I have failed to find any transcendent — that is, artistic — purpose. When the masters painted a nude woman they were merely trying to express in an earthly symbol something of the wonderful, the intangible creativity of God. If this picture is in any way superior to a photograph I'd like to be told how. Here is a pleasant landscape by Monet.

---

[6] Kavanagh, *Collected Poems*, London, Macgibbon & Kee, 1964, p. 74.

There is something in Monet, a touch of childhood nostalgia. His paintings would make ideal decorations for a bungalow in Killiney. . . .

If the purpose of art is immediate sensual pleasure such as we get from drinking a glass of whiskey or smoking a cigarette then these painters have succeeded splendidly. But if the purpose of art is to project man imaginatively into the Other World, to discover *in clay symbols the divine pattern, the Secret,* then the exhibition has failed. (*Italics added.*)[7]

The wider dimensions of the Kavanagh–Higgins clash of world-views would take us through the history of the human mind. In the Irish context, Higgins's view of the real is, of course, a late outreach of the Celtic Twilight mentality. In a central statement of that movement's philosophy in *The Shadowy Waters*, Yeats, through the mouth of Forgael, had been explicit about where real life dwells. Forgael says:

> All would be well
> Could we but give us wholly to the dream,
> And get into their world that to the sense
> Is shadow, and not linger wretchedly
> Among substantial things.

And a moment later, conclusively, with reference to two inhabitants of the invisible world:

> I've had great teachers.
> Aengus and Edain ran up out of the wave —
> You'd never doubt that it was life they promised
> Had you looked on them face to face as I did,
> With so red lips, and running on such feet,
> And having such wide-open, shining eyes.[8]

---

[7] "The New Art Patronage" in *Sacred Keeper*, pp. 129–30.

[8] Yeats, *Collected Poems*, London, Macmillan, 1995, p. 480.

However, by 1947, not only Yeats, but most English Irish poetry had long moved beyond the Celtic Twilight (Gaelic Irish poetry was never touched by it). As far back as the beginning of the century, poets of country life, such as Padraic Colum and Joseph Campbell, had simply shrugged it off and — as Austin Clarke puts it in his essay on the movement — "turned to more mundane matters". As early as 1909, Synge had rejected the Twilight mode, concluding aphoristically: "It may be said that before verse can be human again it must learn to be brutal". After looking at one of AE's faery paintings, he wrote a poem that bade "adieu" to "sweet Angus, Maeve and Fand / Ye plumed and skinny Shee" by mocking them with images of coarse country life:

> We'll stretch in Red Dan Sally's ditch,
> And drink in Tubber fair,
> Or poach with Red Dan Philly's bitch
> The badger and the hare.[9]

Kavanagh, then, was not making history by rejecting the Celtic Twilight poetics as represented by Higgins and unnamed others. His distinction lay in rejecting it on account of the fundamental unreality of its underlying worldview as seen from the standpoint of an opposing, thought-through view of reality. Aware that he might be understood as including in his rejection the leading poet of the Twilight, W.B. Yeats, he was careful to make clear that he could recognise a great poet transcending his own weaknesses. After remarking on how difficult it was for Irish Protestants to be good poets, he interrupts his diatribe to remark: "Yeats got there by being himself, by being a sincere poet. He dug deep beneath the variegated surface to where the Spirit of Poetry is one with Truth. I say this with reservations, but none the less it is largely true."

Higgins's worldview had a second Irish context. Kavanagh was on firm ground — intuitively, on firmer ground than he knew

---

[9] Austin Clarke, *The Celtic Twilight*, Dublin, Dolmen, 1969, p. 49. J.M. Synge, *Plays, Poems and Prose*, London, Dent, 1968.

— when he attributed what he found repugnant in Higgins's poetry to his, and similar poets', Irish Protestantism. What he had principally in mind, and said, was that their Protestantism impelled them to falsity in their attempts to "be Irish". But the historian and Yeats biographer, Roy Foster, has enabled us to see a link between Higgins's otherworldliness and the peculiar mental culture of Irish Protestantism since around the Act of Union. Tracing an Irish Protestant literary tradition that began with Maturin and Le Fanu and culminated in Yeats, AE and Elizabeth Bowen, Foster identifies a Protestant "predilection for the occult" of which these writers were a manifestation. Bram Stoker's *Dracula* was part of it, as were the Japanese ghost tales of Patrick Lafcadio Hearn, the first notable western Japanologist. It was a culture particularly characteristic of the Protestant middle class which, in a period of decline of the Protestant Ascendancy, was feeling marginalised. Foster writes: "The superstition of Irish Protestants was legendary." Recourse to the invisible world and its powers offered a defence against, and a challenge to, both scientific rationalism and pedantic, rationalistic Catholicism. In Yeats, AE and many other Protestants of their generation, this cult of the non-Christian supernatural linked up with international occultism.[10]

To skip forward a few decades, both aspects of what Higgins represented in a culturally emblematic way — the "Twilight" and Protestant otherworldliness — have been neatly fused, and satirised from an Irish Catholic cultural viewpoint, by James Liddy in "A Protestant Mystic". The subject is Higgins's friend, AE (George Russell):

---

[10] Roy Foster, "Protestant Magic" in *Paddy and Mr Punch*, London, Penguin, 1995, pp. 212–32. If we attend to the "scepticism of the rational and tangible" which was an aspect of this Irish Protestant "occultism", the eighteenth-century philosopher Berkeley emerges as a philosophical forerunner. In the pan-European debate on the reality of sensory perception, Berkeley staked out the most extreme idealist or immaterialist position.

Through grass again I am bound to the Lord
He intoned but he didn't really mean it.
How could he when he lived in the city
Where every morning he took a tram
To relentlessly edit the economics journal
So influential in the new emergent nation?
On Sundays instead of praying on the mountains
He kept open house (tea and buns but no drink)
For poetasters who flocked for his wisdom.
Though a saint and helpful to the young
No wonder his verses got woollier and woollier
And his pictures progressively vaguer
Until they were willowy figures in a mist . . .[11]

Kavanagh's "matter transcendent" was orthodox Catholicism. More than that, it was orthodox Christianity. It was the view of the visible world that had been reflected in most of the art, litera- ture, philosophy and mysticism of Western Europe until the seventeenth century. Active, in that century, in Protestant minds, it inspired the greatest Dutch painting and English "Metaphysical" poetry. In Ireland, it had been powerfully reflected since the sixth century in much Gaelic poetry, and was still evident, in Kavanagh's time, in the religious songs and folk prayer of the Gaeltacht. By contrast, in English-speaking Catholic Ireland, this Christian or "incarnational" materialism had rarely found notable expression in any form. Kavanagh's poetry is one of the few liter- ary instances of it.

Many later Irish poets have paid tribute to Kavanagh for hav- ing shown them, when they were starting out, that good poetry could be made out of the unromantic perception of everyday life and its little things. For those among them who shared with Kavanagh a rural upbringing, this revelation had particular force. One such poet was Seamus Heaney. However, it was only in the

---

[11] James Liddy, *A White Thought in a White Shade*, Dublin, Kerr's Pinks, 1987. I am grateful, again, to Brian Arkins for drawing my attention to this poem.

sense just mentioned that Kavanagh's poetry inspired Heaney; he did not accept its worldview. A typical Heaney rural poem is "Blackberry-Picking".

> Late August, given heavy rain and sun
> For a full week, the blackberries would ripen.
> At first, just one, a glossy purple clot
> Among others, red, green, hard as a knot.
> You ate that first one and its flesh was sweet
> Like thickened wine: summer's blood was in it
> Leaving stains upon the tongue and lust for
> Picking. Then red ones inked up, and that hunger
> Sent us out with milk-cans, pea-tins, jam-pots
> Where briars scratched and wet grass bleached our boots.
> Round hayfields, cornfields and potato-drills,
> We trekked and picked until the cans were full,
> Until the tinkling bottom had been covered
> With green ones, and on top big dark blobs burned
> Like a plate of eyes. Our hands were peppered
> With thorn pricks, our palms sticky as Bluebeard's.
>
> We hoarded the fresh berries in the byre.
> But when the bath was filled we found a fur,
> A rat-grey fungus, glutting on our cache.
> The juice was stinking too. Once off the bush
> The fruit fermented, the sweet flesh would turn sour.
> I always felt like crying. It wasn't fair
> That all the lovely canfuls smelt of rot.
> Each year I hoped they'd keep, knew they would not.[12]

There are other Heaney poems ("Churning Day", "Death of a Naturalist") where the materiality and physicality of the visible world, and of language itself, are even more emphatically affirmed. But these verses suffice to show this feature, and the equally typical absence of any suggestion of immaterial reality.

---

[12] Seamus Heaney, *New Selected Poems 1966–1987*, London, Faber and Faber, 1990, p. 5.

After "etherealised matter" and "matter transcendent", the visible world is now presented as "matter unalloyed". That, this seems to say, is all there is. We have moved from immaterialism through a material–immaterial dualism to pure materialism.

That is the "obvious" reading, the one that springs to mind. But on the face of it, there could be others. A rendering of the visible world as "matter unalloyed" is a more than ambiguous poetic statement about reality. Three quite different worldviews, aiming to manifest the real poetically, would use it. Obviously, pure, affirmative materialism would; but so, too, would agnostic materialism — whereof one does not know, one does not speak; and so, too, again, would what might be called the "two-tier" worldview.

The conviction, exemplified in Kavanagh, that reality is a combination of material and immaterial can take another form. Reality can be seen as a two-tier structure comprising a visible world of pure matter and a distinct sphere of immaterial being. No need to go back to deism and the clockwork universe to find an instance. In post-Famine Catholic Ireland the mentality called "gombeen" held such a view of things. The visible here and now of godforsaken matter and treacherous carnality existed for one purpose: to be mastered and possessed in such a manner and degree as would secure survival for self and family during normal life-spans. That was the task until one departed into the other, blessed realm "above", which in the meantime one nodded towards and placated, reverently. Gombeen and poetry are mutually exclusive concepts, but if a gombeenman were to be imagined metamorphosed into a poet, his poems would present the visible world as Heaney's do. On both sides of the dividing chasm the obsessive passion for materiality is the same.[13]

---

[13] This modifies a judgement I made in the Postscript to the American edition of my monograph *Whatever You Say, Say Nothing: Why Seamus Heaney is No. 1*. There I wrote that Heaney "lacks passion", meaning "passion" in the broad sense — strong feeling for life in one form or another — in which the word is often used.

Of these three possible readings of "matter unalloyed" — a two-tiered vision or materialism agnostic or pure — we cannot, as of now, know which of them describes Heaney's own view of reality. We lack the helpful, ancillary information that we had for Kavanagh and Higgins. Heaney has not, to my knowledge, made any direct statement of his worldview in verse or prose, nor does he belong to a poetic "movement" with a well-advertised view of the nature of things. All that we can reasonably do is to deduce how Heaney's image of the visible world as "matter unalloyed" has been read by our age, or more precisely, by its ruling mentality. A poet of the consumerist era (as others were poets of the Victorian or modernist eras), Heaney has been celebrated by the consumerist system of power and honour, and awarded its highest literary distinction. Doubtless his painstaking craft, his sensitive association with the Northern Ireland war, the frequent beauty of his verse, and his amenable personality played parts in this. But the upholders of a system built on the postulate that reality is matter unalloyed would require more than that from a poet to declare him great. They would require him to adhere, at least nominally, to the consumerist postulate. Clearly, Heaney has appeared to them to do that and more. In his verse he has seemed to them to be asserting the postulate vehemently. So finding in him what looked like what they were looking for, the upholders of the consumerist mindset have taken (as did I, naïvely, at first sight) the "obvious" reading.[14]

---

[14] A section of my Heaney monograph is devoted to "The Poetry of Consumer Capitalism" in a first attempt to relate poetry in English since the 1950s to its socio-political environment. It is high time that the generally unnamed period of poetry that succeeded modernism was named "the consumerist era"; the rich critical harvest that the name suggests and encapsulates is there for reaping. Is this sensible decision being prevented by some fear of "sullying " poetry by seeing it in relation to the age that produced it and selectively celebrated it? If so, how can we hope to talk sensibly about the poetry of the last fifty years in the West?

Irish Literary Studies In Italy: A Response

Read in Italian at the launch of The Cracked Lookingglass: Contributions to the Study of Irish Literature by Italian Scholars, *eds. Carla de Petris, Fiorenzo Fantaccini and Jean Ellis d'Allesandro, Bulzoni Editore. The launch took place in Florence University, 17 February 2000.*

My first reaction to this book is astonishment, admiration and embarrassment. I opened it at the Appendix, which is a bibliography of Italian translations of Irish writers, and Italian studies of Irish culture and history, compiled by Fiorenzo Fantaccini. I am astonished at the sheer quantity. I am lost in admiration of the enormous work which Fantaccini put into assembling this bibliography. The translations and the studies demonstrate an active contemporary interest in Irish writing, culture and history not only in specialist academic circles, but in a notable part of the Italian public. I am embarrassed because there is no evidence of equivalent Irish interest in Italian literature, culture and history. Only in Italian cooking — very much — but Italians in person bring that to us!

This has nothing to do with Italy in particular: it is part of a general pattern. Comparatively speaking, European English-language culture, of which we form a small part, shows little active interest in other European cultures. A single, illustrative example: the German TV series *Inspector Derrick*, which was so popular in Italy and was sold to 100 countries, was never seen on British or Irish television. An Irishman who visits bookshops in Helsinki, Copenhagen or Budapest sees how much closer our cultural contacts with the rest of Europe would be if our effort to restore Irish as the national language had succeeded. Those small language-cultures are much more in contact with the rest of Europe than are London or Dublin. Indeed, our anglophone isolation has been increasing since the 1960s. Before that, many Irish intellectuals and artists had cultural contact with continental Europe, especially France. We have become more enclosed in Anglo-American culture, and as a result more uncritical in regard to it. This is one of the reasons why I have chosen to observe the world, and write about it, in Italy.

James Joyce, in the first years of the twentieth century, described Irish art as "the cracked lookingglass of a servant". The editors of this book, in their chosen title, omit the "servant" and describe Irish literature as a cracked mirror. This is an apt description of it. One sees why if, reclaiming the metaphor of a servant to represent Ireland defeated and colonised, we introduce the opposing figure of a princess and tell the following fairy story.

Until the seventeenth century, the mirror of Irish literature belonged to a Gaelic-speaking princess. Then an Englishman hit it with a hammer, and a big crack appeared which was followed by other cracks. The cracked mirror passed to a bilingual servant. She spoke Gaelic and English, but as time went by, mostly English, little Gaelic. In the nineteenth century, because she had become very poor, was often sick and hated looking at herself, the mirror was not kept polished and became misted over, especially the Gaelic part. Then, during the revolutionary years — which occurred in Joyce's lifetime — the mirror passed again into the hands of a princess, this time a bilingual princess. She polished the mirror, made it shine again. She spoke more Gaelic than the servant, but mostly English. Since then the mirror has lost some of its restored shine, and of course it still bears the history of Irish literature in its cracked glass. There is no remedying that.

I think it is important for foreigners who are studying Irish literature and language, and who do not know Gaelic, to know the facts about it and not become the victims of dramatising myths. The Irish, especially when they are talking, like constructing dramatic myths. Donatella Abbate Badin gives a good account of the personal myth about Gaelic which the poet Thomas Kinsella has constructed.[1] It is the story of how one contemporary Irish poet who writes in English solves the problem that he finds in relating to an Irish literary past which is mostly in Gaelic. Obviously, if Kinsella were writing in Gaelic, as about twenty-five contemporary Irish poets do, including two or three of the best — all women — he would not have his problem nor have constructed his myth. He would have other problems.

What I am saying is that Kinsella (he serves as an example) is not supplying factual information about the Gaelic language and literature. Here are three imaginary statements which sound pleasantly dramatic but are untrue: "The Gaelic language and literature are dead"; "In Ireland, Gaelic is the past, English is the present"; "Gaelic literature is accessible to us today only through translation".

The facts are that Ireland today speaks and writes two languages; that Gaelic is in danger of death in this century; and that Gaelic is a slender presence pervading Irish life today. It pervades it from the word *sláinte*, which English-speaking Irish often use when drinking a toast, to the language of the presidential oath of office, and to the Gaelic version of the Constitution to which the judges of the Supreme Court must give precedence when judging Constitutional matters. In the Irish education system during the past ten years, the kind of school which has been increasing most in numbers is, by express request of groups of parents, the *Gaelscoil*, or school where all instruction is through Gaelic. Two of my daughters work on Gaelic television programmes in RTÉ, the Irish RAI; one of the programmes is on current affairs, the other on the arts. And a son is general programmes adviser on a Gaelic television channel. As I said, "a slender presence pervading Irish life today". As it happens, on the train today from Rome I was reading a book of humorous short

---

[1] I am referring to Kinsella's suggestion in various essays and interviews that, for the contemporary Irish poet writing in English, there is a problematic "discontinuity" between Gaelic "past" and English "present".

stories in Gaelic which one of my daughters sent me. [*shows the book, entitled* "Banana" *and says* "Feiceann sibh chomh héasca is atá an Ghaeilge, níor fhoghlaim sibh í, ach tuigeann sibh láithreach í " — *and translates.* "Banana" *is also in Italian the name for that fruit.*]

What is Irish literature, how is it to be defined? In the debate on this matter, Carla de Petris takes a clear stand. She writes: "It is a geographical definition: it indicates writing produced within the island of Ireland." A different definition has been fashionable in Ireland since the publication of the *Field Day Anthology of Irish Writing.* That definition is: "Irish literature consists of writing by Irish authors anywhere." This includes, of course, those many Irish writers who made their careers in England or elsewhere. Naturally, this reclaiming of our exiled geniuses gives Irish literati a certain imperialistic pleasure. However, I would accept this definition only to the point where I would unhesitatingly describe all those exiled Irish geniuses as "Irish", since this is a simple fact. Oscar Wilde was Irish, not English. But when I read the learned essay by Jean Ellis D'Allesandro on the Ciceronian element in Wilde's *The Picture of Dorian Gray,* I do not feel that I am reading about a work of Irish literature. I would prefer the de Petris definition as a basis, while adding some individual writers as circumstances seem to justify it; for example, Edna O'Brien and William Trevor.

Francesco Gozzi writes about how some Irish writers have tried to establish their individual identity with reference to their fathers, biological or literary. This is the first time I have seen this subject treated. Ireland is generally depicted as a matriarchy, like Italy. *O mamma mia!*[2]

Sometimes in Ireland, when the noise of the literary industry wearies me, the following conversation occurs. I say to someone: "Why do we make all this noise about being a great literary nation when in fact, since Joyce's *Ulysses,* we have not produced one single novel that has entered the literary consciousness of Europe

---

[2] "Oh mammy mine!" a very common Italian exclamation.

or even of the English-speaking world?" My interlocutor replies: "Flann O'Brien's *At Swim Two Birds*." And I say: "Well, yes, but only among literati and writers, not generally." And what do I find in Concetta Mazzullo's essay on the influence of *At Swim Two Birds* on Italo Calvino? On page 190 she describes the novel's author Flann O'Brien as "an author who has mainly been appreciated by a restricted group of literati". Thank you, Concetta Mazzullo, full marks! Which is not to say that Flann O'Brien and Italo Calvino were not geniuses.

With evidence of much research and a sensitive eye, Giovanna Tallone analyses intrusions from the world of shadows in two plays by Brian Friel. I am not the only Irish person to wonder why the plays of Tom Murphy have not become much known outside Ireland while Friel's plays have. I would say that, except for Friel's *The Faith Healer*, several of Murphy's plays have more universal significance. One of my great theatrical experiences was to sit for four and a half hours watching the premiere of *The Gigli Concert* in the Abbey Theatre, not caring that I had missed the last bus home. I think that the explanation may be that Friel's plays supply better than Murphy's what the British and Americans want from Irish writers — nostalgia of rural and small-town life, charming marginality and quaintness. And the consequent success in London and New York leads on to interest in continental Europe.

Carla de Petris writes about the poet Patrick Kavanagh. He wrote his poetry from the 1930s to the beginning of the 1960s. De Petris says that foreign students of Irish poetry during this period have a problem. International literary criticism took an interest in Yeats, and then resumed interest in Irish literature only in the late sixties when Kinsella, Montague and Heaney emerged. It took little interest "in following Irish events between the Thirties and the late Sixties". Consequently, according to de Petris, for that period there is a "blind spot", due in part to a "lack of information". At first glance, I did not understand the problem. "Lack of information"? The information about Irish events in that period can be found in libraries, in bookshops. Then I thought that perhaps de Petris is talking about information as distinct from myths and propaganda, and if this is the case, she is referring to a real problem.

It is a problem which exists today for Italians and other foreigners who want to study Irish literature during the period that de Petris refers to — or, indeed, earlier, during the Irish *risorgimento* and the 1920s. Naturally, as good critics, they want to know the circumstances surrounding the literature they are studying. Naturally, too, they will begin by consulting the most easily available Irish publications dealing with pre-1960 Ireland: those of the past ten, twenty or thirty years. And the problem is that many of these publications, as well as a monolithic Irish journalism, provide a mythical and misleading account of pre-1960 Ireland. This is a problem even within Ireland for those who care about historical truth. Last year Brian Fallon, the chief critic of *The Irish Times* newspaper, a man very learned in the arts of Ireland and Europe who had lived in Dublin from the 1930s onwards, published a book *The Age of Innocence* for the express purpose of correcting what is now the dominant picture of those years.

However, like many problems, this one, too, is greatly reduced if one knows about it and understands its causes. These are principally two. Those of you who know contemporary Ireland will have heard of "revisionism". That is one, not quite comprehensive name for the ideological counter-revolution that has taken place there, with increasing force, from the late 1960s onwards. Like all revolutions, its central gospel is that before it began — at one minute past midnight on 1 January 1960 — everything (in Ireland) was dark, stagnant and oppressed by evil forces, and that since then, Ireland is increasingly bright, active, free and virtuous. Combined with this gospel, in the 1990s, is a snobbish disdain of a rich Ireland for an Ireland that was poor.

The other reason why a mythical view of pre-1960 Ireland has become dominant in the country is an Irish intellectual habit which Fantaccini mentions in his essay. He observes it in the earlier nationalist period, but it still persists. It is a tendency to see Ireland and Irish matters in isolation from human affairs generally, that is, outside the relevant comparative context, whether that be the British Isles, Anglo-Saxon culture, European nations, newly independent nations or whatever. Obviously, if you view a human reality in isolation from its context, you can interpret it in any way you like, any way that suits some point you want to make. In Ireland of the past thirty years, this isolating and emotional way of viewing Irish phenomena has been projected backwards onto pre-1960 Ireland. Guided by it, the counter-revolutionary ideology has produced the unreal view of that period which has been dominant in recent decades.

Obviously, as with any myth, the current Irish myth about pre-1960 Ireland contains some elements of truth. As I said, the important thing for the foreign student of Ireland and Irish literature in the period in question is to know that the myth exists and why it exists. After that, it is a matter of sorting out, by research, what is true in it from its overall misrepresentation. In doing so, it is helpful to remember something Robert Musil wrote in *The Man without Qualities*: "The present looks proudly down on the past, which, if it had come later, would look proudly down on the present."

But of course, having investigated the matter with all that I have just said in mind, the foreign student may come to the conclusion that the myth is truth — that this particular "looking down" is justified! But what I have just been saying will nevertheless have been useful, for it will have made you aware that there is a judgement to be made on the matter. I have given you mine.

In this brief response to a book of which everyone concerned can be very proud, I have talked a lot about Irish myth-making. But it hasn't only been the Irish who have made myths about Ireland: all of Europe has done so for centuries — has projected dreams, desires and contempts onto Celtic Hibernia, the edge of the world, the green island, the end of the rainbow, the struggler for freedom, the poor, ignorant, bigoted peasant backwater. A country wrapped in myths of its own making and in myths made by others is likely to be good at producing poetry and other fictive literature. That is probably the principal cause of the abundance of imaginative literature which you and others find in Ireland and enjoy. But because I am speaking in a university, I have been reminding you that myth is myth — not *realtà*.

The Legacy of Pearse

The Irish Times, *2 September 2000*

The Editor
The Irish Times

Sir, — Along with sense, much nonsense has been written under the above heading. The aim of the 1916 leaders as of the subsequent War of Independence was to establish an Irish nation-state. The nation-states of Europe had not been established by democratic or peaceful means. Why should the Irish case be different? To assert simply that it "ought to have been" is as sensible as saying that England or the Netherlands "ought not" to have been created. — Yours, etc.,

DESMOND FENNELL
Dublin 7

Anglo-American Ireland is Becoming Culturally Invisible

The Irish Times, 7 September 2000

It is a pity that Dermot Desmond's multi-storey glass pyramid is not to be built in Dublin docks. A tall, handsome, striking building, it was to contain an aquarium and a simulated tropical forest. Although the architect was American, the promoter like the location was Irish. In a city and country that are fast becoming a derivative English-American mish-mash, it would have provided a note of distinction. And it might have spurred creative innovation of other kinds in Dublin and outside it.

Normally a nation maintains its cultural visibility through a combination of distinctive inherited things — language, religion, man-made environment, customs, arts — and distinctive creative innovations. What Lara Marlowe some months ago called the "Temple Bar Celtic Tiger culture" has little time for the inherited elements of Irish culture. Pushing them to the margins or wishing them buried, it displays its English and American with-itness proudly. Hence the urgent need for creative innovations if Ireland is to remain culturally visible in the world.

I write as one who lives on the Continent, where Ireland figures in the news only as Northern Ireland politics. News of creative innovation (such as emanates from other European countries) never reaches us from Ireland. We do not hear of a new Irish system of urban transport, an Irish reinvention of television, Irish success in reducing abortions or suicides, a new Irish theory of the human brain or critique of feminism, or a ground-breaking Irish foreign policy.

Such things make the country they come from culturally visible. A combination of them reforges and continues a distinct national identity. In a very concrete sense, the lack of such news from Ireland makes Ireland absent from Europe — and in effect from the world.

Europe, the West generally, is an evolving cooperative life in which fresh leads, models and perspectives come now from this country, now from that. In this context of give and take, Ireland is a non-contributor: a taker not a giver, a parasite of ideas and models, not a supplier.

Proud as we are to have the contemporary West — its ideas and ethics, its practices and problems — now at home in Ireland, we assume that they are here simply to absorb or gawp at, not to think about, critically, inventively and with effect. That work, we assume, is for London and New York. Heads bowed in anticipation, we await their next directives.

The result is that, as the distinctive Ireland of modern times — rural, Catholic, poor, struggling for freedom, anti-imperialist, restoring its Gaelic language — passes away, a blank space is replacing it, culturally speaking, on the international scene. "Prospering on massive American investment, a nice place for holidays and week-ends, the home of excellent entertainers and *craic*" doesn't add up to the kind of presence that merits one serious or respectful thought — except from East European competitors for a slice of American investment. People who want English or American life-style know where to find the genuine articles and have no need of Paddy imitations.

To put it bluntly: what is making Ireland culturally invisible is not so much the Celtic Tiger's marginalisation of traditional Ireland as the lack of originality in Irish thinking and practice which preceded the Tiger and which still continues. Originality is another way of saying creative innovation.

Even if we did not know it from personal experience, we could assume that this dearth of originality in Ireland is not due to a complete absence of questioning, freethinking, inventive Irish minds. Presumably, there are at least as many such minds here as in any other nation of our size. No, the absence of originality that can be observed in Irish public thinking and practice is due to effective opposition by Irish society to Irish original thinking getting published and discussed, or having its projects implemented. In this manner, the controlling forces in Irish society effectively compel Irish people to outward conformity and imitation.[1]

I said that creative innovation is needed urgently if Ireland is to remain culturally visible in the world; but it might be argued that there is no pressing need for that. The world can continue to get along without Irish innovatory thinking or action, can even, if need be, find substitutes for its Irish entertainers. In the Republic of Ireland, massive cultural derivativeness and economic boom go hand in hand without apparent contradiction.

All that is true. No imperative requires that we regain cultural distinctiveness. But it would still be a momentous event for Ireland, after all its history, to end up a mixture of Lancashire and Massachusetts. Minimal self-respect demands that we should at least be aware of what is happening, and consciously choose our cultural dissolution rather than drift into it, mindlessly.

---

[1] For more on this matter, see "The Irish Problem with Thought", pp. 222–31.

The Art Problem

The Journal of Music in Ireland (JMI), *first issue, November–December 2000. This venture by my friend Toner Quinn has since developed into Ireland's leading forum for cultural debate.*

In western civilisation as in other civilisations, art was no problem. There were myths, widely believed in or widely known, in whose shadow art could flourish. There were the stories of Adam and Eve and of Christ and his Mother. There were the lives of saints and martyrs, the myths of ancient Greece, the national myths of the European nations, the myths of romantic love, chaste womanhood, the knight errant, the gentleman, Revolution, and the grand myth of the Individual's inner life — the communion of Self and Soul.

These myths and others provided material and incitement for art. They supplied frameworks within which art could be constructed, shared and understood. Without such bonding myths for it to flourish in, art cannot flourish.

Since we rejected the rules and the myths of western civilisation and set out to make a much better civilisation, we have been experiencing this fact. We have an art problem. Abandoning the old myths because they were false or oppressive or incredible was one thing; creating new myths and getting them believed in is another. It has not been happening.

This goes a long way to explain both the withering of art and our industrious attempts to conceal this from ourselves: the proliferation of "arts centres" and arts officials; the constant talk and flurry about "more funding for the arts"; the tendency to call anything in verse-style "poetry" and pat it, uncritically, on the head; and the fact, finally, that "art" can now mean anything so described by a commercial or institutional sponsor who calls its producer an artist.

Because our new civilisation is better, by definition, than anything that went before it — and due to become better still — it must, like any self-respecting civilisation, have Art. And if it hasn't, it must be made to have, because by definition it is the best, and how could the best lack that essential accoutrement?

The busy buzz of arts sections, pages, editors, promotions, centres, festivals, officers, courses and programmes — the hum of an arts industry with regular factories of the arts — show that art, despite appearances to the contrary, is flourishing all around us. Funding, if sufficient, can more than adequately substitute for the missing myths. And by dint of calling anything "art" — a pile of stones, a girl in bed — we can make sure it will exist abundantly and everywhere, not only now but forever more. No civilisation before us thought of that.

I uttered these observations to the Editor of the *JMI* and he remarked, "What you are saying has the current music scene written all over it. Can you spell that out for our readers — apply it to music — for our first issue?"

What he was implying was true. I had been talking about "art" mainly with regard to literature and the visual arts. I had included music by implication — music is art — but not explicitly.

Actually, I was thinking of music when I mentioned "industry" and "factory". It is because everyone says "the music industry" that I have taken to speaking of "the Irish literary industry" — all those readings, launch-parties, workshops, writers-in-residence, reverential interviews and puff reviews. And a Dublin friend who was promoting a new rock-band gave me a telephone number where I could ring her "at the Factory".[1] That's what she said!

---

[1] A building in Barrow Street in Dublin 4, which at the time contained various facilities for the "music industry".

I told the Editor, "Remember I live in Italy. If I were to get specific, I mightn't have much to say that would be relevant to your Irish readers."

But I reflected, doing my best. When I listen to Radio 3 on Italian radio I sometimes hear popular songs of Old Italy, say from Naples or Venice. They strike me as very beautiful. They touch my heart and, even when they are sad songs, lift me spiritually. I believe they were made to be like that — that it's a matter of art, not accident — and that they did for those who made them what they do for me. Again, I hear popular Italian songs of the 1920s and 30s which are witty, charming, flirtatious. They put me in good humour, make me smile. And I'm sure they were meant to do exactly that for those who first heard them. But most of the singing you hear today in Italy is not like that.

The town I live in is on a big lake. When there is a *festa* of some kind, many people gather on a large piazza bordering the lake. They never hear those old popular songs I hear on the radio nor anything like them. They hear what has taken their place.

There's a platform in the middle of the piazza and a band is making booming, blaring and clanking sound which is electrically amplified. It dominates the space and the people. Some young people stand near, and from their faces I would guess they are experiencing intensity. Most people remain at a distance, for the noise hurts, and it is difficult to talk if you are anywhere near it. Occasionally, moreover, a vocalist, usually a girl, shouts and screeches and gyrates at a microphone. She seems unhappy even when it is a lovely afternoon with the sun glistening on the lake.

I don't blame this production for not being "art", for I think that art is not its purpose. It has another purpose of which those who enjoy it are well aware.

I said that a "band" occupies the platform. In Italy a more common name for it would be an *"orchestra"*. Indeed that is what an *"orchestra"* usually means there now — six or seven musicians and a singer rendering contemporary sound. I switched into a national competition for "*orchestras*" on Italian television, and found that all the competitors were groups like that. Until I got used to it, this surprised me, for an orchestra, in the old civilisation, meant something quite different.[2]

I passed on these memories and thoughts from Italy to the Editor, and he said, "Not bad, you're trying. But if the readers of the *JMI* are the kind of readers I'm hoping to have, they'll be able to do a bit better than that. Let's leave it to them. But thanks."

So I've done what the Editor asked me to do for his first issue.

---

[2] I subsequently discovered that the Italian *orchestra* can also mean what it means in English.

The North's Policing Problem

The Irish Times, 30 October 2000. I have a deep belief that the good ordering of human society requires that every self-defined community — especially nation or ethnic or language group — have a clearly defined "home". See Kapushinski on this concept on p. 62. Hence my joint initiative for cantonisation in the North with Ronald Bunting in 1969 and my repeated urging of a "Belgian-style" reordering of the North into three regions. This article was a late hankering back to that principle, if in minimal form. I wrote it more out of loyalty to the principle than with serious hope that it would find acceptance from Dublin and London, which for their own reasons prefer to treat communities as mere interchangeable individuals, thus overriding their hankering after collective "homes".

In the late 1980s, before I stopped writing about the North, I was stressing the fundamental importance of the policing arrangements in a Northern settlement within the UK. Policing is the area where the State regularly touches the citizen. It can be generally effective only if the police, in their political symbolism and their personnel, are reasonably representative of the society — or at least not the contrary.

I argued then, that for this to be possible in the ethnically plural society of Northern Ireland, it would be necessary to replace the "Irish" structural model as represented by the RUC and the Garda Síochána — a unitary police force for the entire territory — with the "British" model of collaborating constabularies. England has thirty-nine of these, Scotland eight, Wales four. Northern Ireland, with only one police force, is an anomaly in the UK.

The Patten Report, while aiming "to make the police more representative of the society", recommended that they continue to have a unitary structure. But the unionists are opposed to the Patten proposals, and the nationalist parties are refusing to accept

Westminster's version of the Patten scheme. In these circumstances, it may be possible to cut the Gordian knot by amending Patten, superficially, on the British model; that is to say, along regional lines.

As it happens, "regional police services" in the North were suggested to the Patten Commission (Report, 12.7) — and brusquely rejected: "A multiplicity of police services would not lead to effective or efficient policing"(12.8). "Multiplicity" is a testily derogatory way of referring to the two, or at most three constabularies that might be contemplated. Patten fails in fact to cite adequate grounds for departing from the British norm.

This omission is all the more striking given the fact that Northern Ireland has two native communities attached to different and opposed national histories and flaunting different national symbolisms. The communities have, moreover, regional and local predominances: British unionists in the east; Irish nationalists in the west and south; large areas of Belfast virtually exclusive to one or other community.

There was an "obvious" way of making the police service "more representative" of that society. Instead, Patten chose a method which is, on the face of it, odd. He recommended that in matters of symbolism — name, flag, badges and emblems — the police should cease to be representative of the unionists, and in respect of personnel should be much less so than hitherto. Their name would be changed from RUC to "The Northern Ireland Police Service". British symbolism would be removed from their badges and emblems. Their stations would cease to fly the Union Jack. And in the foreseeable future, Protestants, instead of making up more than 90 per cent of the police personnel, would constitute only about 50 per cent. The rest would be Catholics, nationalists, republicans and "others". For the nationalists, on the other hand, Patten would make the police more representative with respect to personnel, while removing the offensively unrepresentative symbolism of the RUC.

In this key matter of representativeness, that was the deal offered by Patten. The nationalists found it satisfactory, the unionists decidedly and understandably not.

At issue now is the British government's version of Patten. The nationalists are opposing it on the grounds that it is not clear about removing the unrepresentative symbols, and that its provisions for democratic supervision are unsatisfactory. The unionists are rejecting it mainly because it threatens them with a police force that no longer represents them. So, one way or other, both sides are motivated in their opposition — the nationalists partly, the unionists mainly — by aversion to the prospect of an unrepresentative police force.

If a formula could be found to reduce this angst decisively, the way would be open for negotiation, and perhaps a common front, with regard to matters of detail and democratic supervision. Is it possible that such a formula might be found in a watered-down version of regional and local policing, British-style? For the sake of argument, consider the following possible arrangements. With respect to personnel, the Patten objective of a roughly 50–50 split between the communities is retained. In Limavady and Coleraine districts and generally east of the Bann, the Northern Ireland Police Service operates under the name of Royal Ulster Constabulary, and retains the other British symbols used hitherto by the RUC.

In the rest of Northern Ireland, the Northern Ireland Police Service operates under that name, and the Patten proposals relating to political symbolism are fully implemented.

In Belfast the four police sub-districts proposed by Patten are divided equally between the two modes of policing I have just described.

News for Dublin 4: God Is Alive and Thriving

The Irish Times, *1 December 2000*

From Italy, where I live, I had come to Dublin to visit a friend and found the key under the doormat. To get up to date, I watched an RTÉ television news and read some newspapers that were lying around. In one of them there was an interesting interview with Bono by a well-known Dublin journalist. He was asking Bono about the new album, a recent chat with President Clinton, Bono's Jubilee 2000 campaign to get World Bank debts to poor countries written off. I read the journalist's comment on the latter: "In an age when organised religion is almost a taboo and talk about spirituality is shunned as sex once was among respectable people, Bono's campaigns for the have-nots are regarded with suspicion."

Actually, I stopped attending when I got as far as "respectable people". On the television news, I had just seen Buddhist women chanting prayers for the dead after an air disaster in Taiwan. An Irishwoman who had survived described her escape as "by the grace of God". When a man was sentenced in a Dublin court to life imprisonment for murdering a prostitute, members of the girl's family shouted "There's a God! There's a God!" Last time I met my youngest daughter in Galway she was due to begin a course in Japanese *reiki* to develop her spirit power. Before that, she had been through yoga.

Agitated by the crass ignorance of what I had just read, I took out a pen, and at the start of the astounding sentence stroked out "In an age when". Instead, on the margin, I wrote "In the cocoon of Dublin 4 Ireland". "Dublin 4" was a rough-and-ready way of describing the smug, snobbish band of preachers and pub-talkers in Dublin and its hinterland who believe that the world is as they are.

For heaven's sake, I thought, in *La Stampa*, the Turin newspaper I buy, I had recently seen a whole page devoted to an essay on the Psalms by Bono! It was to be the preface to a new Italian edition of the Psalms. That very day, in *La Stampa* — it happened to be the Feast of All Saints — I had read an editorial regretting that spiritualist practices were in part replacing the Italian custom of visiting family members' graves on All Souls' Day. *La Stampa*, let me clarify, is in its ideological tendency what Italians call "laicist", meaning non-religious or secularist.

That same morning it had been a major drama for me to get to the airport because, owing to All Saints' being a public holiday in Italy, public transport had been reduced.

In the Europe I had arrived from, that sentence by the Dublin journalist could simply not be written — neither in *La Stampa*, nor in *Der Spiegel*, nor in *Le Monde* — no more than it could be written in the *New York Times*. It would come across as too absurdly naïve.

That it could be written in a Dublin newspaper without causing an outburst of national laughter heard around the world, indicated two things: the self-delusion of the "ban God" brigade in the Dublin media and of their gullible followers, and Provincial Exaggeration rearing its sad head again in Ireland.

It is possible for a class of Irish people, if they really want it badly, to delude themselves that "organised religion is almost a taboo" and that "talk about spirituality is shunned by respectable people". It is possible if they take adequate measures.

They can close their eyes and ears to the contrary evidence that is all around them and being transmitted to them from elsewhere. They can also, insofar as lies within their power, actively prevent contrary evidence reaching themselves or the Irish public.

The local "public-service" television station lies within their power. When tens of thousands of Irish people gather in Knock to honour the Blessed Virgin, they can see to it that the RTÉ schedule is crammed with British soaps. Or in this Jubilee year, when many spectacular and beautiful religious celebrations are taking place in

Rome — as recently, the gathering of two million young Catholics for the Youth Jubilee — they can limit Irish TV coverage to an occasional live transmission at seven or eight o'clock on a Sunday morning!

They can do more. They can ban the weekly *Irish Catholic* from advertising on radio and refuse a broadcasting licence for a Christian radio station (making Ireland the only country in the Western world without such a station.) Or by refusing planning permission "for environmental reasons", they can prevent a group of Catholics in Carraroe, County Galway from erecting a public stone Cross!

By taking such measures, our "ban God" brigade have managed to restrict the visibility of religion and spirituality, and thus assisted their self-delusion that these don't exist. Why the frenzied efforts? Because word has reached them that out there, in some imagined Metropolis that rules the age, God and spirituality are out of fashion. And they are the kind of people — provincial, deeply colonised — whose sense of self-worth depends on being in tune with the Metropolis, and on working hard to be so.

Sadly, such provincial exaggeration is a national characteristic. Way back, when the mini-skirt appeared, and many women in Paris were rejecting it because it didn't suit them or was inelegant, you could drive through Mayo, as I did, and find every single female wearing it.

When word finally reached us, in the '70s, that "sexual liberation" was the in-thing, French *au pair* girls in Dublin were shocked by the indecency of the sexual talk on RTÉ morning radio. And when news arrived from the Metropolis that laws about homosexuality must be relaxed, why, our Parliament made the age of consent the lowest in Europe. And so on.

A cocoon of imposed make-believe is stifling. I was glad, a week after I arrived, to return to a continent where most people are irreligious, organised religion is not taboo, and respectable people talk freely about spirituality. I like fresh air.

Ón Iodáil go Cúil Aodha

30 V. Arco San Biagio
00061 Anguillara
Roma

17 M. Fómhair 2001

Do Pheadar Ó Riada
Cúil Aodha

A Pheadair, a chara,

Tá mé le bheith i gCúil Aodha don 9–11 Samhain. Seo ábhar mo léachta:

Western Civilisation: Its Beginning, Middle and End

A civilisation is an agreed set of rules. From Ancient Rome to Western Civilisation. The West's rules-threatening race for super-power: France, Britain, Germany, the USA. How Hiroshima and the 1960s overthrew the Western rules. How can we deal with our chaotic "postwestern" situation?

Dearbhaigh let thoil.

Do chara, Deasún

A Critical Look at the Charter for Regional and Minority Languages

Paper read to the Third International Symposium of Eurolinguistics, Mannheim, 2001. Underlying this paper is the basic principle about "language saving" that I enunciated in a paper in Glasgow in 1980 (see below 2.3 and note). Both for that paper and for this critique of the Charter, I was drawing radical conclusions from my rich practical experience as a Gaeltacht activist in Conamara in 1969–79. It was a matter of drawing lessons for the general from the experienced particular.

1. The Charter and its operation

I will begin by recalling the main features of the European Charter for Regional or Minority Languages, which was proposed by the Council of Europe in 1992. The Charter defines regional and minority languages as "languages traditionally used within a given territory of a State by nationals of that State who form a group numerically smaller than the rest of the State's population; and different [the languages, that is] from the official language(s) of that State".[1] The Charter also urges protection for "non-territorial" minority languages, such as Romany or Yiddish, that may be spoken in some states; but such languages are not at the centre of its concern, and I shall not deal with them.

The Charter states in its Preamble that the protection and promotion of regional and minority languages, as defined above, contribute to Europe's cultural wealth. Some of the languages, it remarks, are "in danger of eventual extinction". With a view to the protection and promotion of all of them, the Charter proposes

---

[1] The status of Irish as an official language seems to be the reason why the Republic of Ireland has not adhered to the Charter, and why, consequently, Irish is not protected by its provisions.

to the member states of the Council of Europe nine basic and necessary rules of conduct and a large number of concrete measures. It asserts that nothing it proposes "shall be construed as contravening any of the rights guaranteed by the European Convention on Human Rights". States which adhere to the Charter undertake to adopt the nine basic rules of conduct and to implement a stipulated numerical minimum of the concrete measures.

1.1. Rules of conduct

The nine basic rules of conduct are, briefly, as follows:

- Recognition of the defined languages as an expression of cultural wealth;

- Respect for the geographical area of each defined language in the matter of administrative divisions;

- Resolute action to promote the defined languages in order to safeguard them;

- Facilitation and/or encouragement of the use of the defined languages in speech and writing, in public and private life;

- Maintenance and development of links between all groups in the state using the same or nearly the same defined language;

- Provision of means for the teaching and study of the defined languages at all appropriate stages;

- Provision of facilities enabling non-speakers of a defined language, living in the area where it is used, to learn it if they so desire;

- Promotion of study and research on defined languages at universities or equivalent institutions;

- Promotion of transnational exchanges for defined languages that are used in identical or similar forms in two or more states.

Besides these nine basic and imperative rules of conduct, four others are proposed. These have to do, on the one hand, with removing discrimination against defined languages and promoting equality and respect with regard to them; on the other, with "taking into consideration the needs and wishes expressed by the groups which use such languages". With regard to these four rules of conduct — but to no other element of the Charter — a state adhering to it may make one or more reservations.

1.2. Concrete measures

The large number of concrete measures which the Charter proposes fall into seven sections: Education, Judicial authorities, Administrative authorities and public services, Media, Cultural activities and facilities, Economic and social life, and Transfrontier exchanges. States which adhere to the Charter must specify the language or languages which they intend to protect and promote, and they must undertake, in relation to each of them, to apply at least thirty-five of the proposed concrete measures. Of these, at least three must be from the sections on Education and on Culture, and at least one from each of the other sections, excluding Transfrontier exchanges.

1.3. Reports on implementation

Each adhering state must present periodic, published reports to the Secretary General of the Council of Europe. These reports must deal with the state's performance regarding the rules of conduct and the concrete measures. The reports are examined by a committee of experts, and the experts' findings and proposals, along with requested comments by the state in question, are forwarded to the Committee of Ministers. Every two years the Secretary General of the Council makes a detailed report on the application of the Charter to the Parliamentary Assembly of the Council of Europe.

1.4. Adhesion to the Charter

The Charter opened for signature in 1992. After five states had ratified it, it entered into force in 1998. As of this year, 2001, the Charter has been signed by twenty-seven states and ratified by fourteen. These latter are: Austria, Croatia, Denmark, Finland, Germany, Hungary, Liechtenstein, Netherlands, Norway, Slovenia, Spain, Sweden, Switzerland, United Kingdom. Except for Croatia, all these states ratified the Charter without declaring any reservation.

2. Can the Charter achieve its purpose?

I want to examine whether — and if so, in what degree — the action which the Charter prescribes can achieve its declared purpose: namely, to protect, promote and save from extinction languages "different from the official language" that are "traditionally used within a given territory of a State" by nationals who form a minority of the State's population. Although I know a number of languages, I am not a professional linguist. In the academic world, I have taught European history, political science and English writing. In what follows, I draw mainly on experience I have had as an activist in language matters in the Irish-speaking parts of Ireland, and on my knowledge of the fortunes of minority languages in Scotland, Wales, the Isle of Man and Brittany. But my special interest in these Celtic languages has led me to inform myself generally about similar language situations in other parts of Western Europe.

2.1. What the Charter aims to do

The Charter's ostensible aim can be restated simply as follows: *by state action to help the languages it defines, which exist in an intrinsically hostile environment, to remain alive and not to become extinct.* Let us look at two of the terms I have used there.

An intrinsically hostile environment. This arises from the fact that both the central governments of the states, and commerce — the producers for the national market and the sellers in it — see linguistic homogeneity as being in their interest and consequently tend to promote it. In addition, the most powerful mass media, serving both the central governments and commerce, also promote linguistic homogeneity.

An "extinct" or "dead" language. I think there is general agreement that the death of a language means the death of the last native-speaker. A native-speaker is someone who has acquired the language as his first language from people who spoke it as their first language. When the last native-speaker dies, that language becomes extinct, that is to say, a "dead language".

This happened in the 1970s to Manx, the Celtic language of the Isle of Man. The fact that a small number of Manx people have learned the language as adults and speak it to each other does not alter the fact that Manx is extinct. In Cornwall, where Cornish, another Celtic language, died in the eighteenth century, some people have learned Cornish from books and speak it. Similarly, again, in England and other countries some people who have learned Latin speak it to each other in clubs and associations. I have heard even of publications that give reports of football matches in Latin and of a radio station that broadcasts the daily news in Latin. No revivalist activity of this kind alters the fact that the languages in question are extinct or dead languages.

These clarifications, together with the Charter's statement of aim, make the following clear. The Charter does not propose to foster the learning or use of dead languages. Nor does it intend to be of help to minority languages, whatever their condition, which rank as official languages: for example, Irish in the Republic of Ireland, Swedish in Finland, Dutch and German in Belgium, Romansh in Switzerland. It aims to help all the other "minority or regional" languages — for the purpose of this paper "the defined languages" — to live and prosper in an intrinsically hostile environment. It proposes to do this by means of state action.

The defined languages exist in widely differing conditions. They range from "secure" and "terminally ill" to "mortally endangered" languages. Which of these three categories a particular language belongs to is a matter that can best be judged by those familiar with its fortunes.

2.2. Secure languages

Their numbers of native-speakers have been stable or increasing for the last forty or fifty years and seem likely to continue so. Generally speaking, they enjoy this security because they are the vernaculars of *representative units of contemporary European life;* that is, of speaker communities which have a representative range of occupations and facilities such as one finds in contemporary Europe. There are, for example, secondary school-teachers, farmers, printers, lawyers, doctors, police, judges, factory-workers, and journalists in print, radio and television. More fundamentally, the languages in question are secure because their speaker communities have the four attributes required to produce a representative contemporary life in an intrinsically hostile environment:

1. an adequate number of speakers (say, 12,000 or more);

2. adequate social compactness arising from territorial contiguity (say, within each group of 12,000 speakers which the community contains, monthly contacts of varying frequency among most of its members);

3. a collective will to maintain the language community; and

4. the defensive means normally needed to secure such maintenance (adequate legal status, self-governing powers and financial resources).[2]

---

[2] When I stipulate or suggest precise numerical and social prerequisites for "a representative human life in contemporary European circumstances", I do so without dogmatic intention, but as an invitation to discussion about such prerequisites. I take it as a given that, broadly speaking, there can be no realistic thinking

Prominent in this "secure" category are minority languages which adjoin a frontier on the other side of which the same language is dominant. The daily contact with their own language being used as a majority and official language elicits and strengthens in the minority community the "collective will to maintain".

Obviously, some elements of the state action that the Charter enjoins can "help" the "secure languages" flourish even more; but such help is not needed and would have no decisive effect.

2.3. Terminally ill languages

It stands to reason that a shrinking language — one which has been shrinking for the past forty or fifty years — can be saved from death only by its native-speakers; specifically, by their acquiring and using the necessary defensive means — legal, governmental and financial. But they can and will engage in this saving action only if they are determined to stop their language shrinking and therefore to do what this requires.[3] When this collective will to stop the shrinkage is absent, the language is doomed, is terminally ill. Its native-speakers accept that it will ultimately be replaced by the dominant or majority language; and they may even, for practical reasons, want this to happen.

Generally speaking, the will to stop the language shrinking is absent in three kinds of diminishing language groups. The group is critically small — contains significantly less than 12,000 speakers. The group is critically fragmented — divided into separated sub-groups, none of which has the necessary numerical minimum,

---

about the survival of a defined "regional or minority language" without a clear notion of what said "representative life" means in practice. However, I say "broadly speaking", because it is also a fact that a minority language can survive indefinitely in a socially unrepresentative life if it is valued by a small ethnic or religious group as a bond and defence of its cohesion and fundamental "difference".

[3] See D. Fennell, "Can a Shrinking Linguistic Minority Be Saved" in Eds. E. Haugen, J.D. McClure, D.S. Thomson, *Minority Languages Today*, Edinburgh, University Press, 1981.

and no combination of which has adequate social compactness. Or finally, the group still has (or had until recently) adequate numbers and social compactness to form a "representative life"; but after unsuccessful efforts to obtain from the state the necessary means to stop its shrinking, it has despaired of acquiring them — has lost the will to try.[4]

Such terminally ill languages cannot be made to survive by state action or by external action of any kind — except on the rare chance that a "prophetic" intervention revives the decayed collective will.[5] So the Charter is of no avail to them; in its professed aim to save such languages by state action, it is attempting the impossible.

2.4. Why is the Charter attempting the impossible?

The Charter is involved in this absurdity because it fails to discriminate between languages which state action might be able to help keep alive and those where such "help" is meaningless. Moreover, there is no sign that those who drew up the Charter even investigated the matter. I mentioned above that one of the rules of conduct which the Charter proposes is "to take into consideration the needs and wishes expressed by the groups which use [the defined] languages". But there is no sign that those who drew up the Charter investigated the most fundamental and decisive "wish" of the shrinking linguistic groups; namely, whether or not they seriously wish to stop their language shrinking. The answer could

---

[4] This, despite its being an official language, has been the case with Irish. In the years 1969–1973 a campaign by native-speaking activists in the shrinking Irish-speaking districts called for regional self-government and failed to obtain it. Since then, there has been an accelerated abandonment of the language in these districts and no remaining collective will to stop it.

[5] The terminal illness can be halted through the agency of a prophetic individual or group who, emerging from the language community or arriving from elsewhere and identifying with it, awakens its will to save the language. But such an occurrence lies outside the scope of the Charter and of any rational calculation.

have been reliably obtained through a combination of observation, listening and direct questioning.

2.5. Mortally endangered languages

When the Charter refers to some of the defined languages as being "in danger of eventual extinction", logically it is indicating languages which are in danger of falling into terminal illness, with its virtual certainty of eventual "extinction". These languages fall into two quite different groups, one small, the other large. I begin with the small group, which requires some detailed treatment.

These are shrinking languages which, besides having the numbers and the social compactness necessary for a representative contemporary life, also have a body of native-speakers who are trying to acquire from the state the necessary means to stop the shrinkage. If these activists succeed in acquiring these necessary means, their language has good chances of being saved. But if their effort fails, the language is likely — through their loss of the will to save it — to fall into terminal illness. Hence its condition of "mortal danger".

Obviously, in such cases, state action can help. The state can grant the language community the necessary legal status, governmental power and financial resources. The nature of the governmental powers will vary according to circumstances. What they must include is an authority empowered to co-ordinate the promotion of the language and to make discriminatory laws that will defend it and promote its use in the hostile environment.

These laws, which will not permit the injury of persons nor infringement of property rights, will — to cite a few examples —

- give the defined language first official status in the territory and first place in primary and secondary education;

- ensure that the defined language is the medium of communication between employers and employees in enterprises of a certain size;

- ensure that the same language will be the normal medium for communication with the public in places of public resort such as bars, restaurants, shops, sports centres, churches and cinemas;

- and finally, require of outsiders who take up employment as professionals or managers in the territory that they qualify in the defined language within, say, six months.

Insofar as the finance necessary for the language community's self-saving exceeds its resources, it will be provided to the community's governing body by the state.

Here, perhaps, two matters require a word of clarification. I am not suggesting that devolution of adequately subsidised governmental power to the language community will make the language secure. Such action merely represents necessary *help* to the community in question in its endeavour to stop the shrinking of its language and to make it secure. Whether it will be used with success depends on the chosen leaders of the language group, and its members generally, acting effectively.

Again, what I am discussing here must not be confused with the granting of independence or devolved governmental power to a nation that possesses a distinctive language spoken by a minority: say, the Irish, Scots, Welsh, Basques or Catalans. There is no necessary link between such political empowerment and the welfare of the minority language in question.

2.6. The Charter cannot help these endangered languages

The mortally endangered languages, just described, are the only defined languages where state action could help decisively. But the Charter fails to prescribe the *kind of state action* that is needed. It prescribes many kinds of state action, but not the kind — devolution of adequately subsidised governmental powers — that would enable such languages to become secure. Instead of the pages which the Charter devotes to detailed lists of benevolent concrete measures which central governments or existing local authorities might take, it could have stated simply:

> If the speakers of a shrinking defined language show evidence of active will to stop their language shrinking, the state will devolve to them appropriate governmental powers. These will include the power to legislate in defence of, and for the promotion of the defined language, provided that such legislation allows no injury to persons or infringement of property rights. The state will also adequately subsidise those initiatives of the language group's ruling body which that body and central government agree are necessary for the creation of a "representative unit of contemporary European life" in the language in question.

If the Charter had included such a provision, it would have contained the possibility of bringing necessary help to the mortally endangered languages in question. As it stands, it cannot supply such help.

It can be objected that if the Charter had stipulated the effective state action I have outlined, then no state would have adhered to it. The central governments and the commercial interests which produce the hostile environments for the defined languages would have united to oppose any such action. They would see such concession of governmental and, especially, legislative power to a language group as inimical to interests and rights which they regard as sacred, or at least imperative.

This is true, and it may be the main reason why the Charter does not stipulate such state action in any circumstances. But I am not sure that this is the case. There is possibly a deeper reason, namely, the paternalist convictions of those who drew up the Charter and of their political sponsors.

We have already noted that the Charter does not propose that states make an effort to discover what are the will and intentions of the speakers of the defined languages with respect to their languages. If we add to this the fact that all the rules of conduct and concrete measures that the Charter proposes are to be taken by central governments and other existing authorities *on behalf of* the language groups, and never by the groups themselves, the impression of an overriding paternalist mentality is strengthened. It is possible, in short, that those responsible for the Charter believed they knew better than the speakers of the defined languages what these languages needed in order to survive and flourish in a hostile environment; and also believed that agents other than elected members of the language groups were the best agents to take the measures required. If so, then there lies at the root of the Charter a serious ignorance of the dynamics of minority languages in an environment hostile to their existence.

2.7. The other endangered languages

I said above that there is a second group of endangered languages, larger than the one I have just discussed. These are shrinking languages which combinations of native-speakers and well-wishers, with the latter often predominating, are trying to save by applying the paternalist kinds of state action that the Charter proposes, or by calling for their application. To describe these languages, collectively, as "mortally endangered" is to speak approximately, for some of them are already terminally ill. What is certain is that, insofar as they are not already in that condition, they are in extreme danger of finishing thus, given the intrinsic inefficacy of the state action being used to "save" them.

3. What is the Charter's real purpose?

In this paper I have taken the Charter at its face value, as an effort to contribute decisively to the survival and vitality of regional and minority languages of the kind defined. Because I am no longer active in this field nor conversant with the current writing on the matter, I am not aware whether this is the general view now taken of the Charter in such circles. Perhaps it is not generally regarded as a serious effort to accomplish its ostensible purpose. For myself, after examining the Charter and finding it virtually useless for its ostensible purpose, I incline to the view that its real purpose may be something quite different.

3.1. *To show respect and concern?*

The Charter may have been drafted and offered for acceptance in order to show respect and concern for regional and minority languages. In itself, given that these languages have been created by human minds and lives, that is a good thing to do. It is also, given the current ethical emphasis on minorities and on respect for cultural diversity (provided the culture is not Islamic!) a fashionable thing to do. On this reading, the Charter is primarily an exercise in fashionable virtue — and, I would emphasise, nonetheless virtuous for that. Among other things, this would explain the Charter's avoidance of any content that might prove seriously unacceptable to European states or to business, whether national or international. On this reading, its purpose was an exercise in fashionable virtue in which not only the proposers of the Charter, but all power holders without damage to their cherished interests, could share.

3.2. *To make language deaths less painful?*

Again, it is possible that, combined with that purpose, there was a subordinate one. The Charter does in fact offer honour and respect to the speakers of its defined languages. And it is in fact inducing governments of states, if they have not already done so, to translate that honour and respect into concrete measures. These measures, in many spheres ranging from schools, courts and administrative practices to radio and television, render the languages more present in the public life of their territories than they have been for generations. All this doubtless gives comfort and pleasure to the speakers of regional and minority languages, even when they assume, as probably most of them do, that their languages will eventually die.

I am reminded of a visit I once made to a government minister in Dublin[6] to complain about the inadequacy of the government's measures for "saving the West". The West of Ireland has long been a problem area economically and has been losing population — in that sense also "shrinking" — due to emigration from it. The government, and in particular this minister, had taken many measures "to save the West", as the phrase had it.

I told the minister that these measures, including his own, were all very well, but that they would not stop the West from dying. "That may well be true," said the minister, "but these measures will make the death less painful. And that is something positive, isn't it? I'm sure you would agree." I think that with regard to most of the languages which the Charter is concerned with, that same positive purpose may have been, at least subconsciously, in the minds of those who framed it. But whether it was or not, the Charter is certainly making the deaths of most of the defined languages less painful than they would be otherwise.

---

[6] Mr Charles Haughey.

September Eleventh

Magill *magazine, October 2001*

The alternative to a Jihad against Islam

During the television reporting after the terrorist attack on the Twin Towers, an incident related by a New York doctor made me think. He told of encountering near the burning building an almost naked woman whose skin was hanging from her body. It brought back to me an unforgettable image from an account I once read of the aftermath of the atomic bombing of Hiroshima: a group of naked Japanese women crossing a bridge with their skin hanging down in strips.

That image had remained with me because it was the first instance of "skinning alive", as a method of warfare, that I had come across since I read of the ancient Assyrians — who were notorious both for massacring populations and for skinning prisoners alive. At the time, I thought it was a peculiar effect of an atomic blast, but the doctor's account from New York made me realise that other explosions can cause it.

At all events, that accidental recall of Hiroshima set me thinking about the fatal gaps of mutual understanding that exist in the world today; gaps similar to those that occurred, through many centuries, between the English way of seeing themselves and the Irish perception of the English.

In the first place, there is the gap between how westerners are taught to see themselves, and how most of the world sees the West. President Bush talks of a terrorist attack on "democracy and liberty", and Colin Powell adds "civilisation". But many non-westerners, who have observed or experienced western "democracy and civilisation" in action in non-western countries, see them not as decent and civil things, but as imperialistic, cruel and arrogant — and therefore hateful to right-thinking people.

As a result — sad to relate — many non-white people from China to Morocco, quite regardless of the statements of their governments, felt satisfaction or pleasure when New York and Washington were hit.

As for western "liberty", it appears to much of the world as America's self-given liberty to wield its power as it pleases — ignoring both its own inherited rules of conduct and those which have been agreed among the nations. How else to understand the unrepented American massacres from Hiroshima to Panama City; American bombers sent to kill Gaddafi and actually killing his daughter; American and British airmen who, with no United Nations mandate, patrol and bomb Iraq and kill Iraqis, and in the name of western humanitarianism destroy Serbia from three miles up?

In particular, reasonable Muslims must perceive American "liberty" as lawlessness when the US supports its proxy Israel, in its decades-long ignoring of Security Council resolutions, and equips it to continue killing Palestinian civilians as if they were badgers infesting a farm. And the judgement of those reasonable Muslims that the West lives by blatant lawlessness is compounded when the US, and its proxy Israel, do as they please with impunity.

In this light, a "terrorist", Islamic or otherwise, is not a "specially evil and ruthless killer". He is distinguished from other killers merely as Brendan Behan distinguished him: "the fellow with the small bomb", emphasis on *small*. Or at least, he was so distinguished until some malevolent genius thought of transforming passenger airliners into the equivalent of cruise missiles.

Then again, when this happened — when some Arabs decided that American impunity must end, and ended it dramatically — another fateful gap of understanding was evident. "Why are they doing this to us? Why do they hate us so? Why are they murdering innocent Americans?" ordinary Americans wondered. No one has explained to them why. Their leaders have kept them unaware of the culpability in which, precisely through their own democracy, all Americans participate.

So they see evil in "them" only; not also in "us". They see it only in those young Arabs who murdered thousands of Americans. And the Arab *shahids*, for their part, believe they are executing virtuous punishment on Satanic America for what the US and Israel have done to them and to people dear to them.

Ordinary Americans, instructed by their president that this is a war of "Good against Evil" — of American "Good" against Terrorist, but in fact Islamic "Evil" — hope that America will strike back hard. Bush promises he will do so, will rid the world of the Devil. So on the world scene as in the microcosm of Palestine — where the Jewish offspring of an Austrian's dream fill the role of "westerners" — the tit-for-tat of mutual slaughter and destruction looks set to go on.

It need not, of course, go on, and it would be very much to the benefit of the Israelis and the Americans that it should not. These two peoples have become linked to each other fatefully. In a future beginning now, this link will acquire a fateful dimension. The fundamental welfare of each will depend on the rulers of both pursuing quite different policies than they have pursued hitherto.

The fundamental welfare of a nation consists in its having a secure life. The policies of successive Israeli governments, but of Sharon's in particular, have led to Israelis living in fear of eating in a restaurant, leaving children to school, or even walking along a street. In other words, their Zionist leadership has, through its policies towards the Palestinians, failed to provide what Zionism promised: "a secure haven for Jews".

Henry Siegman, an American, writing recently in the *International Herald Tribune*, put it plainly: "By now it should be clear to everyone in Israel that trumping every Palestinian act of violence and terror with Israel's superior ability to punish Palestinians does not provide the security that Israel's citizens are demanding.

And providing such security to its citizens, Siegman emphasises, is the fundamental condition for a government's legitimacy.

The title of the article stated what needs to be done: ISRAEL SECURITY MEANS LEAVING THE TERRITORIES AND SETTLEMENTS. In other words: providing "a safe haven for Jews" means doing what the long-ignored Security Council resolution, and international law generally, demand. Siegman concludes as follows:

> The ending of the occupation would enable Israel to assist the new Palestinian state to develop a viable economy and a stable society. There is no more important condition for the security of Israel than a viable and successful Palestinian neighbour.

Turning to the US, there is general agreement that the assaults on New York and the Pentagon were a response to American behaviour towards Israel, the Palestinians and a number of Muslim countries: Iran, Libya, Syria, Sudan and Iraq. Unlike the failed Israeli pursuit of security, this American behaviour was not aimed at making Americans secure (what in fact its muddled aims were is a matter for separate enquiry). But its end result has, in American terms, been exactly the same: namely, to introduce pervasive insecurity into American life.

Henceforth, nervousness will accompany office-work in the upper half of skyscrapers, especially when a plane is heard flying nearby. In airports, any Semitic face, many a brown face, and any sudden or ambiguous gesture by their owners, will excite apprehension. There are seven million Muslims in the US, moving in every sphere of life from colleges and corporations to spectator stands at baseball games. To passengers on commercial flights, any scuffle, anything remotely suggesting a hijack, will simultaneously suggest collective death. On the ground, fighter-pilots will stand ready to act swiftly and ruthlessly. And now that all Americans realise that Fortress America is indeed vulnerable, fears and rumours of bacteriological and chemical attack will regularly occur. Americans have been told often enough that Saddam Hussein and Osama bin Laden have a special penchant for such weapons, and vast stocks.

How will America's rulers try to combat this new, pervasive insecurity and restore both a sense of security and actual security to American life? Many articles have already appeared predicting the minutely controlled police state that will now develop in the Land of the Free — giving new shape to the "liberty" that Bush says is under assault. That is certainly foreseeable for the home front.

Abroad, the predictable and even promised course will be an all-out attempt to "destroy terrorism wherever it can be found". Translated, this means an intensification, with respect to selected Muslim countries, of the kind of action that led to the *shahid* massacres of 11 September and the resulting American insecurity. To bombing, missiling and sanctions will be added the new lawlessness invented recently by Israel: assassination of political leaders and terrorist suspects in their cars, offices and homes.

But just as Sharon's cruel battering of the Palestinians failed to bring security to Israelis, these courses of action, domestic and worldwide, would fail to restore security to Americans. People who have been taught to seek the avoidance and postponement of death, in any form and at all costs, cannot win against men who actively aspire to a death that gives glory to God and entrance to Paradise. Greater slaughters than the one the Americans have just experienced would occur — making their insecurity even greater.

Given that the Palestinian question has been the root cause of Islamic antagonism to America, the first realistic move towards restoring American security lies in Israel's following the course recommended by Siegman: complete withdrawal followed by support for "a viable and successful Palestinian neighbour". So the first realistic American move towards restoring American security would be to ensure that Israel does this.

The second would be for the US to withdraw from its irrational and hostile interventions in the affairs of Muslim nations, leaving them to pursue their destinies as they choose to do, and offering inducements for their benevolence.

On the face of it, it does not seem likely that the US will follow this wise and truly self-serving course. Americans, especially of the WASP variety, have shown only too clearly that they need an incarnate Satan to oppose (Khomeini, Gaddafi, Saddam, Milosevic) as much as does bin Laden.

However, even if, as seems likely, the US drags Europe further along the arrogant, self-righteous course that it has pursued hitherto, it is useful to know that another wise course was possible, and that it remains so. For one thing, this knowledge preserves marginal people, such as we Irish are, from any misplaced enthusiasm.

Western Democracy is not
"The Best Possible Society"

The Irish Times, *4 January 2002*

Gone are the days when humane Europeans explored other civilisations — Ottoman Turkey, Arabia, Persia, Japan, China — and described their strange, non-western ways with respect and occasionally wonder. Even when there was an assumption that European civilisation was the best, Europe took for granted and respected the cultural pluralism of mankind.

Now Europe has succumbed to the new intolerance issuing from the USA that proposes the package called "western democracy" as the only right way for people to live. In the public voice of the West, respect for diversity has been replaced by a constant patronising and carping criticism of societies that diverge from that western "norm" in their political system, laws or customs. In particular, this denigration of diversity points its finger at Muslim nations. In Ireland, "live and let live" — if the "different other" is not hostile or oppressive — has long been part of our culture. But here, too, our mass media and political class have fallen into line with the new cultural fundamentalism of the America-led West; and many educated people take their lead from them.

While this is likely to remain the case, it is important, I believe, to point out two things. The notion that "western democracy" is the best possible society and therefore an appropriate model for mankind is a delusion. Insofar, moreover, as our ruling and preaching classes believe it, it will have negative consequences for the quality of Irish life in the years ahead.

"Western democracy" is superficially advertised as a system having parliamentary elections, freedom of expression, recognition of "human rights", equality before the law, etc. But that is not an account of what a "western democracy" is in practice, and therefore not what the non-western world perceives it to be.

Leave aside that, for much of that world, "western democracy" means arrogance towards it, contempt for its civilisations, economic and military imperialism, and big bombers enforcing western interests from three miles up in the sky. Consider the day-to-day actuality of a "western democracy".

The Republic of Ireland is a not untypical example. It is a society so constituted that a number of positive and negative consequences follow. People vote every few years in parliamentary elections. The rights called "human" are enshrined in law and upheld by the police and the courts. Murders of every kind have been increasing, but in particular of children by their parents.

Referendums are held on major issues. Real pluralism among political parties and media organs is a memory. In matters of public policy, the parties function as if they were a single party with a number of factions. On most issues, large and small, the media teach and preach in unison. Out of deference to values considered superior, the civil law largely ignores God's law.

Men and women have equal legal rights. Because of threatening violence, the spaces in which women and children can safely move have been decreasing. Supermarkets are crowded at weekends with people who have money to buy the goods on offer. More and more girls who have engaged in reckless sex are getting abortions.

Access of the poor to good health care is improving. Many teenagers blow their minds with drugs and practise binge-drinking. Young men killing themselves has become a countrywide epidemic. Public tribunals investigate and expose political corruption.

That, more or less, is what a western democracy amounts to in practice. It is the "package" of features, positive and negative, that follows from how our society is at present constituted. More precisely, since many of the features are of recent origin, it is the package that follows from how our society has come to be taught and organised during the past twenty or thirty years.

Obviously, while it has much to be said for it, it is not the "best possible" kind of society nor one that could seriously be offered as a model, say, to Iran, Saudi Arabia, Iraq, Libya, China or Japan. Leave aside that it is obviously a society in which many young people suffer from desperation and find life senseless; it has too much violence and deliberate killing — of self, of others, and even of the unborn — to be considered exemplary.

Singly, of course, these ills are lamented, and heads scratched for what to do about them, singly. But that the ills, along with the good things, flow from how the society as a whole is constituted — that insight is barred by the ruling delusion. It would mean, if admitted, that the problem lies in the general set-up; *ergo,* the society could be taught and organised better than it is, so that at least the desperation, violence and killing might be progressively reduced.

But that thought cannot be admitted by the ruling belief that, because the Republic of Ireland is a "western democracy", it is a society that cannot be better constituted! That smug delusion blocks any attempt to discover what is faulty in its make-up.

Regarding Mark Patrick Hederman

There were two preludes to our public exchange of March–April 2002

Anguillara
20 December 2001

To Mark Patrick Hederman,
Glenstal Abbey

Dear Mark Patrick,

Not having met you, I'm not sure by which appellation you are normally called when at home! When I phoned you some time ago to check on the final year of *The Crane Bag*, you mentioned three books recently published or in the pipeline. So when I was in Dublin a few weeks ago, I asked Toner Quinn of Veritas about them and he gave me *Kissing in the Dark*. Here are a few reactions to it just before leaving for five Christmas days in Vienna.

I connected straightaway when I read on the first page that when you were nineteen you "planned to understand the world I was born into", that you have since pursued that effort and are now offering some of the fruits of it. This is more or less the theme, *mutatis mutandis*, of the autobiographical book *The Turning Point: My Sweden Year and After* which I have just published. My own central endeavour has run parallel to yours.

I admire how, as you unfold your worldview, you integrate into it the essential truths of Christianity, if not their accidental European clothing. You argue that, from the point of view of human wellbeing, European culture/civilisation has been a mistake — the root of which you find in its reliance on ancient Greek notions.

My impression, however, is that, if we take the specifically European civilisation as having been born in Western Europe around the year 1000, what you are criticising is mainly the inheritance from the (not Greek-inspired but certainly Light-inspired) Age of Reason; and in particular its later "Victorian" formulation that was finally overthrown only in the decades 1940–70.

As you develop your critique of a worldview centred on an angelic, light-filled view of man, and recommend attendance to the dark side, it strikes me that in recent decades, in literature and the arts generally and in the various forms of mass media, we westerners, Irish included, have been having our noses rubbed in the dark side.

When you argue that European culture/civilisation has been a mistake, I, for my part, see your thesis located in three contexts. First, the rejection of historical Europe as "bad for man" by the eighteenth-century intellectual elite; the emergence of the dream of replacing it by a civilisation friendly to man — what I call the "dream of non-Europe"; and the political expression of this dream in the American and French revolutions. Second, the many-faceted assault on the values, rules and practices of European/ western civilisation — led by Americans and contributed to by French philosophers — which has occurred since the 1960s. Third, the successful overthrow of western civilisation by the West's rulers in alliance with ideologues endorsed by them, which has occurred since the mid-1940s. (The seminal act was the approval by the West's rulers, in 1945 and subsequently, of indiscriminate massacre of great numbers of people as an optional method of warfare. This founded the current, "postwestern" ethics.)

In other words, I see your arguing of a "case against European civilisation", on the specific grounds you state, in the context of a long and ultimately triumphant arguing of that same case, on diverse and often anti-Christian grounds, by many western intel-lectuals and rulers. Of course, the particular "postwestern" form that the West has now actually taken is not the postwestern form that you would have desired or are arguing for in your book. But it is the form that the mainstream "case against European civilisa-tion" did dream of and work for.

(Let me interject that the mainstream argument since the eighteenth century for a civilisation "more friendly to man than the European" has been, in its subtext and understandably, an argument for a civilisation more friendly to western man in particular. And consequently, when this argument criticised the traditional values, rules and practices of western civilisation on the grounds — among others — that these obstructed human beings in achieving rightful mastery of themselves and the world — and should therefore be replaced by values, rules and practices that allowed this dual mastery to be realised — it had western human beings, collectively and individually, primarily in mind. So it was inevitable that, when the argument was transformed, in our own time, into fully realised fact, it should result in a collection of new values and rules that both allow westerners to be superpowerful, collectively and individually, and justify them in so being.)

Finally, I am much in sympathy with you, emotionally, when you exhort your readers to work for a culture different from the inherited one, which would be friendlier to man in the manner you indicate. You rightly say that it is people who make culture and, from that, argue that "collective will" could remake our present defective culture. But which collective will — that of the rulers (those who exercise shaping power in our world) or of the ruled? You seem to have the collective will of "the ruled" in mind.

Until the early 1980s I believed that, by forming, even locally, a common mind and combining their action, the ruled could do that. But I no longer believe it. I think that, in the times of the Soviet Union, neither you nor I would have considered it realistic to suggest that "the ruled", in that system, might successfully "change the culture". After all, the Soviet "culture", such as it was, had been shaped to suit, in the first instance, the power and interests of the rulers, and they had the capacity to keep it shaped that way. I believe that the same is true of our present western "culture" from Los Angeles to Stockholm and Palermo. Only a change of mind on the part of the rulers, or a change of rulers, could make things substantially different than they now are.

There are other matters in your thoughtful book that I could respond to. Incidentally, I admire your ability to use illustrations based on precise knowledge of the material and bodily worlds — I never did "science" of any kind! But that will do. And I hope that when this reaches you, you will be having a happy Christmas season.

Yours sincerely
DESMOND FENNELL
Anguillara

Hederman, in a brief reply, thanks me for my comments and reminds me that we had indeed met, years previously. I hasten to apologise for my lapse of memory. In early February 2002, I procure a copy of Hederman's book The Haunted Inkwell, *and am astounded by its wild misrepresentations of my Seamus Heaney monograph. With copies of the relevant pages enclosed and marked, I write to him, pointing out his misrepresentations and regretting that he had failed to quote me honestly and then argue against. Receiving no reply, I decide to make my protest public. The following Letters to the Editor appear in* The Irish Times.

Hederman, Heaney and Fennell

The Irish Times, *18 March 2002 (I had headed my letter "No Argument")*

Sir, — *The Haunted Inkwell*, a book on literature and criticism by Mark Patrick Hederman, was published a few months ago in Dublin and has just reached me here. I note that Fr Hederman, a monk in Glenstal, disapproves strongly of my account and estimate of the poet Seamus Heaney in my pamphlet *Whatever You Say, Say Nothing: Why Seamus Heaney is No. 1* (1991).

What a pity, then, he doesn't argue with me! I mean, quote or fairly paraphrase things I wrote which he disagrees with, and then show, with arguments, that they are untrue or unjust. Instead, alas, he does the typical Irish Catholic thing when disagreeing with the views of a fellow Irish Catholic (practising or post). He denigrates me.

He represents me as a self-righteous, ignorant and malicious person who (1) uses abusive and offensive language about Heaney, Americans, Harvard and Oxford professors; (2) tells Heaney how he "should" write poetry; and (3) hectors Heaney about his religious belief and moral life.

I owe it to Heaney and myself to state that this is nonsense, unsupported by any words I have written. Actually, in Hederman's various quotes of me, the difference is obvious between my humane and measured language and the invented rantings he imputes to me.

Much of the misrepresentation occurs because Hederman quotes from my section headed "What Good Is Poetry to People?" without giving its context — mainly Heaney's discussion of the social usefulness of poetry and the poet in his Inaugural Lecture at Oxford on "The Redress of Poetry". So that when I am discussing what Heaney says, theorisingly, about "the poet, his art and the world", Hederman represents me as discussing Heaney and his art!

What sort of writing is this? Does it pass in Ireland for literary criticism?

To make matters worse, Hederman makes it impossible for the reader to look up his quotations of me and read them in context. In his Notes he refers the reader to my Heaney essay as published in the English poetry magazine *Stand*. But in his subsequent page references to quotes, the page numbers are not taken from *Stand*, but [without this being stated] from the pamphlet version of my essay (first edition), which is paged quite differently!

I'm not angry. I've been through this sort of inter-Irish bitchery before. I'm only sad that, once again, reasoned debate did not occur and I am robbed of the pleasure of a good argument. Incredibly, in four pages, Hederman fails to counter with argument anything I say. He merely makes rude noises and caricatures me. — Yours, etc.,

DESMOND FENNELL
Anguillara

Hederman, Heaney and Fennell

The Irish Times, *22 March 2002*

Sir, — Desmond Fennell (March 18th) asks me to quote or "fairly paraphrase" what he wrote about Seamus Heaney in his pamphlet "Whatever You Say, Say Nothing. Why Seamus Heaney Is No. 1". Perhaps you might give me space to do this?

He begins with a quotation from Alan Bold in *Marxism Today,* which sets the tone and the agenda for the rest: "Eliot is, in my opinion, a greater poet because his poems, finally, say more about the human condition than Owen's do."

With poetry encapsulated thus, he turns his attention to Heaney's *oeuvre*. With a keen eye for poetry as commercial enterprise, Heaney sold his poetry in an American marketplace, Fennell says. The Irish were never consulted when the Nobel Prize was being orchestrated for Heaney on the East Coast of America. There was a correspondence between New England prudishness and Heaney's taciturnity: "This world of theory, especially on the East Coast, accommodated his kind of poetry. If it wanted puritanism, the cool chastity, emotional restraint and guilty introspection of his work supplied it." Heaney's job as poet is "clear light thrown on the human condition, or a voice raised memorably to exhort, decry, console or celebrate".

"What good is poetry to people?" Fennell asks. "This, naturally, raises questions which will not go away. What good to people is this goodness of poetry? Has poetry, has the puritan lyric, any intelligible social function, and if so what? How can the poet who 'says nothing', and leaves the world in darkness, do good socially? In a civilisation which prides itself on its social concern and its democratic culture, these are pointed questions. They concern Seamus Heaney not least because he would like to believe that his work does good to people and in particular to those Six-County Irish whom he keeps looking back at over his shoulder and feeling guilty about."

Fennell imposes his view of what poetry is or should be and takes issue with what he believes to be Heaney's view of the poet's role.

"Heaney seems to me to envisage the poet's beneficent social action on the analogy of the monk in an enclosed religious order, who, Catholics believe, helps to atone for the world's evil — to assist Christ in the world's redemption — by his detachment from the world, his chastity, and above all his life of meditation and prayer. Heaney's repeated injunction that the poet must reflect the affairs of the contemporary world in his poetry — but in his own way and without intervening — corresponds to the monk's promise, much prized by the faithful when they receive it, that he will 'remember' or 'include' their worldly concerns and 'intentions' in his prayer.

"Given belief in God, in the efficacy of prayer, and in the sincerity of the monk's dedication, it is easy, and indeed logical, to believe that, through the processes of the spiritual economy, the monk's prayer effects good in the world, atones for evil, stays the punishing hand of God. It is not so easy to believe that, with no part in it for God or a spiritual economy managed by Him, a man of no proven virtue, perhaps even a bad man, effects social redress — corrects the world's imbalances — by meditating and delivering verses which 'contain the coordinates of the surrounding reality'."

Fennell is saying to Heaney: if you think you can get away with an irrelevant poetry of mutism which says nothing at all by persuading your friends in Oxford and Harvard that you are really a monk performing meaningful rites in the sanctuary, then I'm going to blow your cover. "In short, the poet par excellence becomes a sort of ruminating, groaning shaman, delivering oracles which his academic acolytes interpret to the students within the temple and the heedless multitude beyond the gates." This is charlatanism and/or hypocrisy, says Fennell — and don't quote Simone Weil at him as role model because "Simone Weil was a mystic whose mysticism was intellectually disciplined by Christian doctrine". Here we have "a man of no proven virtue, perhaps even a bad man" (is this not "hectoring about religious belief and moral life"?).

If this is not what Desmond Fennell is saying, then let him disabuse me. If it is what he is saying then it can hardly be described as either "measured" or "humane" and it is part of what I am decrying in my book *The Haunted Inkwell* both as an understanding of poetry and as an assessment of Seamus Heaney. — Yours, etc.,

MARK PATRICK HEDERMAN
Glenstal Abbey

Hederman, Heaney and Fennell

The Irish Times, *4 April 2002*

Sir, — My 20,000-word Heaney essay, an exercise in literary criticism, argues that Heaney is a good but not a great poet, and explains how the overblown reputation came about. Dom Hederman's reply (March 22nd) to my protest about his misrepresentation of my essay is a disgrace. First, he offers no apology for misdirecting readers of his book who might want to look up his quotations of me. Second, he rolls out another travesty of my essay, nearly as bad as the first.

Gone from this new version of "what Fennell says about Heaney" are the more hallucinatory of the rantings which his book attributes to me. For example, "Heaney is a cunning trickster, with a keen eye for poetry as a commercial enterprise, who has had the brashness and bad taste to prostitute his small talent in the gaudy American market-place . . . Heaney shouldn't be wasting the Irish taxpayers' money". Or (this is me, allegedly, speaking to Heaney): "If you are trying to hide in there in the monastic sanctuary in the belief — or the pretence — that you are performing some legitimate function, then come out, you whore, or I'll tell them a thing or two about your private life. Do you realise you have to believe in God . . . etc., etc."

There remain in the new version, as things allegedly written by me but in fact not written: "With a keen eye for poetry as a commercial enterprise, Heaney sold his poetry in an American marketplace"; "He is a man of no proven virtue, perhaps even a bad man" . . ., etc."

There remain, too, those quoted passages of mine about "the poet" imagined as a sort of monk, together with Hederman's false statement that they are about Heaney — despite my pointing out in my protest letter that this is clearly, as any reader can see, not the case.

Why this disgraceful persistence in gratuitous untruths? Leave aside that anyone who has my essay *Whatever You Say, Say Nothing: Why Seamus Heaney Is No. 1,* or who can borrow it from a library, can see that they are untruths. (It was published in Dublin in pamphlet form, with a second, augmented edition; in the English magazine *Stand,* Autumn 1991; in my 1993 book *Heresy: The Battle of Ideas in Modern Ireland* pp. 130–177; and in the US, with a postscript, by Milestone Press, Little Rock, AR, 1994.)

The only plausible explanation is that which I gave in my protest letter, namely, that assassination by smear is a customary Irish Catholic way of combating another Irish Catholic who thinks differently, and Hederman conforms.

Even given a second chance, he has failed to quote something that I have actually written about Heaney, poetry, or whatever, and to contest it with reasons given! — Yours, etc.,

DESMOND FENNELL
Anguillara

Hederman, Heaney and Fennell

The Irish Times, *15 April 2002*

Sir, — Desmond Fennell has been living outside of Ireland perhaps too long to know that his original pamphlet on Seamus Heaney is long out of print and unavailable even through our public library system, which tends to cull such ephemerabilia with a ruthlessness that most of it deserves. Hence my reference to perhaps the one place where it might still be available without having to buy the complete Fennell *Heresy*.

However, any misdirection of the unsuspecting public has been fulsomely redressed in his last letter (April 4th), where he gives full advertisement of his wares.

My reference to his work was not to prompt readers to drink from the source but rather to provide an example of how not to read poetry. Fennell begins with his own view of what poetry should be and then proceeds to assess whatever poetry he reads according to these criteria. He then awards marks or remarks such as "good" or "great" as if correcting an examination paper. "What good is poetry to people?" is Fennell's abiding concern.

As T.S. Eliot says: "Those who demand of poetry a daydream, or a metamorphosis of their own feeble desires and lusts, or what they believe to be 'intensity' of passion will not find much [in this poet]. He is . . . a poet for those who want poetry and not something else, some stay for their own vanity."

In my book *The Haunted Inkwell*, I claim that poetry is original in the sense that it cannot be approached with preconceived ideas about what it is or what it should be. Fennell's attack on Heaney is a useful and amusing example of another, what I might call, if I were being polite, "socio-political" approach.

If any apology is due, I make it to the public who might never have heard of this unwarranted and wrong-headed diatribe if I had not entered this self-promoting and desultory correspondence. — Yours, etc.,

MARK PATRICK HEDERMAN
Glenstal Abbey

There followed a letter from Norma McDermott, Director, The Library Council, assuring readers that my Heaney pamphlet was available in several public libraries "located throughout the country" and "available to users of every library through the excellent inter-library loan system".

The public correspondence had an unpublished sequel — communicated to me by Dom Hederman, who on 18 April wrote the following letter to The Irish Times.

Sir, — You cannot imagine my relief at hearing from Norma McDermott (letter 17/04/02) that at least one Fennell (presumably *Foeniculum vulgare*) has been sighted, not just in its virtual existence on the internet but in its full-blown pamphlet form complete with green covering. My own attempt to establish its survival in these islands, through the Dublin Corporation Libraries, revealed two cases of virtual existence. However, when I followed the trail to a branch in Terenure, I was informed by a very charming and sympathetic librarian that the actual copy had gone inexplicably AWOL.

Could I plead with Ms McDermott, in her role as Director of The Library Council, to check each evening the precious clump on which her guarantee of availability through inter-library loan was based, since the shelf life of even the most hardy perennials is notoriously at risk, and lest it suffer the same fate as my own late lamented personal copy.

Yours truly
MARK PATRICK HEDERMAN

How RTÉ Television
Fails to Earn Its Licence Fee

Media Report, *No. 25, Summer 2002*

Nearly a year ago I wrote to Cathal Goan, RTÉ Controller of TV Programmes, about "public service, licence fee, etc." Some months later, after reading an interview with Fr Dermot McCarthy, Head of Religious Programmes, in *Media Report*, I sent him a copy of the letter with an accompanying note. In view of the fact that I have received no reply from either gentleman, I think it is fair to publish the letter below and to offer it for general consideration.

As the letter shows, I believe that insufficient funding, whether from licence fee or otherwise, is not the principal factor preventing RTÉ from providing Irish viewers with proper public-service television. For years past, the most important factors preventing this have been programme content and editorial policy.

RTÉ's programme content has failed to cater adequately to a popular and defining element of Irish culture, namely, its Catholicism. The editorial policy on public affairs has, in important respects, been persistently partisan rather than "neutral", which in practice means pluralist. More precisely, editorial policy, faced with the plurality of convictions on public matters among the TV public, has regularly favoured only one of those convictions, and that usually a minority one.

I also believe that, in the competitive situation in which RTÉ Television operates, removing these public-service defects would make good business sense. Proper public service would increase audience loyalty and, consequently, advertising revenue. This being the case, while RTÉ fails to remedy its public-service defects

— fails to give the Irish people a proper public service —it has no moral right to ask them to increase their payments to it. And moreover, increasing those payments would alter nothing.

Here is my letter, written from "Anguillara, Rome" and dated

8 May 2001

Mr Cathal Goan
Controller of TV Programmes, RTÉ

Dear Cathal

Re: Public service, licence fee, etc.

When I was last in Ireland, a few months ago, you were quoted as speaking about RTÉ's need for a rise in the licence fee so that it could fulfil its public-service role properly. After living for three years in Italy, I thought: "But at least in one important respect, RTÉ has never fulfilled its public-service role, and on its showing does not deserve a rise in its licence fee." Since I have returned here, and seen further evidence on the TV screens, it has occurred to me several times to put this thought to you — with the proviso that, since I live here most of the time, I have been somewhat out of touch with what RTÉ has been up to.

I'm referring to the fact that RTÉ television, as the public-service broadcaster of a country with a deep Catholic culture, hasn't come near to reflecting this adequately in its programming. My standard of comparison is the six main Italian TV channels — the three RAI ones and three private — in a country which has likewise a Catholic culture, but where religion is practised considerably less than in Ireland.

Leave aside entirely the blanket coverage of every main papal event at St Peter's and abroad, and of all the papal speeches — a sort of "must", partly as a service to TV stations worldwide. Far from considering that "enough", the channels deliver regular peak-hour programming of matters of Catholic religious and cultural interest: drama and documentary on the lives of popular saints or on themes from Catholic history; dramatic soaps with priests as heroes (amateur detective, prison chaplain) — one of these, on RAI I, advertised in the metro stations of Rome; a running series called "Miracles" with Christian miracles and mystics from every part of the world; and so on.

I am not talking about "Religious Dept" material in the RTÉ mould, but about mainline programming for the masses. Once, when I was a fascinated viewer of one of the four main films on Padre Pio that have been transmitted since I came here — it was a two-night affair — I noted the viewing figures: the first night, 12 million plus, the second, 14 million plus — reaching 43 per cent of the viewing public.

Has RTÉ, apart from the independently made *Radharc* reports, ever distinguished itself in religious programming?

I'm not talking ideology. I'm talking "public service" broadcasting, and TV business in the competitive, multi-channel Irish situation.[1]

It is not only the case that RTÉ has failed to operate like the public TV service of a culturally Catholic country; its general coverage of public affairs has won the reputation of having an anti-Catholic bias. And it is a fact that many of those responsible for its programming and presenting have been persons alien to or hostile to the people's religious culture. Those factors, together, do not look like public service in the Irish circumstances, or like a

---

[1] Put differently, I was talking *realpolitik*. In this and similar contexts, *realpolitik* is a matter of exploiting the differentiating factors available to an organisation or a state, regardless of the personal views of those who do the exploiting. Generally speaking, we Irish have been behindhand at doing this. Consider, in an age when all things "Celtic" have been in vogue throughout the West, the failure of the Irish state and its tourist agency to exploit this; to cite only one result of this, the principal international Celtic festival is held annually in Brittany. The same applies to our uncreative use of our neutrality, as compared with Switzerland, say, and even with not quite neutral Norway.

good recipe for winning and holding the loyalty of Irish viewers who have a choice of non-Irish channels.

Add the well-known hostility, during the thirty years of the Northern war, not only to Irish nationalism and nationalists, past and present, but also to other themes of an emotionally and sentimentally national kind. Even with a deliberate effort, that would take a while to change. All in all then, by comparative European TV standards, a rather odd relationship to the nation and culture which RTÉ exists to serve!

Perhaps before talking about more money being needed to compete with British stations on their terms, it might be an idea to invest more effort in winning the minds and hearts of Irish viewers? By giving them more of what no British channel gives or can give them?

I write in total ignorance of your own thoughts and plans. But in that ignorance, what I could see happening RTÉ is what happened the Press newspapers. The *Irish Press* died from imitating *The Irish Times*, and the *Sunday Press* from imitating the *Sunday Independent*. In both instances, the editors/managements thought they were acting in the best competitive interests of the papers. But the fact was that the *Times* and the *Independent* could do their respective things much better than the Press papers could. So the Press papers became second-rate, superfluous and unwanted.

I wish you every success in your work.

> Yours sincerely
> DESMOND FENNELL
> Anguillara

Bush and Iraq

The Irish Times, 9 October 2002. Kevin Myers, the Irish Times *columnist, having reprinted this letter in his column, mocked me for comparing Bush to Hitler. It was ridiculous, he wrote, to suggest a similarity between the two men. In that he was right. In background, wealth, intelligence or charisma, they simply don't compare. But of course I hadn't compared the two men, but rather, their manner of justifying aggression — which, as I implied, is as old as history itself.*

The Editor
The Irish Times

Sir,— Before Germany invaded Czechoslovakia and Poland, Hitler made fiery speeches about the dangers posed by those countries to Germans living within their borders. It is interesting to compare President Bush's speeches about the danger posed by Iraq to Americans living in America. Invasions dressed up as "pre-emptive strikes" are nothing new.

The fact is that an aggressive, militaristic power has appeared once again in the West, and the choice, now as then, is between resistance and appeasement. Once again, a British prime minister is leading the appeasement camp. Yet, how often have we been told that "the next time" an aggressor will be "stopped in time"? — Yours, etc.,

DESMOND FENNELL
Anguillara

2003

The Irish Problem with Thought: Thomas Duddy's pioneering new book

Irish Political Review, *February 2003*

The Irish have a problem with thought. It has got worse since the Anglo-Irish faded from the scene and left the unhyphenated Irish in possession. "The unhyphenated, pure Irish" would be more precise. James Connolly and Patrick Pearse were notable Irish public thinkers of the unhyphenated sort, but they had a saving alienness in their background; Scottish in Connolly's case, English in Pearse's. And they profited from an encouraging intellectual upsurge which a few gifted Anglo-Irish — O'Grady, Hyde, Gregory, Yeats and Russell — had set in motion nearly a century ago.

In other words, and to speak plainly, it is the stay-at-home native or Catholic Irish who have the problem. They had it before that intellectual upsurge and they have had it since then; since that eruption of thought and the revolution it engendered gave most of them a large measure of political independence. Their problem is with thought understood in its strict and proper sense: the human mental activity of looking at life and the world, or some aspect of it, and reflecting on it and coming to reasoned conclusions.

Large numbers of individual cavemen practised it; countless generations of freethinkers took example from them. But centuries of mental colonisation taught the native Irish that thinking, being an activity of grown-up humans, was not for them because they were not grown-up. Their mental activity could not, therefore, unaided, arrive at truth — grasp the object of thinking, which is reality. Unaided, their attempts at thought could produce at worst balderdash, at best fantasy. To connect with reality, the native Irish should use the thoughts of grown-up persons, who lived and thought elsewhere, in grown-up nations, or who came from such nations to live among them, as hyphenated Irish.

The forte of the natives — so the colonising doctrine went — lay precisely in their ability to produce the opposites of thought. Apart from song and dance and comic utterance — things obviously Irish — it lay in fictive literature couched in beguiling prose or delightful verse or witty dialogue. The native Irish excelled in conjuring up, imaginatively, what is not. So it was as entertainers of the thinking, burdened-with-reality nations, and as channels and parroters of their thought, that the Paddies and Bridgets should find their role in the world and triumph there.

Given the brokenness of the native culture and the subjection and poverty of the natives, it was inevitable that they should by and large accept this crippling teaching as true and live accordingly. Except for rare individuals who for the most part emigrated, they suppressed their own thought, used that of their masters, and pleased them by entertaining them, fantastically.

What was not inevitable was what happened when the native Irish had acquired a degree of freedom to manage their own affairs, and wealth in excess of the strictly necessary. Remarkably then, by their own free choice, their culture-shaping elite continued to believe the crippling teaching of the colonisers; and they moulded Irish culture accordingly.

They continued to believe — they still do — that thought is something that Irish minds in Ireland cannot engage in successfully. To connect with reality, beyond solid objects, the Irish must still use imported thought; and to figure in the world they must entertain it. The Irish ruling, moneyed and learned classes have continued to believe this. And they have structured the Republic of Ireland accordingly.

Our singers, musicians and dancers roam the globe. Our State funds institutions, our rich men and local authorities endow prizes, and our publishers pursue policies that promote fictive writing of all kinds and discourage writing that engages, rationally and analytically, with reality.

The Arts Council does this by awarding bursaries and free airline tickets to authors only if they write prose fiction, poems or plays, and also by subsidising publishers only if they publish such work. Aosdána does it by excluding creative thinkers from this putative association of the creative elite, and consequently from the salaries it pays to its needy members.

The Irish State and Irish rich men discourage Irish thinkers by failing to fund even one monthly or weekly journal of ideas. Irish administrators and publishers (except occasionally Wolfhound) discourage them by showing no interest in their thought when it is offered to them. Irish academics do so by ignoring such work of Irish thinkers as does manage to circulate, usually by the author's effort and at his own expense — unless he has found a publisher abroad.

All, finally, academics, publishers, journalists, critics, administrators and clergy discourage Irish thinkers by spreading such a blanket of imported cliché and opinion across the nation as to give the impression that Irish thought about the world and man — or about urban transport or bioethics or the European Union or the condition of women — does not exist.

Faced with this crushing social refusal to recognise or value them, most of the Irish thinkers who don't emigrate to more encouraging climes die prematurely from suicide or drink. Very few, of a particularly strong constitution, manage to maintain their sanity in a semi-secrecy from which they emerge occasionally to take more snubs. Thus, before the world, the colonialist lie about Irish mindlessness is to all appearances verified.

While the world that feeds on ideas hears of no significant thought about anything emerging from the Republic of Ireland, the world that loves stories, poetry and songsters, and jokes and folk or rock music, or the patter of dancers' feet, claps hands and exclaims in unison: "Trust the Irish, there's just no one like them to entertain!"

That is why, whether in Ireland or in the wider world, utterance of the words "Irish thought" evokes an uncomprehending "Irish what?" It explains why your average Irishman, Italian or American, on hearing of a recently published book called *A History of Irish Thought*, expects it to be something like the book (it exists!) called *Irish Erotic Art*: forty blank pages between hard covers, good for a laugh.

But *A History of Irish Thought*, published by Routledge of London and New York, is not like that. It has 361 pages, and 320 of them summarise and discuss the thought of notable and original Irish thinkers from the seventh century to the twentieth. We find Augustin Hiberniae, sometime in the 600s, arguing on the basis of his theory of divine creation that miracles are impossible, and Philip Pettit, in the 1990s, showing how republicanism, rightly understood, is distinct from current liberalism and at variance with it. In between, nearly forty others, most of them from the seventeenth to nineteenth centuries and better known than Augustin or Pettit, are brought alive in lucid prose.

Eriugena, Berkeley and Swift are there; so are Toland, Boyle, Burke and William Thompson. The economist Cairns and the scientist Tyndall figure strongly. Somewhat surprising, I think, for most readers will be the Irish Kantians who helped to establish the German philosopher in English, and the cluster of Irish contributors to the debate started by Charles Darwin.

Inevitably, the author of this book, Thomas Duddy, lecturer in Philosophy at the NUI Galway, ran into the "what, Irish thought?" reaction and had to go to London to get his book published. In his Preface he relates how, when he mentioned to people that he was working on the book, he was met with: "But surely there isn't such a thing as Irish thought — at least not in the sense in which there is English, French or German thought?" No, not in that sense exactly,

Duddy answers. The original thought produced by a nation that has a modern history of "disruption, displacement and discontinuity" does not offer the same kind of story as the thought of a successful "imperial nation". It offers a story of a disrupted, discontinuous kind; but a story, nevertheless, of thought.

"Irish" means for Duddy what it must mean for all of us in the Republic today, now that our direct experience of disruption and discontinuity is over, while we remain willy-nilly the inheritors of that legacy. It means every man or woman who was marked by the Irish story, together with the works, for good or ill, of all of them. So Duddy's selected thinkers are Irish by birth and ancestry or by casual immigration or by acquisition of land or position in Ireland through conquest. The great majority of them are Anglo-Irish. And the thinking discussed here was done only partly in Ireland; rather more, even in ancient Gaelic times, outside it.

Certainly, then, as the author says expressly, reclamation is at work here; the same kind of reclamation as occurred, under Seamus Deane's stewardship, in the *Field Day Anthology of Irish Writing*. Duddy's book is a rightful, decolonising counterattack on conquest; a sovereign, reasonably founded re-ordering of an aspect of our past that equips us better to deal with the present and future. In the short term, retrospectively speaking, it is a continuation of the pioneering work of Richard Kearney as editor of *The Irish Mind* (1985). (It is also an advance on that book both in its more comprehensive scope and in its freedom from the mythical suggestion that the Irish thinkers of fourteen centuries have conformed to an "Irish" mental pattern.)

In the longer retrospective term, *A History of Irish Thought* is a substantiation of the patriotic pride in "Irish thought" that was first explicitly expressed in the nineteenth century, by such Anglo-Irish Trinity College men as Rowan Hamilton, William Graham and Thomas Ebenezer Webb.

*

However, and this connects with my introductory remarks, the reclamation at work in Duddy's book is directed not only against the colonisers, but also against the cultural nationalists of the last century and today. These, he writes, "have been pleased to accept Matthew Arnold's notion that the Celts are distinguished by . . . a sensuous nature and a determination to reject 'the despotism of fact'". Consequently, he continues, they "have been inclined to sing the praises of Ireland's imaginative, especially its literary, achievements at the expense of other areas of cultural activity. The Irish contribution to the history of thought has been marginalised . . ." In my introductory remarks I was illustrating how this colonised neglect of past Irish thought has developed into hostility to Irish thought in the present.

Nevertheless, there is a distinction to be made here which Duddy does not make. The cultural nationalism of the revolutionary period, say, from 1890 to 1921, may not have valued Ireland's heritage of thought, but it valued intellect. It showed this by its richness of reasoned public argument and principled debate and by its conviction that the restoration of Ireland involved, pre-eminently, the restoration of an autonomous Irish mind. Evidence of this conviction can be found from Yeats's stated intentions for the Abbey Theatre and Douglas Hyde's for the Gaelic League to Pearse's definition of "independence" and MacDonagh's speech to his court-martial. It was only after some political independence had been won, that intellectual independence — that is, thought — gradually ceased to be a value for the Irish cultural establishment.

Duddy's overall presentation of Irish twentieth-century thought is at first sight shockingly bleak — even for this reader who believes that the Irish "have a problem with thought"! The only thinkers he selects as meriting extended discussion are, apart from Yeats, the following: J.O. Wisdom, M. O'C. Drury, Iris Murdoch, William Desmond and Philip Pettit. Three of them, even their names, were unknown to me. Except Drury, all of them produced either all their work, or its most important part, outside Ireland; and Drury was born and grew up in England.

Apart from these philosophical thinkers — about matters as various as "the ethics of attention" and the unconscious origins of thought — there are brief treatments of George Bernard Shaw and James Connolly. But the latter, in Duddy's judgement, does "not really belong to Irish intellectual history". In sum, even granting that "the Irish in Ireland have a problem with thought", has the situation since 1900, I asked myself, been truly as bad as that?

My initial shocked surprise was followed by a clarifying insight. The author has special criteria for what constitutes "thought". Given these, his presentation of "Irish twentieth-century thought" could not be very different. Thomas Duddy is an academic teacher of Philosophy, whose criteria for "thought" (as he makes clear on p. 288) are those that go with his profession. It must not only be original, or nearly so, and the product of an individual mind; it must also deal with, or at least connect with, "abstract universals" — ideas that relate to mankind in general.

So *The History of Irish Thought* is, by and large, a book that presents individual Irish thinkers of such orthodoxly "philosophical" thought. By decision of its author, it recognises no other kind of Irish thought as "thought", really. However, in countries with a seriously disrupted history, an important current of creative thinking is of such "other kind": not concerned with "abstract universals", philosophical but not in that standard way. In a nation (not only Ireland) smashed by invasion and colonisation so as to be rendered a formless mass, some thoughtful men — usually immigrants or of immigrant extraction — have often been moved to original, imaginative thought about an "abstract particular", the once and future nation.

Desiring for themselves and their adopted or, occasionally, real kin, a new collective home in the world, they think imaginatively. They become obsessed, intellectually, with the idea of a new, not-yet-existing nation to reincarnate the lost one. They become devoted to this abstract and particular idea to the exclusion of "universals". And they join together with others to work at shaping it.

The greatest Irish intellectual enterprise of the last two centuries has been a co-operative one of that kind, continuing through generations. Its participants, having conceived the notion of a new Irish nation, corrected, refined and embellished it. By the early twentieth century, they had fashioned it into an idea that was passionately desired by the great majority of the Irish population as their new spiritual home in the world. (It was expressed in summary form in the 1916 Proclamation and the 1937 Constitution.)

Thomas Duddy's book cannot, by definition, tell the story of such Irish thought. Nor can it, and therefore it does not, present to Irish readers the welter of intensely held and argued ideas out of which, between the 1890s and the 1930s, an independent Irish State was born. Such thought, together with the reigning ideas and marginal ideas of all the Irish centuries since Augustin Hiberniae, is the stuff of another, as yet unwritten book: an Irish intellectual history.

Duddy's pioneering and, for Irish readers, deeply grounding book gives us some excerpted snatches from that history. But that history as a whole eludes it, for the author did not set out to tell it.

PS. Some Clarifying Words about "Thought"

Irish Political Review, *March 2003*

I return briefly to the matter I was writing about last month: "The Irish Problem with Thought". I return to it because the article was announced on the front page of the *Review* as "Intellectual Thought". That tells me that at least one person misunderstood what I was writing about and that it is therefore likely that others did so too. I believe that the theme I was delving into is important for our self-knowledge as Irish people. So insofar as there was any misunderstanding due to lack of clarity on my part, I want to make up for that. Announcing my article as being about "intellectual thought" suggested that I was dealing with some special kind of thought — very strenuous, very abstract — which the Irish have trouble with.

But I wasn't. I was dealing simply with "thought" (which it goes without saying is an intellectual activity) and saying the Irish have trouble with that. And I tried, but insufficiently perhaps, to make clear that thought is a very ordinary thing.

I defined it unmysteriously as "the human mental activity of looking at life and the world, or some aspect of it, and reflecting on it and coming to reasoned conclusions". To show how ordinary that is, I added: "Large numbers of individual cavemen practised it". By that I meant that many cavemen looked at life in general or some aspect of it — hunting techniques, food storage, procreating children, or propitiating evil spirits — reflected on it and came to reasoned conclusions.

Further on, I made another attempt to convey how ordinary an activity is "thought". After describing how, in the Republic of Ireland, creative thinkers and thinking are efficiently suppressed, I said that the effect of this is "to give the impression that Irish thought about the world and man — or about urban transport or bioethics or the European Union or the condition of women — does not exist".

By listing those few topics, I was illustrating how everyday are the possible subjects of thought. I was arguing that in fact some Irish people do reflect on, and come to conclusions about, such "aspects of life", but that their thought is discouraged and by and large suppressed. Instead, our nation shapes its public language and its life by means of imported ideas.

Should I have extended that list of topics to make even clearer how ubiquitous, multiform and accessible are the possible objects of thought? I will let the late Seán Ó Tuama do so. In his lecture in the Thomas Davis series of 1968–69 on "The Gaelic League Idea" (which he also edited) he said:

As a people, we have few ideas of our own; our model in most cases is still the English (or sometimes American) model. In business, science, engineering, architecture, medicine, industry, law, home-making, agriculture, education, politics and administration — from economic planning to PAYE, from town planning to traffic laws — the vast bulk of our thinking is derivative. One doubts if we have added anything of real importance to sociological or theological, philosophic or aesthetic thought.

Ó Tuama was saying, in sum, that virtually no Irish thought about life in general or about aspects of it was evident, or shaping Irish life, or known to the world. Since 1969 that has remained the case, or become more so.

I think it must now be obvious why I have wanted to demolish the notion that, last month, in "The Irish Problem with Thought" I was talking about some special, high-falutin', tautological thing called "intellectual thought". If I let that go by, I would be allowing some at least of my readers — only too willingly, given our anti-thought culture — to shrug off what I was writing about as "stuff for philosophers and intellectuals".

I have felt bound to make crystal-clear that I was talking about an activity engaged in anciently by cavemen and philosophers, and since then by people in various walks of life, and available today, as always, to anyone.

I know that in thus cutting the ground from under the easy shrug-off, I am being a bit cruel. Because of our colonised history and our resulting mindless culture, even the word "thought" — naked, uncompromising, on its own — frightens us a bit, has an alien aura. I am suggesting, now as last month, that how that is the case, and why that is the case, is well worth . . . thinking about.

Reinventing Ireland

Review of Reinventing Ireland: Culture, Society and the Global Economy, *edited by Peadar Kirby, Luke Gibbons and Michael Cronin, Pluto Press.* *Published in* Sunday Independent, *13 April 2003.*

According as circumstances, desires and challenges change, nations, like individuals, reinvent themselves. In a nation it happens like this. A new alliance of politicians and preachers announces a new set of goals for the nation to aim at. The alliance achieves dominance, proclaims a new national image, and persuades a substantial part of the nation to restructure its mind and society accordingly. The sponsors of the new dispensation represent it as "the good life", and the past that it replaces as "a bad life".

Robert Musil in *The Man Without Qualities* described this latter habit jokily: "The present looks proudly down on the past, which, if had come later, would look proudly down on the present." But the notion that present goodness has replaced past badness is taken seriously by each new set of preachers and rulers in turn.

In Ireland, from 1890 to 1966, the new good life was called "Ireland no longer a province but a nation once again". Irish revolutionary nationalism spelled out what that meant. In the 1960s a new project began its rise to dominance and it achieved this fully in the 1990s. This new good life took its self-description, "The Celtic Tiger", from the American investment bankers Morgan Stanley. It was inspired by American neo-liberalism adapted and propagated by Irishmen.

It is with this latest reinvention of Ireland that the present book concerns itself. In the run-up to the Tiger, the liberal preachers and legislators had changed the rules governing personal behaviour in a manner that favoured consumption of all kinds of goods and sex. Then the state embraced globalisation of the economy, with the result that American firms provided many jobs and large exports, and hamstrung Irish foreign policy. "Social partnership" ensured that wage-earners and those who paid them worked in profitable harmony. Day-to-day regulation and surveillance of the citizens increased, as did suicides, abortions, rapes, noise and imprisonments. Lack of sufficient people to do the work available brought many immigrants from poor countries, to the discomfit of many natives. Statements to the effect that Ireland was a nation, not a province, were treated as boorish or dangerously subversive. The Republic of Ireland became a rich country with high rates of growth and skyrocketing house prices.

In *Reinventing Ireland* ten Irish academics describe aspects of the Celtic Tiger, or question whether it is entirely a good life, or show why it is not. Debbie Ging examines the films it has produced; Lionel Pilkington decries the historical blindness of its rampant anti-Catholicism; Barra Ó Séaghdha dissects Fintan O'Toole; Michael Cronin finds advantages for Ireland in how speed of transport and in the transmission of information has compensated for the country's peripheralness in Europe. Luke Gibbons comes up with the interesting word "post-national"[1] — more, that is, than "post-nationalist". Much of the writing is lucid and courteous, some is turgid in the academic mode.

The long Introduction is comprehensive and meticulous, but, as often happens with introductions, best read after the book has been read or dipped into. Chapter 2 by Peadar Kirby is a good place to begin, because it opens up, argumentatively, several of the recurring themes. He contests the claim, put forward by some, that the Celtic Tiger is simply another, but better invention of Ireland, following in line from the nationalist invention of the

---

[1] I develop this notion in the last item, "Engaging Modernity in a Hi-tech Centre" pp. 255–8.

early twentieth century. Taking the claims of the Tiger's propagandists that it excels in pluralism, egalitarianism, international outlook and so on, Kirby contrasts, point by point, how it stood with such matters in the nationalist period.

What he has to say about pluralism seems to me particularly telling. He lists the great array of weekly and monthly journals of ideas, promoting different and partly conflicting agendas, which existed ninety years ago in Ireland. He adds to them the newspapers that opposed the nationalist revolution. And he comments, truly: "Nothing remotely like this exists in any sector of the Irish media today."

However, he could have still made his point by moving further forward into the past century. Many people alive today remember when the *Press* and *Independent* newspapers and the *Irish Times* put forward different ideological viewpoints. Fianna Fáil, Fine Gael and Labour spoke for ideologically diverse sections of the electorate. Contrast that with our Soviet-style referenda of the past twenty years when, on matters of major national importance, all the print media and political parties, and RTÉ substantially, spoke with the same voice — leaving a third to a half of the people virtually unspoken for. Neo-liberal Ireland is intolerant of disagreement with it.

Peadar Kirby's recall of an Ireland that knew pluralism of thought in its print media bears directly on this book. Here we have eight Irishmen and two Irishwomen, all well-informed, arguing at the length which their themes require — not in mere "opinion pieces" — about matters which are of concern to us all. Pursuing different lines of thought, most of them are at variance, mildly or radically, with the orthodoxy of the Celtic Tiger. But our rich republic has no monthly or weekly journal in which they, and others like them, could offer in the newsstands what they are offering here. They can do so only in a book published in London. That seems to indicate that our rich republic is intellectually and culturally poor.

I find two lacks in the book. There is a general failure to see and discuss the Celtic Tiger phenomenon not only as an Irish phenomenon, but also as an extreme instance of what is occurring generally in European nations, especially but not only in small ones. And the question of "happiness" or the lack of it, though a common topic in the Irish mass media, is not addressed. Surely it must rank as a central topic — more central than "equality", which gets abundantly dealt with — in the assessment of a society's well-being.

The West's Campaign for Mastery of the World

Based on a lecture delivered in the Distinguished Lectures series at the American University of Rome, 9 October 2002 and printed in the Irish Political Review, *August 2003*

> "The nineteenth century was intensely preoccupied with the self, to the point of neurosis. During the very decades of the most sustained campaign for mastery of the world ever undertaken, the bourgeois devoted much . . . anxious time to introspection."
>
> *— Peter Gay*

1

In the history of the West, what we have called "progress" and "modernity" is essentially what Peter Gay in *The Naked Heart: The Bourgeois Experience Victoria to Freud* calls "the most sustained campaign for mastery of the world ever undertaken". Today, with the United States of America in the lead, that campaign continues vigorously and with growing success. In a geopolitical sense, the West mastered the world, superficially, when the Soviet Union exited from the scene. The West's technological dominance of the natural world advances with every year that passes. Because "world mastery" is a limitless thing and the will to achieve it remains strong, this progress is likely to continue on all fronts until internal or external forces end it.

Willy-nilly and in one way or another, the ancestors of all westerners were involved in this campaign. Willy-nilly and in one way or another, all of us westerners alive today have been involved in it and have benefited from its success. For these reasons — for the better understanding of our ancestors and ourselves — I want to examine how the campaign originated and developed and brought us, in America and Europe, to where we are today.

To begin with, a definition. The "world" that confronts any people is the totality of circumstances in which they consciously exist. These extend from their needy, mortal bodies, their feelings and the invisible forces they believe in, to the climate, the lands and peoples that impinge on them, and the heavens above. "World mastery", then, is mastery of these circumstances: the ability to exist and act, maximally, in them and by means of them. To use a pregnant word, it is sovereignty over them.

Such sovereignty is an imperative for human beings. All civilisations strive for it, while conceiving it diversely and pursuing it by various combinations of proactive and defensive methods which can be physical or spiritual. Japan, for example, from 1637 to 1854, attempted world mastery in part by excluding foreigners, except for some Chinese traders and an annual visit by a Dutch ship which brought, among other things, European books and inventions.

In European or "western" civilisation, which took shape in Western Europe from around 1000 AD, the proactive pursuit of physical mastery was for centuries moderated by a defensive effort using supernatural, spiritual methods to "overcome the world". Then, around 1450, that moderation began to weaken as Europeans increasingly desired to achieve collective and individual control of the world by physical and proactive means. In subsequent centuries this passion further intensified until it became Europe's main driving force, at home and overseas. The historical period which saw the campaign gather force and rise to primacy is "modernity", and its successful forward movement is what the West's "progress" has meant, essentially.

For Europeans, as for any people, achieving sovereignty over their circumstances meant increasing their collective and individual power by means of liberations from whatever in their circumstances was unnecessarily or illegitimately restrictive. As physical self-empowerment, achieved in this manner, became Europe's paramount enterprise, the progressives who spearheaded it developed a tacit value system that reflected this. "Good" was themselves, their methods of liberation, and the results of these. Whoever and whatever stood in their way were "evil". And persons and forces that furthered their enterprise were good because they were useful. Obviously this was a value system and an ethics that was in potential conflict with the Christian values and ethics that the civilisation subscribed to.

If Europeans had constituted a single political unit, the sovereignty they desired would have been physical control of the world by that political collective, its sub-collectives and its individual members. In fact, however, Europeans became divided into a number of competing nation-states, and this had two consequences. Apart from contributions by individuals which helped the progress of all, movement towards mastery took place through the agency of the most successful nation-states. And attainment of the goal would necessarily involve one of those nation-states controlling all the others.

However, before that stage was reached, there was much for the campaign to do, much collective and individual power to acquire. The non-European world must be brought under European control. The Spaniards, Portuguese and Italians pioneered this; the English, Dutch and French continued the work. The campaign needed profound knowledge of the physical world. It began to get this with Copernicus, Descartes, Newton, Leibniz, Huygens, Gassendi, Boyle, Euler and Lagrange. It needed many minds trained to operate as like as possible to machines, and then wealth-producing machines in great number. It got the former in the Age of Reason led by France, the latter in the Industrial Revolution led by England.

The progressive political revolutions played a central role. They were spearheading efforts in particular nations which achieved great advances in the campaign. This emerges when we consider the features common to the first American revolution, that of 1774–89; the French revolution culminating in Napoleon's conquests; the second Russian (or Bolshevik) revolution, beginning in 1917; the German national-socialist revolution from 1933 to the early 1940s; and the second American revolution from 1933 to the 1960s. All five of these were progressive group initiatives aimed at liberating a national power from internal and external limitations, so that the revolutionaries, using the augmented power, could promote national and individual sovereignty in three ways.

The first of these was to increase useful individual and collective power within the nation in question. The revolutionaries increased the power — legal, political, economic, technological or ethical[1] — of individuals and collectives who were likely, either by their nature or in response to their empowerment, to support the liberated national power and augment it further.

According to the time and circumstance, the categories of individuals whom they empowered were defined by such attributes as income, sex, class, race, anti-clericalism, the possession of property or the lack of it, membership of a particular doctrinal party or — in the twentieth century — simple ability to earn or receive money and spend it. (The second American revolution empowered, in particular, young people, women, blacks, homosexuals and pornographers, legally, materially and ethically. I reserve for later, in Part 3, a special examination of this revolution which impinges directly on all our lives.)

The useful sub-national collectives which the five progressive revolutions empowered included pre-existing ones — a particular religious confession or secret society or seat of learning, or the judiciary, the police or military, the press, banks, business corporations, or a doctrinal political party — as well as new collective agencies created to serve the liberated national power.

---

[1] Ethical empowerment — the ability to perform without inhibiting moral blame an action previously considered immoral.

The second use which the revolutionaries made of that power was to punish the internal and external opponents or hinderers of their liberating measures — such groups and individuals being by definition evil. Simultaneously and subsequently — their third progressive action — they used the augmented national power to extend their liberating rule to other territories and peoples, and their empowerments to useful individuals and groups belonging to other nations.

In the American revolution of 1774–89, the national power that George Washington and his fellow revolutionaries fought to free from restriction was that of a new nation. They augmented it, initially, by mobilising it as a national congress and an armed force. Thus augmented, they used it to punish an oppressive monarch and hostile Indians and to liberate themselves and their fellow whites, collectively and individually. They did this by establishing a relatively liberal-democratic sovereign state made up of moderately sovereign citizens. This state expanded to include white settlers in Native American territory and it invited Europeans to share its freedoms. In the other four cases, the national power that the revolutionaries increased, distributed and projected was that of an existing sovereign state. Before proceeding to use it in the standard manner, they made it more sovereign still.

In all five cases the progressive revolutionaries were conscious that what they were intending and doing was supremely good, and that this rendered them incontestably righteous. Successively, the revolutionary ideologies — American proto-Liberalism, Rousseauist republicanism, Russian[2] and German versions of national socialism, American fundamentalist liberalism — spelt out why in particular, in "this" case, that was so. Moreover, in the

---

[2] The Bolshevik revolution was a western revolution by proxy. It was an attempt by semi-westernised revolutionaries in a non-western nation, using a western ideology and initially western resources, to take part in a historically western campaign, destined to have a western conclusion.

revolutionaries' minds, the righteousness thus conferred on them entitled them to the national power they seized and augmented, and used to liberate and punish. It was the just due of their righteousness. How much national power qualified as that? How much was "just"? As much as equalled *progressive national sovereignty*; that is, national sovereignty which was really that and which enabled an expandable amount of useful individual sovereignty, in the nation and within its reach.

According to a doctrine that had come to the fore in the eighteenth century and that guided the revolutionaries, such national power, however progressive, had limits. Nations and individuals were sovereign *by nature*, and subject therefore to nature's limits. Their power to act was necessarily restricted by physical nature, and legitimately restrained by the moral law inherent in human nature and self-given by sovereign human beings. In the first American revolution, and in the French Revolution, apart from the Jacobin interlude, that law was taken to coincide substantially with the Christian morality of the West. In sum, the amount of national power to which the progressive revolutionaries felt entitled by their righteousness was limited by those natural factors; but only by them.

As the nineteenth century ended and passed into the twentieth, the revolutionaries' perception of those limiting factors shrank. Accordingly, their conception of the amount of power that was their due — that equalled progressive national sovereignty — grew greater. With each enabling advance of science, technology and wealth, each facilitating new perception of physical nature and of the moral law natural to man, and each permissive weakening of inherited ethical self-restraint, the amount increased. As a result, in the Russian and German revolutions, the national power to which the revolutionaries felt entitled by their righteousness approached power unrestricted, like that of Yahweh, the Old Testament's liberating and punishing God. It included the power to lay down for themselves and others, in disregard of Europe's inherited consensus, which behaviour was right, permissible or wrong. In both those revolutions, this ethical empowerment was transmitted to the very powerful sub-national agencies that they created.

The process, outlined above, which greatly increased the amount of power deemed to equal progressive national sovereignty led to a similar magnification of the amount of power deemed to equal individual sovereignty. Accordingly, the Russian and German revolutions conferred their new ethical empowerments on the hundreds of thousands of individuals employed in their sub-national agencies. Moreover, in varying degrees, in part determined by Party membership, they increased the individual purchasing and technological powers of all citizens. To some degree, notably permission to abort the unborn and to have heterosexual intercourse at will, the Russian revolution empowered all citizens ethically.

True to form, both revolutions worked to extend their empowerments widely: the Russian, by establishing or trying to establish its socialist system in many countries; the German by employing Europeans of many nations in its armies and its subnational agencies and by taking steps to establish a European Economic Community and Common Market[3] under German direction, for the greater prosperity of all its members.

Where the western quest for sovereignty was heading was becoming suggestively visible. It would be an ethically untrammelled and omnipotent western Superpower, ruling over and empowered by superpowerful collectives and individuals. Embodying Good, punishing Evil and extending its empowerments worldwide, it would dominate Earth, and even perhaps, encroach on the Universe.

---

[3] These terms were first used by the Nazis, who made some effort to establish the entities in question.

2

In 1895, in his Inaugural Lecture at Cambridge, the English historian Lord Acton said:

> Soon after 1850 several of the most intelligent men in France, struck by the arrested increase of their own population and by the telling statistics from Further Britain [the USA], foretold the coming preponderance of the English race. They did not foretell, what none could then foresee, the still more sudden growth of Prussia, or that the three most important countries of the globe would, by the end of the century, be those that chiefly belonged to the conquests of the Reformation.

They would also, all three of them, be nations of Germanic origin. Historically, then, they were sister nations. They were also partners in the West's campaign for physical mastery of the world. But given that goal, they were simultaneously competitors. It was a race, spurred by Darwinism, which only one of the three could win.

It was also a race which would necessarily strain against western civilisation and ultimately, if persisted in, overthrow it. "World mastery" is a limitless goal. A civilisation, on the other hand, is limited by moral and customary rules which together define "civilised behaviour" for the rulers and people in question. In Europe's case, these limits derived from the foundation of the civilisation on Christian principles modified by aristocratic and middle-class usages, and fused selectively with the ethical heritage of Ancient Rome. They restricted legitimate physical action.

It was, then, inevitable that the tripartite western drive for physical mastery of the world would, in time, strain against the fundamental rules of behaviour of European civilisation. And ultimately, if the rulers of the racing governments judged world mastery to be a value superior to that of the fundamental rules, they would see these as intolerably restrictive and disregard them. More precisely, they would replace them with "post-European" rules of behaviour which allowed greater power to themselves, and to other collectives and individuals insofar as seemed useful for their enterprise.

In the course of the French Revolution, during the period of the Terror and the cult of the goddess Reason, there had been a notable if brief display of what such rules could mean. This was particularly the case with regard to the rules, fundamental to all ethics, about killing people. Clothed in the "virtue" (a fashionable revolutionary term) of the Republic of Reason, the rulers considered themselves justified in killing whomsoever they regarded as hostile or obstructive to the liberated nation and its liberating laws. Thousands of civilians were slaughtered by hangings, shootings and cannonades, by the new, quasi-industrial guillotines and, industrially, by the mass drownings carried out at Nantes. A Paris city official asked the chemist Fourcroy to investigate gassing. But after less than two years, new French revolutionary rulers condemned the Terrorists and rejected the new ethics of killing they had attempted to introduce.

Bolshevik Russia, after 1917, would provide a more comprehensive and long-lasting example of post-European ethics openly propagated and endorsed by rulers. Because the Soviet Union's basic inspiration was western and its techniques of forging and using sovereign power were imitable, its example influenced the West in various ways. It affected particularly Germany and America. But by definition, not being historically European, Russia could not compete — could at most intervene — in the West's campaign for world mastery. The race to decide which western nation would reach the coveted goal by non-western rules and, by remaining there, lead the West into a "postwestern" condition — that race was between the three powers which Acton identified. In the end, as things turned out, it was between Germany and America.

Modern European culture evolved mainly through a succession of national cultural leaderships: first Italian, then French, then

French and British in the eighteenth century, and finally German, from the nineteenth century into the twentieth. Because the campaign for world mastery was Faustian, it was appropriate that, as it reached its culminating phase, Europe should pass the baton, so to speak, to the nation that had created the Faust legend.

A German high creative period began in the last decades of the eighteenth century. By 1800 it was supplying art music, Romanticism and philosophy to the West. Subsequently, the German universities, reorganised as machines for producing knowledge, yielded models of academic method and masses of new learning, in every traditional field and in new ones. From the second half of the century to the first decades of the twentieth, in physics, chemistry, medical science, pharmaceuticals and military science, Germany led the world. Marxism, a German ideology that offered inspiration and method for the seizure of power by the working class, acquired mass adherence throughout Europe. Theodor Herzl pointed the way for Jews everywhere, after two millennia of diaspora, to reconstitute themselves a nation. Freud and Adler were leading the conquest of a part of the world — man's subconscious and unconscious — which had previously eluded the West's campaign. In the 1920s, while German liners won prizes on the North Atlantic, German film directors showed the world what the new art could do, and Berlin's production rivalled Hollywood's in size.

With Germany's loss of her overseas colonies in World War I and the political weakness of the Weimar Republic, many Germans were pained by the contrast between their nation's cultural predominance and her political status *vis-à-vis* her two main competitors. The desire to liberate the nation from the Treaty of Versailles, economic distress and the perceived menace of Bolshevism led Germany to make a bid for world mastery by postwestern rules. That bid took the form of the national-socialist revolution led by Hitler. In the course of its brief span, Germany's rulers rejected and attempted to replace many of the values and ethical rules that characterised European civilisation at home and overseas.

As in the French and Russian instances, the most fundamental aspect of the willed replacement had to do with the killing of human beings. The Nazi rulers sponsored euthanasia for "useless mouths", and mass killing by industrial and quasi-industrial means of persons deemed noxious or hostile. However, because these practices were carried out more or less surreptitiously, the ethical principles invented to justify them were not proposed to the German people as societal rules, let alone accepted by them as such. After the defeat of Germany, the new German rulers and the West, generally, rejected those Nazi ethical principles outright and condemned the related killings as grossly wrong.

In the practice of warfare, the Nazis had engaged in indiscriminate bombing of cities, at first occasionally, then, with the use of flying bombs against London, systematically. Prior to their use of atomic bombs, the victorious Allies had practised this method of warfare to a much greater extent and for deliberate massacre by "area bombing". The rulers of the West did not subsequently condemn such warfare as immoral; we will come later to the postwestern rule they established in this regard.

In the Nazi, but essentially Hitlerian scheme for world domination, Germany was to be made the leading power in Eurasia. Germans, along with selected Aryan peoples, would become in fact as well as theory the "master race". Hitler's principal candidate for Aryan partnership was Britain; but Britain having refused the offer in favour of an American alliance, Germany was left to pursue her ambition virtually alone.

Britain's decision to opt for an American alliance had several important consequences. Because American power was much greater than Britain's, it would be the main western force ranged against Germany's bid for supremacy. Thus the final contest in the West would be essentially between America and Germany. And because America — given Russia's decisive contribution —

would inevitably win, Russian power would replace Germany's in much of Europe. Finally, the West's world hegemony which West European states, collectively, had exercised for two centuries would pass from them. It would pass to what Acton, thinking less insularly, might have called "Further Europe"; more precisely, to the greatest power of Europe Overseas.

3

> "We still have a special weapon, don't we? A weapon that will change everything?"
>
> — *Walther Funk, German Minister for Economics,*
> *to Albert Speer in the last months of World War II*

> "There were whispered arguments between our parents while we watched TV — arguments about changing the rules, we gathered, that applied to all of us, the dads and moms as well as the kids."
>
> — *Naomi Wolf on San Francisco in 1970*

The national-socialist revolution in Germany was contemporary with an American revolution which, in ideological terms, might be described as "liberal" with a small "l". That was how its ideologues, fundamentalist individualists, described themselves. Their aim was, by a combination of greatly augmented state power, advancing technology and ethical preaching through the mass media and the schools, to render individuals utterly equal, free and sovereign. Their programme was therefore a utopian collectivist individualism.

This Second American Revolution, which took place in three stages, extended from the early 1930s to the 1960s. Consequently, the culminating battle for supremacy in the West, that between Germany and America, was a clash between two revolutionary movements, each of them regarding the other as evil incarnate. The clash occurred when the American revolution was completing its first stage. Throughout its course, the state class that directed it was so convinced of its righteousness of purpose and being that it regarded nothing, not even the American republic of the Founding Fathers or western civilisation, as entitled to stand in its way.

The revolution began in 1933 when Franklin D. Roosevelt became president and launched the New Deal programme, which required a great increase of the power of the central government. Its immediate purpose was to liberate millions of citizens from unemployment and poverty; its measures were inspired in part by Mussolini's Italy and Stalin's Russia. When eleven of these were declared unconstitutional by the Supreme Court, Roosevelt, in defiance of the separation of powers, threatened to appoint extra judges who would do as they were told. The liberal press mobilised public opinion. Eventually, by means of legitimate new appointments, the Court was rendered compliant. Between 1937 and 1946 it reversed thirty-two of its earlier interpretations of the Constitution, extending back over a period of 150 years. Thus the decks were cleared for the overthrow of semi-European Old America and the building of its replacement.

In disregard of American precedent, Roosevelt was three times re-elected. (His period in office coincided almost exactly with Hitler's.) Unknown to the American public, which did not want war, he decided to contest the German bid for world supremacy. By provoking Germany's ally, Japan, into war with the USA, he secured the German declaration of war that he needed. In the course of the war, the American "Big State", whose creation he had directed, mobilised the national resources as never before and used them to liberate and punish in Western Europe and the Western Pacific.

In 1942, Roosevelt launched the second act of the revolutionary process. The Manhattan Project was a highly financed collective of scientists and engineers devoted to putting the indiscriminate explosive power of the atom at the disposal of the United States. When, three years later, that power was acquired, Roosevelt's successor, Harry Truman, used it twice as a "weapon of righteousness"[4] to punish Japan.

Truman repeatedly justified these massacres. The American people, with few dissenters, and Europe acquiesced. The verbal endorsement passed into action: the West armed itself thenceforth with weapons made to kill indiscriminately. Doubly, therefore, the rulers of the West, with popular support, overthrew the ban on massacre that was a central rule of western ethics, whether Christian, gentlemanly, military, or Liberal in the classical sense. That ban, though often breached in practice, had expressed the high value the West placed on the human individual, the West's Christian regard for mercy, and the special consideration for women and children incumbent on western men.

By the late 1940s, on the basis of Truman's justifications, the new rule had been tacitly formulated and generally accepted: "If it is believed that killing any number of civilians in their homes and causing a much greater number to die slowly will shorten a war, save soldiers from death in battle, or prevent Russian control of Western Europe, it is right to kill the civilians, immoral not to do so." In the American Declaration of Independence, there is a contemptuous reference to "the merciless Indian savages, whose known rule of warfare is an undistinguished destruction of all ages, sexes and conditions." The West's contempt for such warfare had been replaced by enduring approval of it if deemed useful.

Truman, by performing and justifying atomic massacre, had established the world's first superpower. He had also, as revolutionary Pope, begun the West's replacement of its fundamental ethical system. About fifteen years later, that would continue spectacularly. By then, Truman's successor, President Eisenhower, was sufficiently equipped with superbombs to reverse the creation of the planet.

---

[4] ". . . merely another weapon in the arsenal of righteousness" — Truman at a Columbia University seminar, 1959.

The culminating revolutionary effort had celestial and terrestrial dimensions. It occurred in response to the launch by the Soviet Union, in 1957, of the first earth satellite and to further subsequent evidence of Soviet superiority in space technology and long-range missiles. The USA intensified its military space programmes and established NASA to pursue civil projects in space. First, earth satellites in growing numbers, then manned capsules were launched. President Kennedy asked Congress for a large vote of funds for the space programme, and committed the nation to landing a man on the moon by 1970. He also requested increased funds for defence, including a tripling of expenditure on nuclear fallout shelters.

To raise the money for these growing expenditures, there was need for an unprecedented growth of the western economy, and specifically of civilian consumption. A boom was already beginning, helped by the foundation of the European Economic Community in 1958. The West Europeans shared the American sense of urgency about the Soviet threat, all the more so because it was brought close to them by the large Communist parties in Italy and France and the repeated Soviet demands relating to Berlin. The idea of demonstrating, strikingly, what liberal capitalism could do for people attracted them.

So on both sides of the Atlantic there were pressing motives for maximising a boom which was in the joint interest of the rulers and the businessmen. All were aware of the potential for this purpose of the liberal ideologues, the preachers of state-sponsored individualism. Rich Sweden was offering a much-publicised example of what giving them their head could do. So the rulers of the West endorsed them from Los Angeles to Bonn and Rome.

The result was the joint venture of rulers, businessmen and preachers of liberation which was later called "consumerism". With the various national states assuming a greatly augmented role in the economy and private life, those collaborating partners facilitated and encouraged two things simultaneously: the increasing acquisition of money by men, women, youths and the poor, and the avid consumption by everyone of all kinds of goods and sex.

In furtherance of such consumption, they discredited the fundamental western rules that stood in the way and pilloried (punished) the authorities — parents, fathers, men, clergy, teachers, local communities — that upheld them. New individual rights, especially to the facilitation, incitement and performance of actions arising from desire, were promulgated and enforced by law. Much as Mao Tse-tung in China mobilised the youthful Red Guards to overthrow the "Four Olds", so now, in the West, and for a similar purpose, the passions of youth were harnessed by flattery, by marketing directed at teenagers, and by reducing the voting age. "Permissiveness" was a common description of the new dispensation: the media preachers (including the commercial advertisers) and the collaborating rulers "permitted" people to do things previously forbidden.[5] But it was only a partially apt description, for the permissions were increasingly accompanied by new, liberal do's and don'ts. These, in combination with the permissions and with surviving old rules, produced ethical chaos.

The combination of measures succeeded: the western economy boomed as never before. In 1969, the USA landed the first man on the moon. Consumerism, having proved its effectiveness and popularity, became a standard feature and description of the American-led postwestern system.

The principal consequences of the Second American Revolution can be summarised as follows. Liberation from the ban on civilian massacre made the emergent New America a military, political and moral superpower which maintained and increased the world supremacy of the West. Liberation from many of the other

---

[5] During this phase — which extended into the early 1970s and had delayed effects beyond that — permission was given to mothers and doctors to kill unborn babies if the mother so chose. This was an instance of a "new right" that "facilitated actions arising from desire".

European ethical restraints helped to generate, throughout the West, economic superpower. This great wealth and productive capacity served two purposes. More immediately, it paid for the growth of the military power and for the related and expanding space technology. At the same time, progressively, with the help of new rights and regulations pouring from the legislatures, and consumer by-products of the new military technology, it empowered westerners individually.

They became richer, physically healthier, more long-lived, bigger spenders, more equipped with legal rights and ethical permissions, able to do more things and at the same time more regulated, than a population of their size had ever been before. The world had not previously seen so many superpowerful and, by a seeming irony, homogenised, easily manipulated, minutely administered and efficiently spied-on individuals. But there is no irony really, only a correction of a common illusion. Successful revolutions restore the previously existing stability by reducing diversity and making the increases in collective and individual power proportionate to each other. More powerful individuals need more collective control. And the greater the individualisation of the society the more necessary this is — and the easier.

In terms of every kind of physical mastery of the world, the West's long campaign had outstripped any similar effort before it. Space vehicles launched on interplanetary journeys probed the hidden recesses of the Universe. Scientists identifying and tabulating the human genes opened vistas for the manufacture of human personalities. The only remaining political obstacle, the Soviet Union, removed itself thirteen years ago. As for the change of rules that made the great breakthrough possible, it has become an established fact. Hundreds of millions of westerners grapple with a chaos of behavioural and judgemental rules which, in many instances, differ fundamentally from those subscribed to by their immediate ancestors.[6]

On the face of it, an American cultural leadership succeeding the German one would have been in the order of things. It would have been a continuation of the succession of national cultural leaderships that had characterised the European world, at home and overseas, for centuries. However, two factors combined to make it, when it did occur, qualitatively different from its predecessors. By the fact that it was propagating a fundamental change of ethical rules, it was not only a cultural leadership but also a civilisational one. And by the fact that it involved a political and military overlordship, complete with military bases throughout Europe and armed interventions there, it has had an imperialistic dimension. The victory of the US in World War II brought into being the second or new American empire with the nations of Western Europe included in it as client states: or what the Romans euphemistically called "friends and allies".

As a result of this subordination to the postwesternising transatlantic power, not only has "Europe" as a civilisation ended: Europe has ceased to be what its history had made it be — *a distinctive cultural and political community of interacting and competing autonomies, which in the continual recreation of itself shaped and reshaped surrounding world*; a classical Ancient Greece on a larger scale. Europe has become a ghost still named "Europe", subsisting as a unified paralysis, its thousand-year-old civilisation replaced by a post-European ethical chaos emanating from its most powerful self-extension overseas.

Postscript on "ethical chaos": In recent years, as the US shows unwillingness to be bound by international treaties or legal juris-

---

[6] The possibility of transforming the ethical chaos into a new civilisation is discussed in my *The Postwestern Condition: Between Chaos and Civilisation*, London, 1999 (out of print but available in libraries).

dictions, and its Middle Eastern proxy, Israel, breaks many international laws and conventions with impunity, this chaos is reaching an extreme degree. In both instances, the "right of a desire to
its enactment", already widely implemented in interpersonal
relations, is being claimed by collective entities with the backing
of overwhelming power.

Engaging Modernity in a Hi-tech Centre

The Irish Times, *28 May 2003*

I have just reviewed a Celtic Tiger book by a bunch of academics and here comes another of them, *Engaging Modernity*, published by Veritas. You know the sort of thing, I let it speak for itself. "*Engaging Modernity* provides a new appraisal of Ireland's engagement with the phenomenon of modernity. The path we have travelled from being a rural-based, religious, traditional, insular country, to a secular, highly prosperous economic hi-tech centre has brought in its wake both problems and advantages".

Two things cry out for saying. The first has to do with the notion — ignorant but it's in vogue — that during the Celtic Tiger decade Ireland finally stopped being "traditional" and became "modern". (The book I reviewed, called *Reinventing Ireland*, went on about "modernisation" as something that happened here in the 1990s.) I have just taken down off the shelf, to check the title, Joe Lee's book *The Modernisation of Ireland 1848–1918* — and Lee writes as a professor of history and a careful user of language.

But I don't need any book to tell me that the Irish engaged with the French Revolution when that was the most modern thing around, and before that with the Protestant Reformation when that was, and centuries earlier encountered and adopted Norman stone castles, body armour and courtly love, and much further back Christianity, the latest thing from Rome, and a very long time ago, when the novelties first arrived from the Continent, iron swords and ploughs and pots and pans, to replace the bronze ones.

What is "modernity" but the latest thing in vogue in the power centres, which subsequently spreads to the provinces and is eagerly adopted by the provincials, led by their fashionable elites?

"Modernisation" has been happening in Ireland since prehistory. Far from its being a case, now or ever, of "modernity versus tradition", the Irish have a long tradition of modernisation; it is part of our traditional way of life.

A more recent Irish tradition is that, in every generation since Daniel O'Connell, journalists and academics tell us that modernity has hit us, and discuss the pros and cons. The Celtic Tiger academics will be followed, in due course, by others who will tell us how Dublin is modernising when, in expensive London and New York restaurants, people are eating prime Al Qaeda Terrorist meat.

In short, with some historical awareness and care for language, Eamon Maher and Michael Böss, the editors of *Engaging Modernity*, might have added "in the 1990s". Granted, it would have sounded banal, but the truth is.

The second thing that cries out to be said is, yes indeed, we have "travelled from being a rural-based, religious country to being a hi-tech centre"; we have heard that before *ad nauseam*. But what happens now and who's discussing that? What do we do with our final achievement of that indistinguishableness from our neighbours which — with some deviation in the post-revolutionary decades — has been the aim of successive Irish elites for centuries?

Getting rid of "rural-based" and "religious" — actually "Catholic" was the trouble — has been only the tail-end of a process which, again, is illuminated by history. It began in the sixteenth century when our top people, with the rest following later, began abandoning Irish law, dress and cuisine for English law, dress and cuisine (there was such a thing then). It continued two centuries later, when our new middle class, strong farmers and gombeen persons, feeling still too recognisably Irish because of the sounds that came out of their mouths, abandoned Irish language for English language, and the lower ranks, trailing as usual, followed suit.

Finally came the 1960s and '70s, and a new bourgeoisie felt uncomfortable that their country, by being "rural" and "Catholic", still stuck out on the surrounding landscape. England wasn't rural or Catholic, nor was America. So those Paddy marks, too, were disposed of.[1] Now at long last, the self-image we project abroad, and like looking at in the domestic mirror, is Ameranglian to a T and free of Paddy marks.

But mission accomplished, we do not need to be told and told again, in self-congratulatory tones, that it has been accomplished and how free it makes us. Free for what?

Animals which change their natural colouring to adopt that of the surrounding vegetation have, so to speak, rational purposes. They wish to protect themselves from attack or to facilitate their own attacks. Have we such purposes in mind? Or was stripping ourselves of our distinguishing clothing our particular, very daring and desperate way of becoming a rich country? And if it was, how will it serve us if we cease to be rich? Have we a project in mind for our post-national future? If there existed in the Republic a serious cultural debate, these are the issues our culture specialists would be attending to.

Europe, or at least its anthropologists, will be watching what we do next. For, ironically, in making ourselves indistinguishable from our Ameranglian surroundings we have made ourselves unique among European nations. In Ireland alone, modernisation — to return to the theme — took this nationally self-obliterating turn, and so resolutely that it continued after political independence.

---

[1] In a letter to the Editor, Jaime Hyland objected to this as "not history but crude invective" against persons such as he who, had "chosen to live without religion", not as part of any Dublin middle-class fashion, but out of personal conviction. It was unworthy of me as a reputed "humanist". In a reply, I conceded that he had a point — that I had used "shorthand". However, I was sure that in each of the "abandonments" I had referred to there was a minority who were not acting out of conformist angst but who had "well-thought-out reasons". It was the "overall pattern of national self-obliteration" that interested me — that, and what we would do with the result.

Alone among the nations, we Irish had sufficient self-hatred and sufficient daring to transform our nation into a *tabula rasa* and post-Irish space on which something culturally quite new and post-European can be built. But only if we stop hating the notion of being different . . . Anthropologically speaking, we are an experiment.[2]

---

[2] As I read the proofs of this book in Anguillara, I am intrigued to hear that a book has been published by Manchester University Press called *The End of Irish History?* Good question, good title!

Epilogue

The Author as a Dublin Liberal Problem

In the Preface, personally to the reader, and in the subsequent pages, to a variety of publics, I have been speaking as I am; that is, in real life. I have been talking to readers who are interested in what I have to say on things, or at least on some things. I have assumed that, from page to page, you were agreeing or disagreeing with me, or at least thinking critically about what I was saying. It has been, in other words, a normal writer–reader situation and relationship.

At the same time, most of you know that besides this real-life man who has been speaking to you with these assumptions, there exists another mythical person to whom my name is attached. At the very least, you have bumped into some puzzling remarks or references that seemed to suggest his existence. He is an urban, more precisely Dublin, legend. In the last chapter of *Heresy* and *The Turning Point*, respectively, I had something to say about his creation from the early 1970s onwards. Around the time *The Turning Point* was published, two years ago, John Waters wrote a penetrative essay on the necessity for creating him and on how his continuing existence is managed by his creators. That was in a collection of essays called *Desmond Fennell: His Life and Work*, edited by Toner Quinn. Waters pointed out that because of the dangerously subversive things I write in reasonable language, and my harmless-seeming, real-life character as a pipe-smoking, smiling, conversational fellow with a respectable education, I presented a problem to those in Dublin who control the public Truth. I was not fit material for a liberal Bogeyman. So to deal with the problem, in the public interest, they were obliged to tag my name with all the liberal booh-words, thus creating a straw figure who was by definition and quite obviously Wrong. And having thus established Fennell's Wrongness and immersion in Error, they took reasonable prophylactic measures lest his Error spread.

Waters's account is literary art in an ironic vein. But the matter has become such that it demands more precise exposure than either he or I have hitherto given it. The impersonating mechanism set in motion by my influential opponents thirty years ago still comes between a substantial sector of the public and me; its workings mislead even some who find meat in my writings. Most seriously of all, those workings are now implanting biographical falsities about my life and work. These are urgent and sufficient reasons for presenting the precise exposure that follows. By backtracking to trace the origin and nature of the mechanism, and by illustrating, from a few examples, how it has been working this very year, I want to enable people not only to identify it at work and to discount it, but also to suspect the possibility of its presence whenever there is a reference to me in Dublin journalism or in a footnote to an Irish academic work. Such, over a thirty-year period, has been the spread of the infection, and you will see presently that I do not exaggerate. At the same time, I am aware that my experience of this illiberal phenomenon is part of the ideological and political history of Ireland since the 1970s. Its significance extends beyond my particular case. So my secondary motive is to provide a precise historical record for those who will wish to have a comprehensive understanding of what was happening in Ireland in this period.

In *Books Ireland*, last January, John Kirkaldy, an Irishman with whom I have never had any contact, reviewed two of my books. His review, while complimentary to me as a writer and thinker, was broadly disapproving of the views the books express. By a happy chance, his article serves several illustrative purposes at once: it indicates the background out of which the impersonation sprang and exemplifies some of its present workings. In his introductory paragraphs, having listed the variety of subjects on which I have written, Kirkaldy writes of me:

> Nearly all his comments and ideas have gone against the conventional norms of the dominant liberal ideology that has tended to set the agenda for debate. For years he has been the Man You Love to Hate of Dublin 4.

That is true, and I find the verb "gone against" — rather than, say, "opposed" — particularly apt. The fact is that, from the late 1960s into the '70s, when it all began, the liberal agenda in its broadest sense — including its centralist, anti-nationalist and London-directed aspects — was clashing with my own agenda, which was the completion of the Irish Revolution. An Ireland democratically self-governing in all its parts, economically self-sustaining, intellectually self-determining and culturally self-shaping was my goal. Inasmuch as Dublin liberalism was also then beginning its assault on the people's religion, I was irritated by this, but on national grounds mainly; for my own, actually Catholic reasons, I supported the proposal to remove the Catholic Church's "special position" from the Constitution. All this is evident from the selection of *Sunday Press* articles I published in 1972 as *Build the Third Republic* — and indeed from that very title which once caused me trouble with British soldiers at the border! From what I have said in the Preface about my subsequent writing and activities until the late 1980s, it will be clear that, first in Conamara, then in Dublin, the Dublin liberals impinged on my concerns mainly as a counter-force to my agenda; that is to say, as the Counter-revolution.

Be that as it may, from the Dublin liberals' point of view, I was clearly an opponent and a dangerous one, in part because my *Sunday Press* column had given me a large all-Ireland following. But some knowledge of the world, as well as mental agility not possessed by doctrinaires, were required to reply to me and eliminate me by argument. So instead, the tagging of my name with the liberal booh-tags got under way. Essentially, it was a matter of pub-talk and party gossip in the RTÉ–UCD–*Irish Times* triangle and its dependencies, in Dublin and elsewhere, in journalism, academe and publishing. Those who engaged in it were the middle-rankers, the liberal cadres; the kind of people who, in any party, form along with the footsoldiers the, so to speak, standing army. Non-practising Catholics who had found a new, imported faith which gave them self-esteem and a sense of being a cut above the ordinary Irish, they felt threatened by the articulacy with which I challenged those precious acquisitions. To choose the tags they hung on my name, no mental effort was required; or rather, as little as is required for anarchist demonstrators to call the police "fascist bastards". Sufficient for them to believe that they were the latest wave of enlightened progress; two centuries of such waves had supplied a stock nomenclature for opponents, and to hell with what the latter might actually be standing for, even if they were stating it in plain words. So this particular opponent got the conventional, mindless tagging treatment of self-imagined new-wave "progressives". And as "nationalist" and "Catholic" also became liberal scare-words, those tags, added, made him a proper sight to scare the liberal crows and their wavering converts.

In short, the aim, rather than to contest me and defeat me with argument, was to neuter or, so to speak, airbrush me. Once my pseudo-persona had been established by the tagged figure passed around, it went without saying that no self-respecting liberal — and liberals generally respect themselves — could publicly agree with me, or even publicly discuss anything I might say or write.[1] Thus I became, in pluralist, tolerant, diversity-respecting Dublin liberal circles, something not unlike Hiroshima in the public discourse of the contemporary West. By dint of the cadres' constant

---

[1] It was not considered a breach of liberal discipline to misrepresent something I had written, and to comment on that fiction. That would be a rare enough occurrence, but see, for example, pp. 206–216. And neither was it a betrayal of the party to indicate my continuing existence by occasionally publishing an article by me in a liberal organ or displaying me beset by the right-thinking on RTÉ television. Quite on the contrary. In Stalinist Russia, when Trotsky was airbrushed, literally and figuratively, out of the historical record and public discussion, his haunting ghost was maintained as a warning presence of radical Wrongness — and of the disaster which would follow if the dams built against him were to break.

watchfulness to suppress my real existence, I acquired an importance for them which I have retained to this day.

Fast-forward through thirty years, during which the Fennell-impersonating mechanism did its work by nudge and whisper until word of the tagged impostor reached John Kirkaldy and lodged in his mind as "conservative, old-fashioned bigot". In two quite contrasting ways, his article shows this. In the first instance, because he is writing after having read two books of mine, that implanted image dissolves and I come through more or less real. In the second, because Kirkaldy hasn't the relevant reading material to hand, the implanted image makes him write untruthful nonsense about me.

In the first instance, because *Books Ireland* has asked him to review the two books and he has agreed to and read them, he writes:

> Conservative, old-fashioned and bigot — all are unfair or inadequate descriptions. He speaks several languages (including Irish); he has travelled widely and lived in several countries (he currently lives in Italy); and his writings and speech are littered with philosophical references (which, unlike some, he has obviously read). Although his views are very emphatic, they are usually delivered in a reasonable tone. At his best, he writes in a clear and well-argued fashion. There is a touch of Swift about him but also a little bit of Malvolio and Eeyore.

It is a curious feeling to read someone describing you, more or less factually, in a tone of surprise! (In passing, let me clarify that I do not accept the smearing connotation which our liberals have given to "conservative" in Irish public language. If my own inclination has always been to imaginative innovation[2] — Seamus Deane once

---

[2] More precisely, "imaginative innovation respectful of the past". As for conservatism, it is precisely the dire lack of it in our modern centuries that has caused the cultural self-stripping to the point of national nullity that I describe in "Engaging Modernity in a Hi-tech Centre", pp. 255–8.

suggested "pathologically so" — that does not prevent my being aware of the positive value of principled resistance to it.)

In the second instance, because Kirkaldy has not checked my writings from the 1960s to the 1990s, the implanted image rules and he writes of me:

> He has gone against the stream on abortion, divorce, contraception, economics and the current political mores. He has opposed much of what has taken place in Christianity since the 1960s, especially in the Catholic Church.

It is deeply disturbing to read such a highly inaccurate "biographical note" about yourself written with such confidence. If by "against the stream" Kirkaldy means against liberal opinion, it's an odd choice of expression, but let's assume he means that. I cannot remember writing anything about liberalising the law on contraceptives in the 1970s — the issue as such never excited me and I had competing concerns. Regarding the liberal push for divorce legislation, in two newspapers I briefly suggested a pluralist solution: two available marriage contracts, one indissoluble, the other dissoluble i.e. open to divorce. True enough, I have been repelled by the Dublin liberal campaign of winks and nods in favour of permissive legislation on abortion. I have written that to condone abortion is to condone the killing of a human being, and that if, in any country, the law in fact permits it, it should restrict it to the first three months of pregnancy and have strict limiting conditions. The liberal stream on economics and current political mores? I'm not sure what is meant; but if the latter item is a reference to the investigative tribunals, I took almost no interest in them and was, anyhow, mainly abroad. As for the Catholic Church since the 1960s, in that decade, as many people can recall, I was editing *Herder Correspondence*, an international Catholic magazine known for its strong support of the reforming programme of the Second Vatican Council. That indicates the general line of my writing on Catholic Church matters then and since.

It's really pretty shocking, isn't it? But it also provides remark-able evidence of the staying power of the liberal implant which Kirkaldy had received. After reading the two books, he seemed liberated from it; but here he is on the same page giving a fictional account of my working life that is inspired by it. The "pig-headed conservative" notion governs it.[3] And unaware that my differ-ences with the liberals were marginal to my concerns, he has me all wrought up about *their* central concern, their "liberal agenda" as they called it, on sexual matters and abortion, and contesting it indiscriminately every inch of the way. (It was their central con-cern because victory on those issues would signify victory over the Catholic clergy and replacement of them by themselves.) And he has me continuing this absorption with them right through to the 1990s and the tribunals! Mere assumption stated as fact runs right through it all, and I could fault him severely for the careless-ness and disrespect of this — he's dealing with my life. But at the same time I see him as one among many victims of the campaign of nudge and whisper directed against me by the liberal hacks, and that softens my anger.

Let me add, to finish with the matter and because I have promised to be precise, that I have indeed protested against, and depicted with scorn, the bullying methods and contemptuous tones with which the Dublin media liberals have conducted their successive campaigns, whether on their central agenda or on other matters. I have done that as one who believes in representative democracy and pluralism. In particular, I have come down hard on the liberal-sponsored "Soviet-style" referenda of the 1980s and

---

[3] An alternative to "conservative" was "traditionalist": another latest-wave-of-enlightened-progress booh-tag dating from the eighteenth-century battle of Reason against Tradition. In the Dublin liberal context, oddly — say, in Fintan O'Toole — "Tradition" has been located only in a rural, never an urban milieu. "Traditional-*ist*", when spelt out, has meant an excessive valuation of the habits of Irish small farmers and their families between 1870 and 1960; that is to say, of the mythical "rural Ireland" discussed on pp. 119–34. Applied to me, it was for obvious reasons a damp squib, impossible to accompany with an illustrative reference.

'90s which I described on page 234. But those referenda concerned European Union matters as well as items of the "liberal agenda". With regard to those items, my stated positions, when there were any, have been as I wrote above.

Before returning, finally, and on a different note, to Kirkaldy's valuable article, I want to illustrate how an academic who broke the liberal rule on not discussing my writings was nevertheless misled by one of those reports passed on by the comrades. Also this year, only a few months later, Vincent Twomey, who teaches Moral Theology at Maynooth, published a book *The End of Irish Catholicism?*. In the course of it, he drew, with quotations and fair paraphrase, on some of my writings. In a note, after referring to the book *Desmond Fennell: His Life and Work,* he writes:

> As the contributors point out, Fennell is an original thinker who rarely fails to stimulate and, in almost equal measure, rarely finds agreement.

"Rarely finds agreement"; it appears there as a factual description of my writing career. Obviously, the report that had reached Twomey in Maynooth College from the RTÉ–UCD–*Irish Times* triangle and its dependencies was to the effect that "no one" (meaning no one who matters, no right-thinking, liberal person) "agrees with Fennell". Twomey, thoughtlessly or because he lived in academe and lacked competing information, understood it literally; but because he himself happened to agree with some things I had written, he modified it with "rarely" and wrote what he wrote. But because the implanted image, thus modified, remained, his guiding light with regard to the person concerned, he imagined, when he read the book of essays about the latter's life and work, that the contributors, all of them, were confirming the implant, modified by "rarely". In other words, he read that statement into what Waters and the others were saying. I say "imagined" and "read into" because in fact none of the contributors writes any such thing! It is a fascinating example of how a pre-implanted image — it is a common occurrence in all our lives — can shape our understanding of something we see or read; and all the more fascinating because here we see it happening to an intelligent, clear-thinking man.

At all events, the net result was that Vincent Twomey delivered to the world and posterity, as a fact attested to by himself, and seven others who knew me well, that few people had ever agreed with anything I had written. Again, it is a very unsettling experience to read such a ridiculous untruth about your working life stated as a vouched-for *fact*. As happens, allegedly, in the moment of death, your mind races back through your life to those years as an art critic in Dublin in the 1960s and — fast-forwarding to the pamphlet you published about the overrated poet — passes through the *Herder Correspondence* years, the Gaeltacht revolution years, the *Sunday Press* years (both stretches of them), all that long involvement in the decentralisation campaign and the search for peace in the North, *The State of the Nation* selling like hotcakes, and those articles in the *Irish Times* which so often brought you "thank you" notes. All those successive episodes of happy in-tuneness with publics, substantial or quite large, to be cancelled from the record by one lapidary sentence! And as happened when you read that nonsense written by Kirkaldy, you thank God that it is not in fact the moment of your death, so that you are still around to write these words of indignation at a printed and circulated lie about your work and life.[4]

These two examples suffice to illustrate why in Ireland today *any* brief description of an Irish writer or thinker — other than a certified liberal — must be treated with scepticism and checked out. I am not of course suggesting that, in references to me, such misrepresentation always happens. In Twomey's book, obviously

---

[4] Readers will recognise at work here the Orwellian principle: "Whoever controls the past, controls the future." Compare this minor instance of misrepresentation of the past by Dublin liberal methods with the broader instance of the same phenomenon which I discuss in my response to the Italian book, pp. 164–6.

it does not, since, apart from that bloomer where he is in fact an incautious victim, he reports and quotes my work with accuracy. I am talking about the casual, cocksure, indoctrinated common-place, which is the most insidious form of misrepresentation. And I am pointing out that when my stance on life is, occasionally, characterised correctly — or when, simply, the liberal booh-tags are declared invalid — the writer does so in a tone of some sur-prise and of consciously challenging orthodoxy. We have seen this in Kirkaldy's momentary rejection of the particular implant he had succumbed to. But just before that, he had performed an even more sweeping rebellion with "Fennell fits into no neat little box". Stepping a moment into the Internet, I find there an Irish-American whose father I knew, Mark Gauvreau Judge, writing about me with a wide knowledge of what is written and said in my regard in Ireland. Trying this way and that to fit me into the American and Irish ideological schemes, and failing, he summa-rises: "thoughtful, full of surprises" and then, with that rebellious edge — for he is aware of the tags — "impossible to categorize". More to the point, he quotes "Irish Book reviewer Bill Sweeny" — should that be *Irish Book*? — calling me "a staunch, if not always lucid defender of his own personal take on the human condition". That is stark rebellion: I am just, what in fact I happen to be, a thinking man! But to return to where we were: No, I am not sug-gesting there is no variety in the characterisation of me in print in Ireland. I am talking about the casual, cocksure, Dublin-liberal-indoctrinated commonplace, which, with a thirty-year tradition behind it, is pretty common.

Generously, and with the best intention, Kirkaldy writes:

> I should make clear that I am opposed to much of what Fennell stands for, but would argue that he has made a substantial contribution to discussion and argument. Life would be much duller without him!

Pray, Mr Kirkaldy, "a contribution to discussion and argument" *where?* You are a normal man who believes that when a known intellectual publishes new, thought-through ideas on matters of general interest, his fellow intellectuals, in his own country, will grab at them and kick them around, uttering cheers, caveats and anathema. It is what would happen, say in England, or in Holland or Lithuania. But, Mr Kirkaldy, you live in a country where a thinking man can make all the "contributions" he is capable of, and the normal does not happen! I could give notable examples, beginning with Tom Barrington, Raymond Crotty and Ivor Browne. With regard to my own "contributions", as you call them — the latest in *The Revision of European History* — Irish liberal party discipline has not been the only impediment. There are also the limiting, Ameranglian paradigms within which our academics toil. And there are other historical conditioning factors that I won't enlarge on, because I have dealt with them in the last chapter of my Sweden book, and in this present book in "The Irish Problem with Thought". In short, Mr Kirkaldy, if intellectual life in Ireland would be "duller without me", it is in truth, for a combination of reasons, as dull as that.

I have always believed that in the matter of tagging people with regard to their worldview or partisan zeal, the same etiquette should apply as in the matter of tagging them with a nationality. In the latter case, by general agreement, one should do so only with the person's consent. One does not say "she's Irish" or "you're German", if the person in question, in the first instance, says she is British or, in the second, a Dane. To do otherwise is plain boorish, with an imperialistic taint. I am aware that, in the matter of the other kind of tagging, these niceties are often ignored; polemical passion or the desire to do down by name-calling often overrides. But I have stated my own principle on the matter, and I try to make it my practice. In these pages, for example, I have not called the Dublin liberals "illiberals". I have called them "liberals" because that is what they call themselves and like being called. On one occasion, true, I called their operation with regard to me "illiberal"; but that's a different matter, it's not personal, and it's patently true. Other, cruder terms would equally apply, but on the assumption that my readers possess an adequate vocabulary, I leave them unsaid.

*

As this book goes to press, *The Encyclopedia of Ireland* has appeared (General Editor Brian Lalor, publisher Gill and Macmillan). Apart from abundant information about Ireland and Irish persons from ancient times onwards, the *Encyclopedia* contains several hundred entries about persons who did something notable or something minor — often in fictive writing or traditional music — during the past forty years. Unfortunately, in matters of thought, writing and politics, the selection of these contemporary entries reflects the liberal-revisionist ascendancy, including its intolerance of disagreement with it. That I am not mentioned goes without saying; but more interesting and instructive is the good company in which I find myself. Two random examples of the selection pattern: Roy Foster is in, Joe Lee out; Fintan O'Toole is in, John Waters out. Succinctly put, all those are missing who have prominently pursued agendas which were at variance with the liberal-revisionist agenda — or who have notably opposed some facet of it. Further examples of the excluded are Raymond Crotty, Anthony Coughlan, Tom Barrington, William Binchy, Damien Kiberd, Ruairí Ó Brádaigh and John Robb. This general airbrushing of persons who have been notably in disaccord with the reigning ideology results in a picture of the Republic in the period 1965–2003 as a community of orthodox liberal believers, without intelligent or argued deviance. It is also, therefore, a serious misrepresentation of Irish intellectual history during this period.